VOICE

A Multifaceted Approach to
Self-Growth and Vocal Empowerment

Laura Stavinoha

Author: Laura Stavinoha
Editing: Jessie Mannisto
Publisher: Leessst
Cover illustration: Roel Iken
Illustrations and book design: Sander de Haan
Photo cover: Tim Hillege

ISBN: 9789491863745

Foreword by Lotte van Lith

As a professional speaker, I'm used to paying attention to my voice. It serves as a mirror into how I am feeling, and it signals whether what I'm expressing is authentic and interesting—and therefore worthwhile to the audience. When I speak about topics like positive disintegration, my voice tells the emotional story that my body has lived through. Even more than the content of what I'm saying, the sensitive musicality of my voice is vital to the quality of my performance. And even though I have wrestled with crippling stage fright in the past, I've always appreciated the artistic fine-tuning that is possible with our voice as the core instrument.

I'm both an emotionally excitable person and a life coach, so I recognize the power that tone of voice has to directly influence others' feelings. By actively shaping my voice, I can create and express a broader emotional repertoire. Through this practice, I can more easily demonstrate values such as compassion and responsibility. Because my voice conveys the multilevel world I internally inhabit, it co-creates a safe space for another human being to sense his or her needs and values.

When I first encountered Laura's work, I saw an equally driven creator. The online presentation of her work as a voice coach piqued my curiosity, and I happily shared her offerings within my network. My intuition turned out to be valuable for myself as well. Laura has coached me in individual and group sessions, and every time I've worked with her, I've been struck by her ability to stay present and focused, mild yet direct, knowledgeable, and approachable. On top of this, she combines her artistic expression and development with a fascination with and experience of psychological growth. This fusing makes her expertise truly relevant and vivid.

The same qualities are evident in the way she approaches psychological development in the book you are about to read. Creativity, roughly speaking, is the ability to make new connections between apparently remote topics—connections that are useful, beautiful, and engaging. To me, this work is a wonderful example of creativity: a combination of impressive expertise, considered insight, and innovative perspectives. Laura weaves together an impressive amount of theory and practice. While you are reading the book, it feels as though she is speaking to you personally. There could be no better recommendation for a book on multilevel vocal development!

I know Laura as a curious and mindful person, and this is reflected in her writings. Her ability to explain technical and emotional information in a transparent, direct way while at the same time honoring the storytelling quality makes reading this book both engaging and informative.

The bundle of perspectives and theories that are combined in this work include, for example: the theory of positive disintegration, polyvagal theory, mindfulness, and acceptance and commitment therapy. You will also find scientific, philosophical or practical insight by, amongst others, Antonio Damasio, Lisa Feldman Barrett, David Bohm, and Deb Dana. In this work, Laura draws on lesser-known theories and shares up-to-date understanding of topics such as emotions and personality development. Taking an embodied approach while sharing the intellectual fruits that theory offers us, she actively invites both the reader's mind and heart to learn. Because Laura dares to share her own creative and emotional journey, the reader's threshold to integrate the learning process will also be lowered.

As a coach, trainer, and teacher with a long-lasting relationship with humanistic developmental psychology, I am also grateful to Laura for creating this paper space for Kazimierz Dąbrowski's work to be shared with a broader public. His theory of positive disintegration may not be considered mainstream, but the insightfulness of Dąbrowski's multilevel understanding of emotional development is nonetheless manifestly clear to me. By connecting artistic growth, conscious vocal development, and embodiment and validation of the voice with Dąbrowski's insights on emotional development, readers will find themselves encouraged to compassionately understand their suffering and recognize the developmental potential inherent in it. All the practical exercises root the theory in everyday life choices, offering small challenges to take yourself seriously and to explore and embody your talent, values and vision.

Laura's written voice will surely encourage you to tune into your wisdom and vocal freedom. Even more so, the book will inspire you to be gentle to your own emotional "beingness," to strengthen your autonomy, and to express what in you is truly authentic and valuable to others. I would like to end with a quote by Dąbrowski:

> Our understanding of human behavior and human development cannot be complete without the study of emotional development. [Human life] lose[s] meaning if the emotional component is taken away.[1]

What better representative of this truth is there than our own (inner) voice?

---

1   K. Dąbrowski *Multilevelness of Emotional and Instinctive Functions* (1996, Towarzystwo Naukowe, Lublin) p. 5-6.

Introduction

Voices can touch us deeply. When a particular voice has really mastered this, we say that singer or speaker has a talent or a gift. People generally believe that you're either born with an amazing voice or you're not. And if you're not, well then, too bad for you.

This is a major misunderstanding. Perhaps there are singers and speakers to whom it just comes naturally, but this certainly does not apply to most people who have mastered their voices. We typically only see someone's success, not what they did to get there.

I've been a singer since I was young, and I've struggled with my voice for a long time. It was never in shape. There was always something in the way that prevented me from sounding the way I wanted. I also had serious stage fright and didn't feel accepted in the music business. For years, my voice was a source of frustration. Looking back at the journey I undertook, I have many memories of hard work, disappointments, but also the drive to *just keep on going*.

What I didn't know back then was that my voice reflected the struggles, frustrations, and insecurities I was dealing with in other parts of my life at the time. Gradually, I dealt with these struggles, and I noticed that as my life grew less conflicted, my voice did too. Today, I no longer feel limited by my voice. In particular, I don't fear what others will think about it—and that, paradoxically, has led me to a place where I've even received compliments for it, as others tell me they can hear this sense of freedom in my voice. I feel free to sing whatever and whenever I want to, and I've discovered a wealth of vocal sounds and timbres I didn't know I had in me. Meanwhile, I no longer rely heavily on daily practice to keep my voice in shape. Somehow, I can always count on it when it's needed.

Singers usually become vocal coaches for other singers; I was no different there. Gradually, however, I also began coaching those who were seeking help with their voice in other ways, including professional speakers and others who just wanted to overcome something they didn't like in their voice. While I do offer my clients voice and breath techniques, what has turned out to have the greatest impact is guiding them through the developmental processes that I went through myself. Through this work with my clients, I've learned even more about the voice. It's a wonderful experience to have such an up-close view of my clients' personal and vocal development and to explore how I can contribute to their journeys. I believe that the struggles people have with their voices are not talked about enough. Without more conversation around this, people won't know what they can do with their voices, if they want to. That's why I decided to share my approach to working with the voice in this book. I illustrate theory and practice with examples from my personal life, as well as my clients' lives, and the voice-stories of a couple of renowned singers and speakers.

Overall, this book is an invitation to see your voice as a starting point for introspection and development. This means that my advice is not just beneficial for speakers or singers. My method points to ways your voice can help you to grow as a human being, thereby contributing to personal transformation. Consequently, you won't find any quick fixes here. I don't offer tricks on how to lower your pitch for a sense of authority, nor a checklist for a kick-ass presentation style. It is my mission to put the voice in a broader perspective and to create awareness for the role it plays in safety, connection, emotional expression, and personal development.

In Part 1, *Voice &...*, I look at the voice through the lens of two theoretical frameworks: the polyvagal theory and the theory of positive disintegration. Based on these theories, I will guide you through the many levels from which you can look at the voice. I explain why your voice reflects so much of your inner world and your behavior and why you can perceive voice as either a powerful or vulnerable quality of yourself. This vulnerability that the voice reflects is discussed in Chapter 1.

In Chapter 2, on safety, I'll introduce you to Stephen Porges' polyvagal theory. Porges' work sheds light on the impact that the autonomic nervous system has on the voice. It talks about the role of the vagus nerve in emotion regulation, social connection, and the fear response. Through our own voice and hearing the voices of others, our nervous system communicates with us about danger and safety. This means our voice is a barometer for our autonomic nervous system, just like our breathing or heart rate. Problems in these areas indicate that you feel unsafe. It's true that speech is a form of human behavior, and we can influence it through the use of voice techniques. However, if we only work with the voice on the level of behavior, nothing will change on the level of the nervous system, which is where the problems often lie. That's why certain voice problems keep on coming back to us in moments of stress. To address this, we have to look at what lies underneath speech, at the role it plays in the autonomic responses of our nervous system.

The second theoretical lens I use in the book is psychological. Following my own experiences with the voice and those of the people I've worked with, I've found no better framework to illustrate the role of our psychology on our voices than Kazimierz Dąbrowski's theory of positive disintegration. I believe this theory of personal, emotional, and moral development can help us to understand not only personality development in general, but also how it affects the voice.

In Chapter 3, on personal development, we'll read about how I connect the developmental process of my voice to the process of positive disintegration. Chapter 4 discusses Dąbrowskian developmental potential, which is a great way of also looking at the potential of our voice: What part of the voice comes from one's physiological make-up, what part is influenced by one's environment, and can our voices be more than the sum of these two parts? After that, we'll dive into the so-called overexcitabilities, the most well-known element of Dąbrowski's work. Here I argue that these overexcitabilities manifest through the voice, just as they do in the other behaviors through which Dąbrowski observed them. A lesser-known element of the theory is called *dynamisms*; Chapter 6 will introduce them. These transformative inner forces are often present in people who experience voice problems with no physical cause. Through the stories of four of my clients and one famous singer, you'll learn how their voices became counselors in their development processes. Since they have such a huge impact on the voice, Chapter 7 takes an extra deep dive into the world of emotions. What are they, and how do they come into being? I'll argue that everything we feel, think, value, and believe is rooted in the physical experience of our own bodies.

In Part 2, *Work with Your Voice on a Deeper Level*, I offer practical tips, exercises, and advice based on the theoretical frameworks discussed earlier. Here I also combine the physiological and psychological levels of the voice. Chapter 8 talks about the basis of any good voice: breathing. Chapter 9 promotes body awareness and offers exercises to help you embody your voice while you use it. By now you know what emotions are, but how do you make sense of them, and how do you regulate your nervous system? Chapter 10 gives answers to that. Along the way, through emotional development, it's inevitable that you'll shift your perspective on your mind and thought process; tools for that are offered in Chapter 11. The same goes for your perspective on your sense of self. To help you become aware of your behavioral patterns and develop your ability to change them, Chapter 12 is about self-awareness, meditation, and contemplation.

The book is written in such a way that it is possible to read any chapter on its own. To get the most out of it, however, I recommend that you begin with the polyvagal theory and certain principles of positive disintegration as they are discussed in Chapters 2 through 5.

I would like to say a few of more things about the theoretical frameworks mentioned above. "Theory," which is rooted in the Greek word "theatre," originally meant "to view." According to theoretical physician and philosopher David Bohm, a theory is primarily a form of *insight*. It is a way of looking at the world, not necessarily a description of all of reality. Forms of insight are ever-changing; they point into a reality that is possibly implicit and unmeasurable—that is, not convertible into evidence-based science. I approach the polyvagal theory and the theory of positive disintegration exactly in this way—as valuable and inspiring ways of looking at the voice. They have helped me and the people I work with to make sense of ourselves and our voices.

I do not attempt in this book to give a complete overview of the polyvagal theory nor the theory of positive disintegration. Both theories are complex; it would be beyond the scope of this book to discuss them in depth. From both frameworks, I chose to discuss the elements that are relevant to my subject of the voice, and what you will read here is my personal interpretation of them. This especially holds for positive disintegration, which does not talk about the voice or voice issues in its source texts. The fact that I came to connect personal development, developmental potential, overexcitability, and dynamisms to the voice is entirely the result of my qualitative experience with the people I work with and their voices.

Above all, this book is the result of my personal exploration into the world of the voice. Most research projects that people undertake have a personal motive. This one is no different. My curiosity about voice, personal development, the nervous system, and how they all interact comes from a longing to make sense of my personal experiences in life and has resulted in my desire to write this book to share my insights. Equally, it comes from a desire to restore or evoke vocal expression and meaningful communication in myself and in others. It is my hope that this will ultimately lead all of us to genuine connection with ourselves, our loved ones, and with the world.

Part 1
Voice and...

1. Vulnerability

As a young child, I felt completely free to express myself. I could sing. I could dance. I was not at all concerned with whether I was good enough, or what others thought of me.

At some point, however, I developed self-consciousness. This put an end to my free expression. I vividly remember the moment when I suddenly realized that everything had changed. It was when I was fourteen. I was giving a solo performance at school with piano and voice. Performances like this were not new to me; I had even given one in a renowned concert hall at the age of nine. This time, my song was Billie Holiday's *God Bless the Child*. I had played it over and over, and the music was one hundred percent integrated into my muscle memory—my hands could find the right piano keys even with my eyes closed. I was really looking forward to performing; it had never occurred to me that anything could go wrong.

But when I was invited to the stage and sat behind the piano, something happened to me that I had never experienced before. To my surprise, my hands began to tremble and sweat. My mouth became dry and I felt palpitations in my chest. I searched for my first chords, but I pressed the wrong keys. I was cut off from my muscle memory. I don't exactly remember how I did it, but somehow, I made it through the song with a thin and trembling voice, hitting a fair number of wrong keys on the piano. After the performance, I cried, overwhelmed by complex emotions that were hard to put into words at the time. I now remember it as a combination of relief, ecstasy, failure, shame, and feeling exposed and vulnerable.

Looking back now, I don't think I gave an extremely bad performance; I even got some positive feedback. But my performance that night was nothing close to what I was capable of. It did not show how meticulously I had prepared myself. Most of all, feeling those overwhelming physical stress sensations before the performance—and the heavy emotions afterward—came as a profound shock.

From that moment, I couldn't trust myself anymore. Stage fright haunted me. Because I never consciously felt this type of fear, however, it took me a long time to recognize that that's what it was. I wasn't aware of my underlying emotions. All I knew was that, for some reason, when I performed, my body showed all the sensations connected to fear: heart palpitations, shallow breathing, sweaty palms, tension in the throat, a trembling voice. It was incredibly frustrating. I had a strong urge to get out there—to share my art in front of an audience. But when I did, I was always disappointed with what I delivered.

1.1. The Origin of Stage Fright

What I didn't know back then is that performance nerves are completely normal—and they don't just affect artistic performers. Stage fright can occur in any situation where all eyes are on you: in the meeting room where you give a presentation, during a job interview, or even when you introduce yourself to a new group of people. Most people hate moments like this. Some even say they would rather die than speak in public. And yet, acknowledging this is a taboo. No one likes to talk about stage fright—not even at schools for the performing arts.

So is there anything you can do about stage fright? If you look for help on the subject, you can find some well-meant tricks and advice—*know your material, make sure you are well prepared, and stop scaring yourself with thoughts about what might go wrong*. Well, that's not really an epiphany. It goes without saying that I, a person who always wanted to do well, prepared myself thoroughly in order to make a good impression. Now that I'm a voice coach, I frequently help my clients unpack this same unhelpful advice.

Beyond a certain point, preparation of your material is not the path to a good performance. Overpreparing can even make things worse if it's at the expense of rest and self-care. But what can you do instead? Here's the first step: *be open to your nervousness*. Yes, it's inconvenient, but ignoring it won't drive it away. Your body is telling you something with this dry throat and sweaty palms! So start listening to its message.

Being fourteen years old and making an entrance on stage, I was fully aware of my environment and the difference between success and failure. Although I didn't realize it yet back then, I cared a lot about what other people thought of me, and I was trying hard to prove myself to others. And it's completely normal to care about what others think of you. In his book *The Righteous Mind* social psychologist Jonathan Haidt tell us that everyone, even those who say that they're not affected by others' opinions, show strong declines in self-esteem when confronted with disapproval by others. Yes, we are all concerned about other people's opinions about us, even if not on a conscious level. But we don't like to admit this—sometimes not even to ourselves. In order to navigate our daily lives, we learn to hide our vulnerabilities; we don't want to come across as weak. If you're sensitively wired, you care even more about what others think of you, so your emotions will be even more obvious when you feel like you're being judged.

Consequently, the problem we call "stage fright" isn't limited to staged performance. It comes up in any situation where you want to come across as confident, engaging, persuasive, or decisive, like when you have to sell yourself or your product. It's also a factor in any situation where you want to share what you think, believe, feel, or value, like when you need to set boundaries. Why is that? Your voice is a unique and personal instrument emanating from your own body. The muscles around the voice box are in close contact with the nerves that activate when you're stressed—as you are when you set high expectations for yourself, share vulnerable or emotionally charged information, or fear failure or judgment. Your voice reflects your physical state, thoughts, and emotions. By sharing your voice, you share an intimate part of yourself. This is especially true for singers, who can't hide behind an instrument. For me, it feels much worse to sing a note out of tune than to hit a wrong note on the piano. If someone criticizes your voice, it can feel like a commentary on your deepest self—*ouch!*

Sadly, this is a common experience. Maybe you remember moments when you were a child—I know I do—when you expressed your joy by singing, and there was this grown-up or classmate who told you to shut up because, "It sounds horrible," or, "You can't sing." For a lot of people, this is enough to never sing again, or to restrict their vocal expression to the bedroom or shower where no one can hear them.

Consider what happened to Maya, a lecturer in a design program at a university. She came to work with me because she didn't feel comfortable talking in front of a group. It was her wish to become more persuasive as a lecturer. Since childhood, Maya had disliked being the center of attention. Moreover, when she gave lectures, she was extremely sensitive to her audience's response. She especially lost confidence when she shared her own ideas and theories about design. When students seemed bored during her lectures, she got nervous. Her voice started trembling. She didn't enjoy giving lectures anymore; instead, she wanted them to be over as soon as possible.

Because her trembling voice was making everything worse, I offered Maya voice techniques for word stress and intonation, which she performed flawlessly. She displayed a great sense for language and was highly capable of communicating in an engaged and expressive way. Technically, there was really nothing in her voice to work on.

Then Maya told me a story. As a child, she sang in the church choir. One day, the choir director told her—and not in a considerate way—that she sang too loud. This critique made a profound impression on her. Since that moment, she no longer dared draw attention to herself.

Now Maya and I understood why she couldn't stand being the center of attention—even when she was expected to make her voice heard. To cope with this, she meticulously prepared her lectures and tried to keep everything under her control. That meant she couldn't lower her guard. And that meant she couldn't create a sense of flow during her lectures.

A criticism does not need to be *about* the voice to *affect* the voice. Critique of a fundamental part of your identity or of the things you value in life, especially if this critique is given by a person who's important to you, can leave a profound impression. This was another part of Maya's struggle. Though she otherwise came across as a fun, playful person, she completely hid these qualities when she performed a sample lecture for me. Suddenly, she transformed into a deadly serious person with a dull, theoretical style. She failed to connect with me, just as she had failed to connect with her students. As Maya realized during one of our sessions, her uptight, serious style might stem from her father's disapproval. He did not consider design a serious university subject, let alone a useful contribution to society. Despite the fact that she was now an adult, Maya still felt she needed to defend her career choice to her father—and she brought this into practice every time she lectured her students. She spoke to them as if she were proving herself to her father: uptight and deadly serious.

1.2. The Inner Critic

Negative feedback from your environment emboldens your inner critic. If that critic is too bold, then while you speak or sing, you judge every sound you make, labeling it "right" or "wrong." Every wrong sound feels like torture. You get so scared of making mistakes that your voice gets tense or even stuck. Teachers often want to solve this by putting extra focus on technique, but in those cases, this only makes things worse.

After I graduated from high school, I decided to study jazz at the conservatory. But somehow, in class, my singing never sounded as easy and relaxed as at home. There was always a lot of critique from the teacher: "You hit a false note, you sing too high, you sound too thin, this music does not suit you, you should rather sing this or that...." I became so painfully aware of all the things I had to learn—and of my weaknesses—that I couldn't hear anything else. I became terrified of making mistakes, even during exercises. I grew critical of my own voice. Slowly, I lost all joy in singing. And I didn't improve at all, so, after a year, the conservatory was done with me.

If you're like most of my clients, when you're stuck in a downward spiral like this, your strategy is to try to increase control over your voice. This, however, won't lead to better results. By focusing on control, you lose your connection to the words and emotions that give meaning to what you're saying or singing. The desire for control will also lead you to strain the muscles in your throat and jaw, which should be completely relaxed in order to make free-flowing, easy sounds. When you feel that your voice is stuck, there's a good chance that nothing is wrong with your voice itself. Rather, it's your negative beliefs about yourself that are holding you back: "I can never hit this high note," "My voice is not deep and warm enough," "People won't like my voice," or "My voice is in bad shape because I have a cold". The influence of these negative beliefs on your voice—and how your environment plays a role in shaping them—is not always acknowledged in voice training for singers and speakers. For better vocal results, recognizing these beliefs is essential in escaping the downward spiral.

I see this struggle in a lot of my clients and I deeply recognize what they are going through. But unlike me all those years ago, most of my clients are aware of what is happening to them—and brave enough to share it with me. Consider Kasper, a spoken word performer. It was clear that he had a trained voice. We briefly started with some voice techniques, at which he was excellent. When I asked him to recite one of his pieces, however, something changed. His voice suddenly became flat and monotonous, and he struggled to get into the flow of the piece. After a few lines, he couldn't continue. Kasper was overwhelmed with the situation: His eyes teared up and he couldn't give words to what he was going through. After we sat down together for a while, Kasper said that he thought this had happened because he was supposed to perform in front of me, the teacher. He really wanted to do it right—and show himself at his best during this first lesson. But he didn't realize how vulnerable he would feel while doing so.

Sarah was another client who struggled with her inner critic during her lessons with me. To my ears, Sarah has a very smooth and pleasant voice—she's quite a joy to listen to. But she didn't think so herself. Whenever she sang a song in class, she suffered not only from nerves, but also from extreme self-consciousness. Every time she sang a note that didn't come out the way she wanted, her facial expressions would speak volumes—they showed such strong disapproval of herself. Because of the strong emotions our classes evoked, she gradually grew reluctant to attend.

In Sarah's case, it became clear that it didn't make sense to work with her on technique. Her singing was fine overall; she could depend on her natural musical talent. The issue was that she wasn't enjoying singing anymore because her negative self-talk completely dominated her experience. To restore her singing, we had to address those negative beliefs—so we worked on changing her relationship with her thoughts. We did this through an intervention called defusion. You'll read more about this later; for now, I'll only note that you often end up laughing about yourself and your thoughts. In the best case, the thoughts are still there, but they don't hurt you anymore; instead, you see them as ridiculous. A couple of weeks later, Sarah sang one of her favorite songs in class—without the torture she'd been putting herself through before. She could now focus on the song, the meaning of the lyrics, and the performance in the moment. The negative self-talk was still there, but it didn't pull her out of her performance.

1.3. Your Vulnerability is Your Strength

For me, Maya, Sarah, Kasper, and many others, our voices play an important and vital role in our lives. Precisely because of that, working with the voice can be utterly frustrating. The things that you value the most are the spots where you're most vulnerable. To feel more confident about your capacity with your voice, it does help to some extent to learn voice or singing techniques. When I start working with someone, this is often where we begin. But no matter how well you know or practice these techniques, if your inner critic is at the steering wheel, they're not going to save you in the moments that matter most.

I lost count of the number of clients who reported voice problems but were perfectly able to reproduce voice techniques from my sheets with exercises. Whenever they read from paper, they can direct their voice as they want. The problem occurs when they have to get away from the exercise and speak spontaneously and intuitively about something they value, in a situation where they can be judged. Then thoughts and emotions take over too much of their conscious processes, leaving no room for the delivery of the message. In those cases, it's not voice techniques but work on other parts of yourself that will make you a better speaker.

One of my clients came up with a metaphor for this process. He said that he realized that voice coaching is not only about maintaining the car: You have to maintain the driver as well. It's usually not sufficient to work with your voice in a technical and instrumental way. We have to consider the owner of that voice, too: What's going on in your inner world? Are you overwhelmed by emotions or unable to connect with them? Is your inner critic producing unhelpful negative thoughts? Do you have so many different thoughts, feelings, and ideas that you find it challenging to give words to them?

There are many possible reasons why finding your voice and making yourself heard the way you want is difficult or challenging. More often than not, feeling vulnerable—that is, the need for safety—lies at the core of this. While some people think of vulnerability as a weakness, I argue that it is a strength. Acknowledging that you are vulnerable means acknowledging your emotions, feelings and needs. That is an act of courage. If you have a growing awareness of your inner world, you are increasingly able to identify your personal values, make conscious choices, and respond accordingly. This is where you can grow and develop as a human being.

There is a famous quote from Rumi about love: "Your task is not to seek love, but to look for the blockades in yourself that you have built against love." I have learned that you can apply the same principle to your voice because it can—like love—feel like such a vulnerable part of you. In order to find your voice, you have to look for the blockades in yourself that you have built against expressing yourself freely. In the chapters that follow, I will introduce you to theories about the nervous system and emotional development, and I'll explain how your voice is connected to all of this.

2. Safety

We need to remember that we live in a culture where people say, "It is really what I say and not how I say it that's important." But our nervous system is telling something different to us: It says, "It is not really what you say—it is how you say it."[2]

— Dr. Stephen W. Porges

While I was on a concert tour in Mexico City, I was nearly robbed. It was late at night, and some friends and I were walking from one club to another. Two boys ran past us, and one tried to grab my bag from my shoulder. I didn't let go—and so I was knocked down onto the street, still holding tight to my bag. Fortunately, the boys ran away without fighting for it.

After they were gone, I felt the adrenaline raging through my body. I was totally awake and alert, my heart was pounding in my throat, and suddenly, though I'd had a few drinks, I was completely sober. That night, though my conscious mind felt relief that I had escaped unscathed, my body was still on high alert, and I couldn't get to sleep. Although I had some more drinks to calm down and eventually took two tranquilizers that I hoped would help me to sleep, my body's reaction overruled all the substances I took. The booze and the tranquilizers didn't help me calm down; they only made me feel nauseous.

In the week after the attack, mentally and emotionally, I was doing fine. I actively processed the almost-robbery, dealing with the thoughts and feelings it evoked, so I quickly got over any fear of going outside on my own. Nevertheless, I felt extremely tired. What's more, my digestive system had been thrown off, only allowing me to eat cooked rice.

The following week, I underwent a two-day treatment by a curandero, a traditional Mexican healer. I had planned this treatment long before the attempted robbery because I was suffering from inflammation in the form of rashes on my arms and legs.

I didn't tell the curandero about the incident straight away. After the first day, however, he asked me a question:

"Do you lead an extremely busy life? Are you under a lot of stress?"

"No," I said. "Compared to others, my life is quite tranquil. I'm not that busy, and I generally feel quite balanced."

---

2   S.W. Porges *The Pocket Guide To The Polyvagal Theory – The Transformative Power of Feeling Safe* (2017, W.W. Norton & Company, Inc., New York) p. 148.

He frowned, as though he didn't believe me. "I'm asking this because your nervous system seems extremely active and alert," he explained. "It's something I see a lot in people who are under a lot of stress."

"More than a week ago, I almost got robbed on the streets. Of course I was very stressed afterwards. Is that maybe what you mean?"

"Well, yes, that's probably it," he replied. "But your nervous system is active on a level as if that robbery happened to you yesterday."

I don't like to admit it, but he was right. One week after the incident, I had still not physically recovered from the stress it had caused. That session with the curandero made me realize clearly how differently my body and mind deal with stress. My mind is extremely swift in comprehending and processing the things that are happening to me; my body is not. My body seems to have a completely different agenda, and my mind has no authority over my bodily state. On a conscious level, I quickly got over what had happened. But unconsciously, I apparently needed more time to heal.

This truth, moreover, applies not only to negative things like facing criminals. It applies to anything that causes arousal, even when it's something positive, like performing on stage, or a fun night out with friends. Good or bad, they all send me quickly into that state of arousal—and it takes an extremely long time for me to come down from it and feel relaxed again. It seems to take me much longer than most other people.

So what does this story have to do with the voice? That's simple: Your voice reflects your inner world, it reveals the current state you are in. Some even call the voice a window into your soul—and as ethereal as this may sound, recent insights in neurology and psychology suggest that there's something to this belief. In this chapter, I'll discuss the science of arousal and how it affects our sense of safety. Then I'll explain why this arousal comes through in your communication—for which your voice is only one medium—and how you can develop a conscious awareness of this process.

2.1. The Polyvagal Theory

The first thing you should understand is this: The idea that the mind and body are separate is out of step with modern science. All of our personal experiences and means of expressions are complex interactions between mind, brain, nervous system and body—which are all parts of one system.

This means our psychological, physical, and behavioral responses are all dependent on our physiological state. This is the basic argument of Stephen W. Porges' polyvagal theory. According to Porges, a psychiatrist and neuroscientist, the state of the body has a major impact on the brain's processes, whereas the impact is lesser in reverse, going from the brain to the other organs in the body. Moreover, the polyvagal theory explains how risk and threat can make your physiological system shift out of a state of safety into one of defense.

This concept of safety is at the core of Porges' work. His most important message is that feeling safe is emphatically *not* just about the absence of threat; it is about being able to engage socially. Our sense of safety, therefore, depends on cues we get from our environment and relationships—mostly facial and bodily expressions and tone of voice. If the rhythm and intonation of our voice communicates safety, others are drawn to connect with us and listen to us. Our bodies are processing this type of information constantly, but mostly subconsciously. As we interact with others, we learn who we can trust and who might be a threat. If the cues we get are friendly and positive, our defense system gets deactivated. We detect that we are safe, and this makes us able to engage with others in a relaxing way. Only when our nervous systems detect that we are safe are our bodies able to restore themselves and generate health, creativity, and positive feelings.

The conditions required to feel safe, Porges continues, vary significantly among individual humans. Some people are fortunate enough to have defense systems that don't under- or overreact. But if you look at modern society and how people behave and interact with each other, you have to conclude that there are a considerable number of people whose defense systems are always slightly active. That means they lack an overall sense of safety in their environment or their relationships—and this in turn gets expressed to the outside world through their behavior and their voice. People who don't feel safe are constantly judging and evaluating their environment. This means they can come across as anxious or defensive.

Many voice problems are a sign of such chronically active defense systems. They are induced by ongoing stress; often, however, a person is not consciously aware of this stress. It is worth knowing that your body's slightest sense of unsafety can change your voice, even if you are not consciously feeling unsafe.

Let me illustrate this by telling you about Lauren, an engineer who was referred for voice coaching by her boss. He observed that during presentations for the board, her voice always lost intonation and became monotonous. Learning voice techniques for intonation would give her the tools to change that, or so he expected. During our sessions, Lauren did indeed benefit from learning voice techniques. However, in our final session, she observed that she had actually been applying some of those intonation techniques in some situations already, and therefore, it didn't seem to be her core challenge. So then why did she lose intonation during board meeting presentations?

As we talked about this, Lauren told me that in front of the board, she always feels she has to be on guard. In her company, there's a gap between the corporate experience of the board and that of the people who work on the floor—which means the board doesn't always understand the decisions the people on the floor make. The questions board members pose to Lauren are often critical, making her feel that she has to defend her decisions. Although she doesn't literally experience the board meetings as threatening, Lauren admitted that she also doesn't feel completely safe there. Her stress system gets activated, and as a result, her speech becomes flat and monotonous.

Experiences like Lauren's show why I talk about the voice as the canary in the coal mine or as a barometer for measuring pressure in our lives. To explain how this works, I'll take you deeper into the polyvagal theory, beginning with how your autonomic nervous system works.

The Autonomic Nervous System

The human nervous system is a complex structure that gathers information from all over the body and uses it to coordinate activity. It has two main parts: the central nervous system and the peripheral nervous system.

The central nervous system controls most of the body and mind. It consists of the brain and the spinal cord, which connect most of the body to the brain via nerve fibers.

The peripheral nervous system, which encompasses all of the nerves outside of the brain and spinal cord, has two distinct subsystems. The first one is called the somatic nervous system, which operates with our conscious volition. This system enables your brain to control your muscles and sends sensory information from your body back to your brain and spinal cord. The second one is the autonomic nervous system (ANS), which works involuntarily. This system—and the fact that it is outside your conscious control—is the most relevant to this topic. Situated in the brainstem, you might know it as the "reptilian brain." The ANS controls processes such as breathing and your heart beat without your conscious effort, carrying on while you are asleep or unconscious. It also helps you scan, interpret and respond to danger cues.

We can break the ANS down further into two more subsystems that help us to read and respond to these cues: the sympathetic and the parasympathetic nervous system.

The Sympathetic Nervous System

When we experience danger, stress, or heavy emotions, the sympathetic branch of our autonomic nervous system gets activated and we enter fight-or-flight mode. This indispensable feature of the body keeps us safe when we are threatened. When we're injured, this system minimizes our pain, prevents our blood from draining, and sends extra blood to our brains and muscles so we can focus and flee from danger. It's like hitting the gas pedal in a car. This is what happened to my body when I was almost robbed in Mexico; it's why I could hold on to my bag and why I didn't feel pain when I hit the pavement, though the next day I could feel my bruises.

There's just one problem with the ANS: It treats every stressful event as equally dangerous. This is especially true for sensitive people. It means that fight-or-flight mode will be activated not only when someone tries to murder you, but also when you have to give a speech at your best friend's wedding. To the ANS, it doesn't matter that in the first situation your life is truly in danger, and in the second situation there is no real threat (apart from the possibility that no one will laugh at your jokes). Stress is stress, and in both these situation your sympathetic nervous system will supply you with all the tools to fight or flee, as if your life depends on it. In fight-or-flight mode, your heart rate and blood pressure rise, you get sweaty palms, and your mouth gets dry.

Our voice reveals this state, too. When we're in fight mode, we become defensive and louder. In flight mode, we either speed up our speech so we can get out of the situation as quickly as possible, or we speak softer, with less diction and intonation, as if we want to disappear. Our breathing gets faster, shallower, and higher in the chest.

The Parasympathetic Nervous System

Along with the sympathetic nervous system—that is, the gas pedal—the ANS has a second mode that can get activated. This is the parasympathetic nervous system, and it functions as the brake. This system activates after stress or danger have disappeared—for instance, when the speech at your best friend's wedding is safely behind you. The parasympathetic nervous system stimulates relaxation and restoration. It now sends your organs messages that your heart rate and breathing can slow down. Your muscles relax, your veins get wider, and your digestive system is activated. Your emotions become calmer, too. You become more open to social engagement, and your voice no longer sounds strained.

In parasympathetic mode, the nervous system tells our lungs that it is now safe to start breathing slower and deeper again, into the lower lobes of the lungs. This even works bidirectionally, as a feedback loop: By deliberately breathing deep, low, and slow, we activate the parasympathetic nervous system. Have you ever felt that it's relaxing to take slow and deep breaths? Here you have it. The deeper and more softly we inhale and the slower we exhale, the more our heart rate slows down and the calmer we get. During sleep, the parasympathetic system is switched on automatically. People who always seem to take short, fast breaths into the chest when they are awake magically switch to slower belly breathing when they are asleep.

This is all happening because of the vagus nerve. This very long cranial nerve is the main component of the parasympathetic nervous system, and its branches go all the way from the brain stem to the abdomen. It connects with the nerves in the face, neck and throat, and travels down through the heart, lungs and bowel system. There are two branches to this vagus nerve: the dorsal, which runs down the back of our bodies, and the ventral, which runs down the front. These two branches have the widest distribution of any of our nerves, facilitating bidirectional travel of sensory information: Bodily sensations influence the brain (and consequently how we respond to our environment), and brain processes influence our internal organs. For instance, the vagus nerve sends messages to the heart and the lungs to regulate the heartbeat and the depth and pace of breathing. This activity is referred to as *vagal tone*. You're probably familiar with how your breathing pattern changes depending on whether you're stressed or relaxed, but did you know that the vagus nerve also directly affects your throat? It controls the muscles around the voice box. Whenever we get nervous, the muscles in our throats tighten, making our voices sound strained.

So that's a basic explanation of the ANS—but only that. As it turns out, the metaphor of the gas pedal and the break is a bit simplistic. For instance, according to the polyvagal theory, the parasympathetic nervous system can also get activated by danger cues. And this slightly more complicated understanding matters when we're working on our voices, as I'll explain next.

Detecting Threats and Safety Without Awareness

In the polyvagal theory, *neuroception* refers to the subconscious process by which our ANS detects signs of threat or safety. It responds to cues both from within our bodies and from our environment, including our interactions with others. Since our ANS carries out this detection, it is involuntary; we are not even aware it's happening.

In this process, both branches of our vagus nerve can be stimulated to activate the parasympathetic nervous system—and each responds differently. The ventral branch of the vagus nerve responds to cues of safety in our environment and interactions. It thereby supports feelings of physical safety and secure emotional connection to others in our social environment.

The dorsal branch of the vagus also activates the parasympathetic nervous system, but in a totally different way than the ventral branch. This is where it gets complicated. The dorsal branch doesn't respond to cues of safety, but to cues of danger, just like the sympathetic nervous system. When you are in danger, your ANS initially activates a sympathetic response—fight or flight. When you cannot fight or flee, however, your nervous system might then freeze instead. Freezing is the result of a parasympathetic response from the dorsal branch. In this state, you are pulled away from connection, out of awareness, and into a state of self-protection, like blackout, collapse, or shutdown. If you have ever experienced a threatening situation that left you feeling frozen or dissociated, this indicates that your dorsal vagal system has taken over.

Three Developmental Stages of Response

Until recently, scientists thought that the ANS had two response modes: the parasympathetic nervous system's sense of safety or the sympathetic nervous system's fight-or-flight. In the polyvagal theory, however, Porges describes an ANS with three stages that may have developed as animals evolved from reptiles to mammals. Rather than being binary, these three stages represent a spectrum from safe to unsafe (or from comfortable to uncomfortable, which your body treats as the same thing). They also form a hierarchy of evolutionary stages, as follows.[3]

Social Engagement–Ventral Vagal Response

This part of the parasympathetic nervous system readies us for social engagement by making us feel playful, curious, creative, flexible, resourceful, and connected to our surroundings. This response comes from the ventral branch, which is the most evolutionarily recent side of the vagus nerve. This nerve pathway—which developed as we evolved from reptiles into mammals—controls

---

3   The hierarchy of responses as a result of evolution from reptiles to mammals is not supported by scientific research, and this part of the theory is considered unfounded from a social neuroscience perspective. This, however, has no impact on the clinical utility of the theory, which practitioners recognize as a valuable framework that illustrates how body and mind are one system. According to psychiatrist Dr. Bessel van der Kolk, the polyvagal theory looks beyond the effect of fight-or-flight responses and reinforces the importance of safety and social relationships for overall well-being. It thereby gives us a better understanding of trauma and offers a new approach to healing from it.

The Autonomic Nervous System's Three Stages of Response

REGULATED
RESPONSE MODES
Activated by cues of **safety:**

VENTRAL VAGAL (parasympathic nervous system)	**SOCIAL ENGAGEMENT** Playfulness Resourcefulness Creativity Connection Flexibility Peacefulness Being Mindful Curiousity		

DYSREGULATED
RESPONSE MODES
Activated by cues of **danger:**

SYMPATHETIC	**MOBILIZATION** Excitement Focus Intensity Energy	**FIGHT** *OR* **FLIGHT** Irritation Worry Frustration Anxiety Anger Panic Rage Fear	
DORSAL VAGAL (parasympathic nervous system)	**RECHARGING** Restore Rest Digest Conservation of Energy	**FREEZE** Helplessness Withdrawal Lethargy Immobilization Numbness Dissociation Burnout Depression	

muscles in the throat, the face, and the head. It thereby enables us to detect the affective states of individuals within our species (as other mammals can do within theirs). This is how facial expression, listening, and vocalizing became integrated with the parasympathetic nervous system. Functionally, this integrated connection enabled animals to distinguish members of their species who were expressing cues of safety from those expressing cues of danger. As human beings, it provides us with the ability to signal whether we can make physical contact and create social relationships with other human beings and to interpret how they feel. Imagine your voice while you're talking to your best friend about your holiday over coffee. When you're open, relaxed and comfortable, you'll probably use rhythmic, melodic speech.

Fight-or-Flight–Sympathetic Response

The sympathetic nervous system regulates our heart rate and blood flow. When feeling safe, it mobilizes us to act, move, and meet the demands of the day. It makes us feel excited, energized and focused. The system also helps us respond when we detect danger cues. This causes both fight reactions like rage, anger and aggression, and flight reactions like panic and fear. The sympathetic system can, however, operate in a dysregulated fashion as well, interpreting cues that are not really threatening as dangerous. In these instances, it manifests in feelings of irritation, frustration, stress, chaos, anxiety, and worry. When you suddenly find yourself speeding up and your voice becoming high-pitched during a presentation, this is your body activating a flight response. The polyvagal theory suggests that this pathway was the next to develop in the evolutionary hierarchy.

Freeze–Dorsal Vagal Response

In daily life, this part of the parasympathetic nervous system enables us to restore, rest, digest, and conserve energy when we need to. When this system picks up cues of danger and it's not possible to fight or flee, it causes us to immobilize: freeze, faint, dissociate, collapse, or shut down. This response comes from the vagus nerve's most ancient branch, known as the dorsal branch. Reptiles readily switch into this state when they detect danger, slowing down their heart and breathing rates. Mammals have this capacity as well: Imagine a mouse that has just been caught by cat. It's likely to be "playing dead" between her jaws—an involuntary response triggered by the dorsal vagal system. Like the sympathetic, this response can also be activated in situations that aren't actually life-threatening and operate in dysregulation. This manifests in feelings of helplessness, withdrawal, numbness, depression, and lethargy. Have you ever draw a blank in front of an audience? This is a common example of your voice in freeze response. The dorsal vagal response also activates to protect the body from exhaustion when the sympathetic response has been active for too long. The most common example of this is what can happen to us after we've been continuously exposed to stress or anxiousness: burnout.

The Problem with Regulating the ANS

We need all three of these stages of response to function in life and keep ourselves safe from real, acute danger. Problems, however, occur when your ANS fails to appropriately recognize cues of safety. When there is no acute danger, *fight, flight, or freeze* disables social engagement and takes over your system unnecessarily. To address this problem, we should be aware of three important things about how these systems function.

First, the stage activated by the ANS in a given situation depends on the individual, *not* the situation. For example, imagine you're being interviewed on the radio and the interviewer comes up with a question that you are completely unprepared to answer. How do you think you would respond? Some people would stay socially engaged and trust in their smarts to talk their way out of the painful situation. In other people, this will trigger fight-or-flight behavior, resulting in a slightly more defensive tone of voice or faster speech with a higher pitch. Others may even freeze, totally shutting down and drawing a blank. It's just an interview, as your mind knows very well, but your body can still interpret it as a life-or-death situation. A given individual's response depends on his physical and environmental contexts, like the sensitivity of his nervous system and whether or not he has a history of trauma.

Second, the activation of these stages is involuntary. You cannot control an autonomic response consciously, the way you control your central nervous system. Consequently, it doesn't make sense to blame yourself for being in sympathetic or dorsal vagal response mode. When either of these activate, your body is trying to keep you safe, whether you agree with it or not. Within the body, the ANS bypasses the mind, overruling your voluntary cognitive functions.

Finally, it's worth noting that while 80% of your nerves send sensory information from the body to the brain via the ANS, only 20% of your nerves send sensory information from the brain to the body. This means that it is much easier to manipulate your mental condition through your body than it is to control your body with your mind.

As a result, it's pointless to tell yourself to calm down when you are nervous before an important performance. If you are unable to regulate your bodily state via your ANS, then you'll have difficulty accessing and processing higher cognitive functions. The brainstem doesn't defer to the mental reasoning of the prefrontal cortex. Cognitive therapies can work very well for the treatment of problems with thoughts and beliefs, which are connected more to the cortical and limbic systems in your brain. But—as I came to realize through my work with my clients and myself—since the ANS functions independently from your conscious mind, cognitive therapies usually will not help you to regulate emotions and your bodily state.

So what *can* we do to regulate those things? According to the polyvagal theory, bodily states react to bodily states. This means that we can regulate our ANS with our own body. Even more strikingly, we can also help regulate the bodily states of others. In fact, we predominantly co-regulate our bodily state with those around us in many ways: by the way we look at each other, searching for eye contact or avoiding it; through our posture, whether it's open and relaxed or tense and closed; through our voice, with intonation, vocalization, and rhythm; and how we breathe, whether high and shallow in the chest or deep and slow from the belly. These are all cues that communicate our physiological state to others, and we get the same cues from others. These signals regulate our ANS and make us feel safe or threatened in the company of others. According to Deb Dana, the clinical therapist who translated Porges' theory to clinical practice, co-regulation is the foundation for building self-regulation. This is because, as human beings, we are dependent on our caregivers for safety for a very long time, before we are able to navigate the world independently. She stresses that only when we have sufficient experiences of safe co-regulation are we able to self-regulate effectively.

The Significance of Face-to-Face Interaction

As we've seen, the ANS sometimes interprets the environment as unsafe, even when there is no real threat or danger. Cues for unsafety can be a sharp tone of voice, a certain smell, bad lighting, or a continuous low sound in the background. This happens to people with a highly sensitive nervous system, including (but not limited to) those with autism or a history of trauma. It also applies to people who tend to avoid new experiences and unwelcome emotions. As a reaction to these cues, the ANS then unnecessarily activates fight, flight, or even freeze, in safe situations. As a consequence, a gut feeling may tell you to withdraw from social activity.

Dana says that for traumatized people, social engagement initially might feel unsafe, and co-regulation can be a terrifying experience in the beginning. When you're in such a state, you'll probably want to withdraw from others—but in fact, it's at moments like this when you would especially benefit from social engagement! By nature, humans are deeply social beings. It's thanks to our social abilities that our species now dominates planet Earth.

Here's how the cycle gets going: When we feel a desire to withdraw, our minds tend to interpret cues from the ANS in a certain way. We make up cognitive narratives to explain why we don't want to interact with others. We might say that we don't 'click' with someone—that we don't like him, or even that we don't trust him. We might tell ourselves a story about how we prefer to be alone, that we just don't enjoy events like birthday parties. We like to think of ourselves as 'independent'.

The thing is, the more we avoid social contact, the less we are able to co-regulate our bodily state with others—and the harder it will be for us to start interacting with people again. It's a downward spiral leading to social anxiety. That's why, *especially* if you have a tendency for social anxiety, it's important to stay socially connected despite your impulse to withdraw. Engaged connection with other people is supposed to make you feel calm, safe, and maybe even loved and trustful.

In today's society, however, human interaction—face-to-face or over the phone—is gradually being replaced by technological alternatives. Even if there had been no pandemic, we increasingly buy all of our things online, without interaction with a real person. If something is wrong with the product, we often can only approach customer care via a chat window, where our questions are answered by a bot instead of a human being. It seems that children spend more time playing games on their iPads than running around with their peers. And overall, people seem to prefer communicating through email for business, and through chat and dating apps for personal matters. If we do interact with humans face-to-face, we prefer to do so with the people we already know. In many places around the world, talking to strangers on the street, on public transport, and in bars, cafes, and clubs, is far less common now than it used to be only decades ago.

Connectivity is easier to establish than *connection*. We can't take face-to-face contact—including *vocal* contact—for granted the way we used to, especially in interactions with strangers. In today's digitally-focused narrative, truly social behavior is not treated as supportive, but disruptive. If this trend continues, it is my guess that a growing number of people will develop social anxiety, losing their ability to activate their social engagement system by co-regulating in the presence of others. As a result, they will withdraw even more from social activity.

Fortunately, there is an alternative: We can relearn the value of real human interaction—and the role our voice plays in all of this. I'll repeat once again, that feeling safe depends on cues we get from others, such as facial and bodily expression, and tone of voice.

Now let's talk about *how* the voice and body language interplay with other means of expression and your inner world in face-to-face communication.

2.2. Four Means of Expression

When we communicate verbally with others, the *voice* is only one of four means by which we express ourselves. The others are the *words* we speak, *body language*, and *attention*.

Voice

The vocal folds are folds of tissue in the throat that enable us to make that particular, complex range of sounds we call the voice. The voice is not the same as spoken language, however. We can use our voice to convey language, but we can also use it to express ourselves in ways that are outside that culturally structured system. In fact, this is the first thing a newborn baby does when he enters the world: he expresses himself vocally through crying. Moreover, our voice can communicate information beyond the content of the words we speak through subtle cues about intention and emotion. These are hard to get across in written language, demonstrating the additional power of the voice. Take, for example, a sentence like "Wow, that's really interesting". You can say this with a tone of voice that communicates sincere interest or one that communicates sarcasm. Just like body language, the voice conveys cues of threat and safety, and contributes to co-regulating each other's nervous systems.

Spoken Language/Choice of Words

Spoken language is a structured system of communication. It is a cognitive ability—an aspect of the mind. Unlike body language, which is a subconscious expression of our sense of threat or safety, spoken language is a cultural tool that we actively have to learn. Through the words we choose, we communicate information not only about our environment, but also our feelings, thoughts, desires, and ideas. We do this through a system of auditory symbols produced by our voice. Through spoken language, we can convey to others information about the past and future, and about things that are not present. If I say "cat" to you, you can imagine the animal I am talking about without it being in front of you.

Body Language

Body language is all of the nonverbal signals that we use to communicate with others, including facial expressions, gestures, and other postural signals. Animals depend on body language for most of their communication—and we too are animals. Although we've developed spoken language, body language still makes up a great deal of the signals we convey to others and detect in turn from them, giving and receiving cues of safety and threat to regulate each other's nervous systems. Imagine two people sitting in front of you, one sitting stiffly, with crossed arms and crossed legs, the other with an open, relaxed posture. Who makes you feel more comfortable? It goes beyond the scope of this book to dive deeper into body language, but Chapter 9 offers tips on how being more present in the body helps the voice.

Attention

Voice, spoken language, and body language obviously belong on this list, but you may ask, what has attention got to do with this? Our authentic voice—that is, that voice that can really connect with people—is most powerful when we're feeling safe and tuned into our intuition, with our attention in the present moment. When our attention is consumed by thoughts or memories, we're not present. Having our attention entirely and intensely in the now means that we're tuned in with our five senses, connected and responsive to what's going on around us. When we achieve this sort of presence, our intuition will give rise to the right words, and our voice and body language will naturally enable us to connect with our audience in an authentic, powerful way.

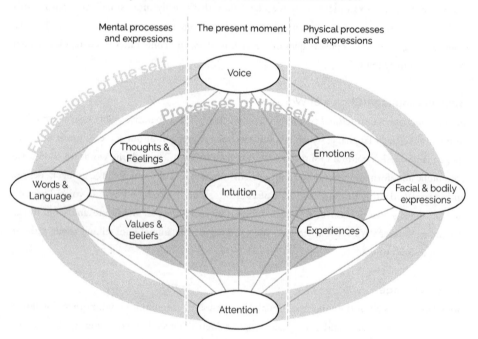

Aspects of the Self in Verbal Communication

What Do We Express?

What exactly is it that we express with these four means of expression? When we say we express *ourselves*, what is this *self*, anyway? When we think about our sense of self, we refer to an ongoing process of experiences, emotions, feelings, thoughts, beliefs, values, and intuition. Let me discuss each one of them briefly with you:

Experiences are all the events from your past that stay with you. Some become memories, but most of the information we retain is unconscious. Your body, however, remembers the way it reacted to these experiences. In that sense, you can say that memories are stored within your body.

Example: "When I was young, people would make fun of me while I was singing."

Emotions are instinctive physical responses that helped early humans survive their harsh environments. We feel emotions consciously after we identify the physical reaction as an emotional concept. Sadness, anger, fear, joy, and disgust are examples of emotional concepts. However, we don't have to be consciously aware of emotions in order for them to influence our thoughts and behavior.

Example: "When people make fun of me, I feel tightness in my chest and throat and I feel sad."

Feelings are the conscious experience of emotions: That is, they are the specific mental translations we make out of our physically felt emotions. This process of translation is individualized, and its product can be quite refined.

Example: "When I sing, I get nervous and uncomfortable."

Thoughts are mental concepts about ourselves and the world around us that come in the form of language, images, ideas, predictions, and fantasies.

Example: "If I sing, people will make fun of me."

Beliefs are particular thoughts that we repeatedly think. Such a thought becomes an assumption we make about the world and ourselves that we hold to be absolutely true.

Example: "I'm the kind of person that is not a good singer."

Values are guiding principles that we intuitively find important to live and act upon. Values guide people's actions and behavior and form their attitudes towards things.

Example: "I find it important to be modest about my ability to sing."

Intuition is a sense of direct knowing without conscious deliberation. It is a semi-conscious coming together of loosely linked facts, concepts, experiences, thoughts, and feelings, so it is at the center of all the other processes.

> *Example: "I don't know why, but I just need to sing."*

The processes and expressions of the self are ever changing, with no fixed elements. Thoughts and feelings are things that you have; they are not what you are. That means you can work with them and learn to regulate them. In my model, all aspects of the self are connected to each other, and they influence each other constantly. Overall, your voice is at its best when you're not dominated by thoughts, feelings, or emotions, but rather, have all these processes dynamically balanced. Since we're human beings, however, this isn't often the case, is it?

Given what we've learned from the polyvagal theory, it shouldn't come as a surprise that all these ongoing processes of the self enter your awareness via both mental and physical sensations. Language, thoughts, feelings, values, and beliefs are cognitive: You become aware of them in your mind. Compare these to facial and bodily expressions, emotions, and previous experiences from your life; we can call these physical functions, since you become aware of them via physical sensations. You're probably familiar with those moments in life when your heart starts racing and your breathing gets shallower. This is how you notice that you're scared or angry—possibly even before you become consciously aware of it.

Experiences from your life also leave traces in your body and can return to your awareness through sense perception. Have you ever experienced how a smell can transport you back to a time and place in your memory? This can be something happy, like the smell of your grandmother's perfume—but it can also be something that triggers another response of your nervous system. One of my clients told me that the sound of a meowing cat always makes him freeze. He discovered that this originated in the moment he had found his father, who had suddenly passed away, lying dead in his armchair. At the moment of discovery, his father's cat had been meowing. Trauma gives us a powerful illustration of the connection between memory and the physical body. In a split second, a certain sound or sight can send a trauma survivor back to the physical experience of their trauma, bypassing the conscious mind.

2.3. How You Can Regulate Your Nervous System

Although there's no such thing as a quick fix for nerves or anxiety, there are some things you can do to calm your nervous system and activate its ventral vagal response mode when you're feeling stressed or anxious. Dana says that, first, you must recognize the response state you are in. Are you in fight, flight, freeze, or social engagement? What are the signs from inside your body that give you information about this state? How do you feel, what do you think, and how do you behave? It's also helpful to be able to recognize these response states in others. In voice coaching, for instance, I'm attuned to body posture, facial expression, language, and of course, the voice, especially when I meet someone for the first time. If someone makes a restless impression, speaks quickly and unclearly, doesn't finish her sentences, and is uncomfortable with silence, this is an indication of sympathetic response mode. If someone is not emotionally expressive, lacking facial expression and intonation in the voice, I know this could be related to dorsal vagal response mode.

The second step in Dana's process is to identify our particular cues of danger and resolve them. To give you some idea of what cues of danger might look like, I'll share some of mine: being cold, places that are dirty, too dark or too bright, and people who disconnect or withdraw without explanation.

Simultaneously, we must identify our cues of safety and actively invite them into our lives. Here are some of mine: sunlight, being warm and comfortable on the couch with a blanket, adjusting the lighting, the smell of coffee beans, drinking and holding a warm cup of tea, seeing a smiling face, hugging someone, connecting with friends, cuddling animals, listening to music, watching penguins, or walking in nature.

If we can resolve our danger cues and invite safety cues into our lives, this will help us to regulate our nervous system. What are your particular, personal cues for safety? For those who find it hard to identify them, therapist and psychiatric nurse Lia Jaeqx suggests that the following activities are generally safety cues for most people:

- Eating or drinking
- Shaking all parts of your body to loosen up
- Focusing on sensory experience instead of the content of your mind
- Being playful, laughing, and having fun
- Dancing slowly; moving your body from side to side as if you are being cradled
- Social contact such as hugging, cuddling, or eye contact
- When you are in freeze state, just see if you can move. If this seems hard or impossible, wiggle your toes and see where that takes you

Now I would like to highlight some other activities that activate ventral vagal response mode and that are related to the voice.

Singing

Have you ever experienced how singing with a group of people can make you feel powerfully connected to each other? That's because one of the best ways to regulate your nervous system is to sing. When you sing, you use breath control: You vocalize as you exhale air and extend your exhalation. This slow, controlled exhalation triggers your ventral vagal nerve's calming effect on your heart, throat, and voice box. On top of that, you actively use the muscles in your face and mouth to enhance pronunciation and intonation. These practices will reduce your stress levels and makes you feel calmer. Add in a group to sing with—to co-regulate each singer's nervous system—and you have the best possible neural exercise. If you prefer, playing in a wind ensemble will have a similar effect.

Breathing

If you'd rather not sing, breathing exercises are also a great way to regulate your nervous system. In this book, I devote Chapter 8 to the breath and its interactions with your voice and ANS.

Listening

Your ears are another tool for regulating your nervous system, as listening plays a central role in detecting cues of threats and safety. When you listen to someone who has an engaging, rhythmic, and melodic voice, she makes you feel comfortable. You become interested in what she is saying and want to interact with her. Her voice calms you down, and your sense of safety is switched on by her ventral vagal response mode. In return, you use more melody in your voice as well. This way, you both activate each other's ventral vagal response modes. Similarly, you're probably less interested in getting to know someone who speaks in a monotonous voice, without rhythm and in short sentences. Her voice gives you cues that she doesn't feel safe, so intuitively, you don't want to get close to her.

Given the power of these voice cues, listening to a podcast by someone with a pleasant voice can actually help you when you feel stressed or anxious. It could help you for the same reason that babies are more likely to fall asleep when people are softly chatting in the background. Personally, I enjoy falling asleep on the couch with the TV still on, preferably listening to a calming voice like that of the BBC's David Attenborough. (You can be sure that award-winning broadcasters like Attenborough have mastered the art of the voice!) It's worth adding that even when it doesn't include a human voice singing, music can also influence your mood and your nervous system. Relaxing, low-tempo music activates your ventral vagal response mode and makes you feel calmer.

Intentionally Activating Sympathetic Response Mode

All this talk of how to calm your nervous system may give the impression that you should always strive to stay relaxed and in ventral vagal response mode. This, however, is not the case. If you have an important task to execute—say, a meeting, presentation or performance coming up—you don't want to feel one hundred percent safe and relaxed. You need to focus—and mobilize! To meet that goal, you need the alertness that comes from the right amount of healthy stress. That means you want to activate your sympathetic nervous system just enough to prepare for your performance.

So if you want to become more focused and alert, how can you allow a little more sympathetic energy in a regulated way? Here are a few things to try:

- Listening to energetic, high-tempo music
- Refraining from food or drink

- Jumping, running, or fast and energetic dancing
- Playing sports or working out
- Taking a few fast and shallow breaths in the chest

Generally speaking, to mobilize your nervous system, you do the opposite of what's needed to calm it. In order to prepare herself before a presentation, Jaeqx says she always goes for a walk with her dogs with energetic music on her headphones, dancing along with it.

Intuitively, you probably already use some of these tactics to regulate your nervous system when you feel the need. You've probably also noticed that moving your body is a recurring theme here. That's because while you are in sympathetic response mode (whether intentionally or not), your body is releasing cortisol and adrenaline to build up energy for fight or flight. If your conscious mind has no intention to fight or flee—for instance, during a performance—you'll still have this energy excess in your body. If you don't release it, your muscles will tighten, making you feel tenser. Movement is the most natural way for your body to expend that energy. When you have an important meeting, presentation, or performance, you'll do your nervous system a big favor if you use gestures and keep your body gently moving. This will help you avoid becoming stiff and tight. On the other hand, if you're the type of person who's already all over the place during a performance, then try pacing yourself. Are you able to keep your movement relaxed and gentle on stage? Then, afterwards, engage in physical activity to release energy. Have an energetic work out, or dance all night if you like!

Training for a Balanced Nervous System

I must add one caveat: Some of us should be careful when intentionally activating the sympathetic response. Make sure you don't stay there too long, and be sure that you're always able to go back to ventral vagal response.

How long is too long? That's hard to say, because everybody is different. Highly sensitive people, as well as those with autism or those who have experienced trauma, have delicate nervous systems. They have to be careful in this respect, as their threshold for stress is lower than others'. Their nervous system may already produce a considerable amount of sympathetic energy during the day, or they may need more time to return to ventral vagal response.

This is the case for me as well. In Mexico, after the attempted robbery, I couldn't regulate my system back from sympathetic to ventral vagal. Instead, I even dipped into dorsal vagal, which caused me to have digestion problems and to want to stay on the sofa all day, binge-watching *Friends*. It took my body more than a week for ventral vagal to kick back in again. Like the curandero said, my nervous system was still responding as if it happened yesterday. In the end, it comes down to knowing your body and being aware of the cues it gives you.

Having said that, it's important that you learn to influence your nervous system. It's impossible to avoid stress and setbacks. To become resilient and handle what life throws at you, you need to be prepared to face unpleasant situations and unwelcome emotions from time to time. Those who always try to avoid pain and suffering will have an especially hard time when reality catches up with them. Their nervous system will react to minor negative events as if they are major threats. When you have a small window of tolerance for stress, your system enters fight or flight much quicker than necessary.

It's possible to allow a certain amount of sympathetic energy into your system while the ventral vagal stays in charge. This is called the vagal brake. If you train this vagal brake, you can quickly energize or calm yourself, easily switching between engagement and disengagement. The trick is to combine activities that activate your nervous system with those that calm it. Here are some ideas:

- Listen to a playlist that combines relaxing, low-tempo tracks with energetic, high-tempo tracks
- Go for a run, but take intervals where you walk quietly and mindfully
- Do a workout that combines high impact aerobics with periods of stretching
- Practice breathing exercises that combine fast, shallow breaths with slow, deep ones

By actively and intentionally entering fight-or-flight mode and returning to social engagement shortly after, you'll increase your comfort zone and keep your nervous system flexible. This way, you can influence your body's responses to some extent.

In addition to directly training your nervous system, there are other complementary things you can do to build psychological flexibility. For instance, you might change your daily routines, take a different route to work, start a conversation with a stranger on the bus, order a dish you've never eaten before, go to a party alone—anything to engage in a new experience. You can also sing along to your favorite songs and alternate between slow, relaxing music and fast, upbeat music. The possibilities are endless!

The polyvagal theory makes clear how our bodies, more than our minds, determine how we feel. Posture, facial expression, and vocal expression play a key role in relationships with others—how *they* make *us* feel and how *we* make *them* feel. These cues convey a huge amount of subtle but essential information about our state of being—in ways that we often fail to realize. The quality of your voice is about so much more than coming across as engaging, decisive, or persuasive. It is the key to intimate, honest connection to your fellow human beings. And this connection with others is your key to feeling safe.

3. Personal Growth

Consider this observation of Brian W. Hands, a Canadian ear, nose, and throat (ENT) doctor who specializes in vocal problems: "In my experience, over eighty-five percent of voice problems experienced by singers and actors and other voice users, whether amateur or professional, have no basis in any obvious disease of the vocal cords. [...] Rather, they are often related in some way to stress and poor breathing, which in turn relate to anxiety, depression, and spiritual crisis."[4]

As a voice coach, I have worked with hundreds of people. I've also struggled with my own voice. This has given me a similar insight: A request for help about the voice is not just about the voice. It is often about someone's personal inner world and emotional development. Your voice is a barometer, indicating when something is out of balance in another area of your life. Indeed, a vocal problem can be a symptom of inner conflict: opposing values resulting from complex, conflicting emotions. It's an invitation to confront a part of yourself that you're hiding—to start living according to your own values. In this way, the voice can be a catalyst and a guide in your development process.

We tend to label the events that happen in our lives as "good" or "bad." We want to avoid the bad ones at all costs, while we welcome the good ones wholeheartedly—we can't have enough of them. But no matter how cautious and sensible we are, from time to time we are all confronted with setbacks that seem to stand in the way of how we think life should be. We might fail to live up to our own expectations; we might be disappointed in how others treat us; or we might just have to face those unfortunate events in life that just "happen" to us without a perpetrator. This can feel unfair, unjust, or useless. Most of us will try to avoid the related pain, anxiety, and unwelcome feelings by fighting against them. But does this really improve the quality of our lives? Many find that a life spent avoiding risk, pain, and suffering at any cost is boring and uninspiring.

But what's the alternative? Perhaps the struggles and setbacks we encounter in life are neither bad luck nor unfair. They might offer us new opportunities: to learn about ourselves, to become increasingly self-aware, and to find purpose. If we frame it that way, we're more likely to experience feelings of happiness and sorrow as meaningful, in the sense that all our life events, good and bad, provide opportunities for development.

I would now like to share some personal episodes about my voice and creativity and how they have interplayed with my personal development process. It is a story about vulnerability and the need for safety, but also about emotional development and inner transformation. Along the way,

---

4   B.W. Hands, MD *Finding Your Voice – A Voice Doctor's Holistic Guide For Voice Users, Teachers And Therapists* (2009, BPS Book, Toronto) p. 25.

I will introduce you to Kazimierz Dąbrowski's theory of positive disintegration. This theory contributed a great deal to my understanding of my own development, and I believe it will help others to make sense of complex episodes in their lives, too.

3.1. Struggling to Adapt to Society... Seeking Acceptance

As I wrote in Chapter 1, when I was a small child, I felt completely free to express myself. I could sing and dance without worrying whether it was good enough or what others thought of me.

But around the age of fourteen, things changed. I became extremely aware of how others viewed me. I remember the moment when I realized this change: It was the school performance I wrote about in Chapter 1, where I drew a blank and sang with a shivering voice. I had become sensitive to the judgments of others. From that moment on, public failure was the worst thing that could happen to me.

To fight this discomfort, I sought to prove myself to others. Unfortunately, in the first couple of years of high school, I was intensely lonely. I had no deep friendships; and although occasionally other children welcomed me as a friend, these friendships could suddenly collapse, leaving me puzzled about what had happened. Looking back, I think I was trying so hard to fit in and seek approval that others got annoyed by it.

Something else happened to me in those years, though: I developed a strong drive to express myself creatively through music. I had absolutely no clue that people could actually like me for the person I am; I thought they would only like me if I displayed a special skill or gift. So I used my musical skills to draw attention to myself. I sang, accompanied myself on the piano, and started to write songs. This made me somewhat less anonymous at school, but it didn't lead to more connection or any new friends. I now realize that by making music, I mainly wanted to get attention and recognition from others—to be seen. That strategy did not always work, and I was often disappointed.

Meanwhile, my fear of failure was growing. You'll recall that I struggled with stage fright at this time. When I did face an audience, I developed a clever coping mechanism: to deal with stress symptoms like shallow breathing, a tight throat and a trembling voice, I would dissociate from my body and became a "singing head." I was able to successfully suppress my stress symptoms so they didn't sabotage my performances to the extent they had before. Technically, I was now in control. I was singing correctly and hitting all the right notes. But to do so, I had to sacrifice a certain amount of emotional expression. I lost contact with my body—and that, as I would later realize, meant that I could no longer connect with the emotions and intuitions that give singers the extraordinary ability to move an audience—to touch them on a deeper level. I was too concerned with making no mistakes and trying to meet other people's expectations. At the time, my desire to perform was extrinsically motivated, driven by the desire for recognition.

Still, this coping mechanism gave me more confidence as a singer. I had a strong desire to follow the traditional path in music through formal education, so I decided to audition for the conservatory.

I started my music education at Codarts, the conservatory in Rotterdam, with a focus on jazz singing. I was highly motivated to work hard and get the most out of my education. Unfortunately, I didn't click with the singing teacher that was assigned to me. Singing class didn't feel like a safe place where I was free to try, explore, and fail. It felt more like an ongoing audition where I had to prove myself worthy of admission over and over. My voice reflected that. In class, my singing never sounded as easy and relaxed as it did at home. My teacher always had loads of criticism: *You sing too high. You sound too thin. This music does not suit you. You should sing this instead.* Looking back, she was probably trying to challenge me, or to toughen me up a little. If it was the latter, it was a dismal failure. My sympathetic response mode went into overdrive, and I failed the course. After one year, I had to leave the school.

But I didn't want to give up. I tried to reinvent my singing entirely, switching from jazz to classical because I thought it suited my voice better. That meant I had to start from scratch with my training—and this time, I did so with a teacher who offered me safety and encouragement. Her class left me feeling confident and energized instead of insecure and drained. So I gave performance training another shot, this time at the University of Bristol in the United Kingdom. Here, however, I met a new set of problems: a curriculum that was too advanced; culture shock; failure to connect with the other students. And this time, my singing teacher was preoccupied, taking maternity leave a couple weeks before my final exam.

In the face of all these stressors, I once again failed my performance major and returned to Amsterdam. Looking for some other form of music education that could suit me, I enrolled in a BA/MA in musicology. This was a theoretical music course—and here, finally, I passed with flying colors. I recall what a tremendous relief it was to have finally succeeded—and to be able to participate in the world as it is, as a "normal person"—that is, a person who happily enrolled in university after high school and enjoyed student life.

It was at this point that my creative drive faded into the background. I no longer saw myself as creative person. The big dreams and the ambition to be a professional singer were gone. Instead, I invested my energies in developing a social life. Finally, now that I had become a respectable, successful, normal person, I could relax and have fun. This allowed me to develop my social skills, and it became easier for me to make friends. After my studies, I was fortunate enough to find jobs in public broadcasting and later at the renowned Concertgebouw, a concert hall in Amsterdam. At that time, I was convinced that this type of life was the highest possible one for me, given my abilities.

3.2. Discovering My Voice... and Its Vulnerabilities

But I never stopped singing for my own enjoyment. I still wanted to master my voice, even if it was now for my own sake and not to pursue a profession. So I continued my training. I worked with teachers I chose, with whom I got along well. I sang in choirs. I started to sing solo in public again. By the time I was thirty, I was getting some paid gigs as a classical performer.

Still, there was still something off about my voice. There was always something in the way that prevented me from sounding the way I wanted: nerves, sleep deprivation, hay fever, colds, too much mucus production—I could go on and on.

There was one experience in particular where these problems caught up with me: it was when I had a gig singing arias while floating on water in a dress made out of umbrellas. This was the Floating Diva, a collaboration I undertook with a costume designer when we were both trying to build our careers.

That involved performing and preparing outside most of the time, often under less than ideal Dutch weather conditions with wind, rain, and cold. Additionally, the street theater festivals that invited us didn't always offer the hospitality facilities that musicians need in order to prepare themselves for their performance. Dressing rooms—if there were any at all—were often big, crowded tents for everybody at the same time. Most of the time there was no space where I could retreat alone half an hour before the show to quietly warm up my voice, breathe slowly, and focus on my performance. I often changed my costume and warmed up my voice in cars. On top of that, we often had to leave very early in the morning to get the installation for the umbrella dress out of storage. I had to drive to the location and set up the umbrella construction long before the festival started. If my performance was scheduled in the evening, by then, I would be way over my energy peak for the day. Since we performed at different outdoor locations, we were often confronted with unexpected logistical problems that led to uncertainty or even panic, and didn't get solved until minutes before my performance. During especially stressful circumstances, when an important show was coming up or when I had to perform under bad conditions, my voice sometimes completely let me down. I sounded thin and tense, and I failed to reach my high notes.

One day, we were invited to Oerol, one of the preeminent Dutch theater festivals. In the build-up to this event, things were really chaotic. My voice became seriously strained. I knew I would not be able to give a good performance, and I thought about canceling. But my partner convinced me to go—this was, after all, such an important opportunity for our careers.

On the morning of our first performance day, I sat down in my hotel room—I'd negotiated to have it, since performers were otherwise supposed to sleep in tents at the camp site—trying to calm an impending panic attack. I knew I really should have canceled, but now it was too late. I was afraid of disappointing my partner and the festival, so I proceeded to sing with a blocked and strained voice.

My performance was on the bad side of average. Vocally, it was boring. I returned from the weekend completely exhausted.

Hindsight is 20/20, as they say. When I look back on my career as the Floating Diva, it's clear to me now how much my voice suffered from these uncertainties. Energy-draining activities like driving, building the set, and fighting for my needs as a classical singer depleted the reserves I needed for my most important professional role. My fear of disappointing people led me to agree to too many demands—which meant I couldn't perform my most important one.

But it took me a long time to realize it. At the time of the festival in Oerol, I had no idea what was happening to me, and nobody knew how to help me. When something like this happened—and by then, it was happening to me quite a lot—my singing teacher focused on improving my technique and regaining control over my voice. That, however, only made things worse.

Finally, at my wits' end, I ended up going to an ENT specialist. He examined my vocal folds, and told me that my vocal instrument was in perfect health. He sent me to a speech therapist. It was there, to my surprise, that I finally got the information I needed. The therapist knew to ask about stressful events in my life. She was the first professional to make a connection between stress and my blocked voice. This might seem like a no-brainer to you, as you knew enough to pick up this book. But at the time, I had not connected the dots, nor had anyone else.

My speech therapist told me that it was extremely important for me to acquire agency over my performance conditions—and to stand up for myself if my needs were not met. For me at the time, this was a radical change in attitude. I was so grateful that people gave me the chance to sing and perform that I was willing to set aside my own well-being. I didn't set clear boundaries. I was so eager to succeed that I did anything anyone asked of me. I believed that working hard, doing what was expected of me, and toughening up would finally reward me with recognition and success. Experience taught me that this is anything but true.

Once that light bulb had clicked on, the speech therapist's advice resonated powerfully with me. Now that I was aware of the link between vocal problems and stress, I felt an urgent need to change my attitude towards performing and take better care of my self. That was when my voice began to improve. While I still struggled with tightness and other stress-related symptoms in my voice—and I certainly was still critical of my performances—at least now I knew what I had to face.

With that realization, I learned to manage the strain in my voice. My performances improved— and I was pleased with what I'd finally achieved in my musical career. A couple years earlier, I would have never imagined that I would be able to have a performance career in the first place.

But, as so often happens in life, it wasn't quite as simple as living happily ever after. Though I'd established myself a performer, I was experiencing a sense of restlessness. "Is this it?" I found myself asking. "Or is there more to get out of life and music?" It's true that I was having a blast. It was *fun!* But fun, as it turns out, isn't enough. My life was lacking meaning and purpose. I understood already that music was my outlet for my energy and emotion. It was also a medium through which I could get in a state of flow and transcend my sense of self when all of the conditions were right. At the time, however, I was not yet able to effectively convey what I wanted to express through the music I made. I thought of myself only as a musical interpreter, not a musical creator, and that didn't feel ultimately satisfying.

Meanwhile, I had always found myself increasingly attracted to the underground creative world. This made me open to new experiences, new adventures, and new people. There I found people who mirrored my feelings of being different from the mainstream. This felt like living a double life:

By day, I worked at a posh, classical concert venue with a side career as a soprano; when night fell, I joined my fellow nonconformists in creativity, nightlife, and drugs. For a long time, being part of this scene did fill that void and tame my restlessness. When this also turned out to be not ultimately satisfying after all, I realized I needed to start yet another chapter in my life. And so, while I felt increasingly comfortable in my classical career, I went looking for more.

3.3. Reconnecting to Creativity…Letting Go of Everything Else

The problem was, I didn't know what this new chapter was supposed to be. For years, I felt only that restlessness; its purpose remained elusive. I found a compass in a book called *The Artist's Way* by Julia Cameron. Through its introspective exercises, I connected again with the activities I enjoyed so much during my childhood—dancing, writing, and making music—and, consequently, with my desire to create. It appears that the games and creative outlets you're drawn to as child reveal a lot about your talents and potential as an adult. If you find it difficult to channel your creative restlessness or discover what you're passionate about in life, you might find answers by looking at your childhood.

I knew that I wanted to experience the freedom in singing that I remembered from my early youth, so I returned to singing pop and soul music. I also started writing songs again. Suddenly, I was back to what I was doing as a teenager, but with a completely different sound. Because of all my classical training, I sounded like a very polished singer. There was nothing wrong with that, but I was looking for something else: that very original sound of the past.

To achieve this, I would have to consciously unlearn a lot of techniques. I had to trust that I would regain my voice if I started to rely on my musical instinct. My classical singing would become increasingly unstable—and I had to accept that. Now I understood that my highly trained, polished voice was in conflict with the free, authentic sound I wanted to explore.

That was how, fifteen years after I gave up songwriting, I rediscovered myself as a creative person. I still felt hesitation: *Can I really do this? Who am I, that I suddenly want to start doing this at age 33?* But in spite of my insecurity, my desire for purpose, creative expression, and new emotional experiences was growing. I was increasingly confident that this new path would serve me well.

So I kept going. Gradually, I was able to more actively direct my creative development, consciously going in the direction I knew I wanted. This time, making music was one hundred percent intrinsically motivated. I struggled; my choices came at a cost, and I was often unsure. Ultimately, however, I was driven to manifest my ideas, and that made it worth all the hesitation and insecurity that came with it. In the end, I surpassed my own expectations and did something I never thought I would ever do: I released a CD with songs I had written and produced myself. It was a milestone in my life. Suddenly, I was a creative musician and not "just a singer" anymore. And it was a milestone not only in my creative and professional life, but in my personal life as well: by becoming a composer and musical artist, I had rewritten my story—and shared that transformation with the world.

This newly discovered meaning and purpose, however, didn't conquer my restlessness. My new path came with new problems, such as the very real need for self-promotion and the incredible amount of energy that it takes. To succeed in this realm, you not only have to perform as much as possible, you also have to manage your online presence. You must show that you're successful, ideally one hundred percent of the time, and spend an awful lot of time finding new gigs. Maybe you recognize a similar pressure towards continuous connectivity in your own life? To some people this comes naturally, but to me it was energy draining. That's how I found myself spending less time writing new music and more time selling myself on social media. My sense of inner tension returned: This was not the creative life as I had pictured it.

Another problem was the reality of how difficult it was to make ends meet in music. Given this reality, my partner, friends, family, and coworkers did not always understand my choices—and I myself often questioned whether I was on the right path. I took a part-time administrative day job for financial security, but—again—I didn't fit in there and I clashed with my boss, just like I had in jobs in the past. I came to recognize that these conflicts erupted when I took on jobs that didn't align with the talents and interests *that were most important to me*. It turns out that I have great organizational skills—but on its own, organizing is not satisfying or meaningful to me.

Moreover, I took on jobs that were beneath my level of competence. At the time, I thought this was the right choice because it would allow me to devote more time to creative projects outside work. These jobs, however, drained my energy. Now I know that I need challenge, diversity, autonomy, and creativity to thrive in my life, even in part-time jobs. In my creative endeavors outside these jobs, I initiated all kinds of projects and collaborations, but often they failed dramatically or caused conflicts. Partners in work recognized my organizational and problem-solving talents and let me solve problems that other people had caused, but I was never in a position where I had agency over the project or could determine the course.

This frustrated me immensely. It was easy for others to take advantage of me and let me do all the dirty work. What was going on? I just wanted to contribute to the world with an average daytime job, make music, initiate some creative projects on the side, and make a modest living out of this. Was that really too much to ask? The fact was, I was still afraid of disappointing others, not aware of my own value, and not standing up for what I needed. So in the end, even in my dreamed-of new creative life, things never worked out the way I had pictured them.

When I hit rock bottom at age 36, I saw that I was stuck in all kinds of unhealthy patterns and dynamics with the people around me. If you have been at such a place yourself, you probably know how this feels: Like you're a lost cause, that there is no way out. I lingered there for a while, but there was a growing feeling inside of me that this was not how my life was supposed to be. This time, I really wanted to find out what was at the core of these unhealthy patterns, and not fall back. So I searched for professional help. The key turned out to be recognizing and living through old pains and emotions, developing more body awareness, and listening to the signs my body gave me about people or situations. I had to learn to stand up for what I find important and what I want to do in life instead of pleasing others and looking for validation—even if that goes against the expectations of society.

And so, listening to what my body was telling me, I realized what I had to do: I said goodbye to my professional career as a classical singer. It was only when I auditioned for a role in an opera that I came to terms with that. The role was clearly a good match for me; however, since I had reestablished my connection with my body, the physical sensations of my stage fright—the ones I had suppressed more or less successfully before—now came roaring back. They manifested in particular when I was singing classical music. So of course, I failed the audition.

The problem I had with classical singing is that the singer is participating in an art form with a long established tradition. That means people have very specific ideas about how the classical voice should sound. There's not a lot of space for exploring your own sound and ideas. In classical singing, I had always felt restricted, walking on eggshells in my fear of being out of sync with the expectations of the establishment. When I realized this, I finally recognized that classical music wasn't the right path for me. The fact that I had devoted half my life to classical training didn't mean that I was supposed to do this forever.

With that, I walked away from my career as a soprano—and the whole classical music scene. I said goodbye to almost all the other collaborations I was involved in at the time, including the Floating Diva. I consciously chose to relinquish my professional identity and financial certainty because I felt I had to give up all the things I invested in so I could make a new start. Everything had to be rebuilt from scratch.

3.4. The Tumultuous Years After Seizing Agency

What followed were a couple of years with many ups and downs leading me to a point of no return. During this time, I got a sense of values like connection, awareness, autonomy, and compassion. It was liberating: For the first time in my life I made choices for myself, not with the expectations of society or some other person in mind. It astonished me that it took until my thirties to discover that I had the ability to create. For years, I thought I couldn't do anything like that, but after clearing some blockages, I recognized my own creative capacity. I was also amazed at how I suddenly managed to change certain bad habits, stop procrastination and avoidance, and develop new habits and routines—without it costing me a lot of effort, because they were one hundred percent intrinsically motivated.

This was also the time when I discovered something called the loop station: a pedal that records and layers musical phrases you sing or play, allowing a solo artist to sound like a whole band. I enthusiastically started to experiment with this new way of composing. As I did so, I resolved to no longer fight for a place in the music industry. From now on, the creative process came first. Suddenly, for the first time in years, I was reconnected with my intuition and a strong sense of self-determination. This led me to make other choices that were less rational and more intuitive.

This also affected the sort of music I created. In my lyrics, I began to address social and spiritual subjects stemming from deep self-reflection and meta-contemplations. My personal process was so intimately connected to what I made at the time that the divergent and changing aspects of my personality resonated through my work. To me, this is the intrinsic value of the creative process. I found out that this music was much closer to my own truth, regardless of whether the mainstream audience connected with it.

And, clearly, they did not. The response was stark. Nobody bought my music anymore. And nobody booked my shows. I'll be honest: At first, this made me feel like a failure. But as I grappled with this reality, I also became aware of my need for validation and recognition from others. I came to see how I was still hoping that music and creativity would fulfill those needs, just like all those years before. When I recognized that old pattern, a light bulb switched on for me—and by its light, I could see my inner compass. Suddenly, it was clear to me: *This is exactly what you have to do now. You don't know yet where this path will take you. Not everyone will understand. It may not bring recognition. But this is the only way. Going back is not an option anymore.* I followed my creative instinct and was no longer concerned with what might or might not be successful. Gradually, I developed a more self-aware, autonomous, and authentic style in singing and composing.

In this results-oriented world, it's not always obvious that the personal creative process has value in its own right. After all, it often fails to demonstrate economic value. Sometimes these two forms of value coincide very nicely; sometimes they do not, or not immediately. That, however, does not negate the value that you, as an individual, get from going through such personal development.

What followed for me were some quiet years with a lot of spare time to spend on myself. In a sense, I really needed to rest from the complex and tumultuous years before. I spent a lot of my time alone, journaling, reading, processing emotions, organizing my thoughts, looking back on the narrative of my life so far, and further restoring my connection with my body and intuition. I did yoga and self-inquiring meditations, and I went for long walks in nature. I was receptive to creative ideas and made lots of music.

Around me, everyone was caught up in work and family life, but I seemed to be temporarily disconnected from this part of society. It's true that I didn't earn much money at that time. What I did have were many meaningful conversations with others who mirrored my process back to me. There were days when I didn't do much except practice contemplation. In the beginning, this bothered me a lot, because I wanted to connect with society so badly. This impulse was no longer about recognition; rather, I now felt a strong urge to contribute to whatever needed to be done. At some point, however, I found complete peace with my situation. There was a growing trust that this quiet stage was part of a process I had to go through, and it was impossible to skip this step. Looking back now, this time—which to the outside world looked like I was doing absolutely nothing—was the most valuable time of my life and absolutely necessary for taking my development to the next level. One of my friends used to say at the time I was practicing the Taoist concept of *wu wei*, which means "effortless action."

I remember one particular moment that contributed to this sense of peace. After a long midday walk in the dunes, I was relaxing with my partner on the couch. Usually, when I was in relaxation mode, I would get caught up in mind wandering. But not this time. I had my attention on my breathing, and after a while I noticed that my thoughts had stopped. This was a completely new experience for me, and it lasted the whole evening until I went to sleep. Of course there have been times before when I was not caught up by my own thoughts, like when I'm focusing on sense perception or performing a task. But this time it was different. This time, my attention was not directed elsewhere. In my head there was just silence and empty space. At first, this experience felt quite awkward, even uncomfortable. In the months that followed, I occasionally had more moments where my thought activity suddenly disappeared—always as a result of complete relaxation combined with body awareness. As I grew more familiar with this empty space, I began to recognize it as a state of peace and trust—a kind of foundation where everything was always well, no matter what was going on around me. Since then, I often actively enter that state through meditation.

3.5. Reconnecting with Society—On My Own Terms

Meanwhile, on the level of voice, I underwent a shift that I could not have foreseen. Without consciously working towards it, my voice sounded truly free for the first time. Suddenly, it had connected with my body, facilitating emotional expression. Playing around with my voice and singing in an improvisational choir, I discovered all kinds of timbres and sounds that I didn't know I had in me. This free voice is still developing. I now sing everything I want—including classical—but in my own way. I always used to need to warm up my voice; now I hardly need to. My sound is stable, balanced, and consistent. External influences don't seem to affect my voice anymore, and I can't remember when was the last time I had a sore throat or a hoarse voice. I never feel limited by my voice now, and I'm not afraid anymore of what others might think of it. My voice also improved because nowadays there is much less negative thought activity going on in my head. Generally, the self-talk in my mind has quieted down substantially. Singing from the present moment, where you're not entangled with your thoughts, is the only right way to do it, as I learned.

After my quiet, contemplative years, I gradually succeeded in reestablishing my connection with society. I was already working as a singing teacher, but after the remarkable vocal changes I experienced in myself, the time was right for the next step. I started to offer voice coaching to non-singers as well. It became clear that my knowledge of vocal technique, combined with my new awareness of how stress, thoughts, and emotions influence the voice, would be valuable to share with all those who struggle with their voice, beyond just singers.

At that point, things began to get even better. Like-minded people who were on the same quest for creative or personal development started to cross my path. For the first time, I became part of an international music making community. There, to my delight, I finally felt like I belonged.

One day, after posting an invitation for one of my voice workshops on LinkedIn, I promptly received a personal message in my inbox from a complete stranger: *What fascinating work you do. And what beautiful websites you have: really committed, positively stimulating and creative. I'm happy to share your workshops!* This piqued my curiosity. Who was this unknown person who had made the effort to write me these kind words, endorsing my work without asking me to return the favor?

This stranger turned out to be Lotte van Lith, who you will have met in the foreword of this book. Surfing around her websites, I found myself fascinated by her work. It was on her website that I first heard the term "positive disintegration."

3.6. Dąbrowski and His Theory

The theory of positive disintegration is a personality theory developed by Dr. Kazimierz Dąbrowski, a psychiatrist who faced a fair share of hardship in the first half of the twentieth century. Born in 1902 in Poland, he witnessed two world wars. As he lived through this tumultuous period and other adversities in his early life, Dąbrowski made two foundational observations. First, he noted that humans may act based on lower or higher motives. Think about how, during World War II, some people betrayed Jews while others helped them, sometimes risking their own lives to do so. Second, he noticed that while some people suffer from traumatic events and never recover, others display a capacity for resilience and even post-traumatic growth. For those with this capacity, the traumatic events lead to a transformation, bringing the person to a new level of functioning in which those higher motives consistently direct their actions. Together with the hardships he encountered in his own life, these experiences laid the foundations of his theory of positive disintegration.

According to Dąbrowski, our internal conflicts are the gateway to multilevel personal growth, and emotions are the forces that drive this process. In moments of difficulty or conflict, we come to recognize our personal values, and we see what this means for the way we want to live. As we start to recognize the lower and higher motives in ourselves, however, we also see that it is not always easy to live according to the higher ones. This gives rise to the psychological upheaval that Dąbrowski called *disintegration*, a process he says is necessary for something new to unfold. This process—which is typically intense—reveals what truly matters to you emotionally, socially, and morally. As we pass through this process, we develop a self-created personality structure. Because this process is ultimately positive, Dąbrowski asserts that we should not try to avoid or eliminate inner conflicts. He also tells us that most people will never experience this inner transformation. According to his theory, whether a person will go through this process is influenced by what he called *overexcitabilities*, *factors of development*, and *dynamisms*. (We will discuss all of these later in this book.)

When I read about this theory for the first time, I felt that I had connected the dots of my personal and vocal development. I recognized that, since my thirties, I had been going through an inevitable process of transformation. I'd found it hard to put this process into words; others around me had not always understood what was going on with me. But here was a Polish psychiatrist who, many years ago, described exactly what I was going through. It was a discovery of tremendous importance. Dąbrowski's work made me feel acknowledged and supported in my process, and affirmed my intuition that I was on the right path. The struggles I encountered in my life were not merely because I'd messed up; they pointed to me a new direction. I no longer looked at my struggles as failures, and gradually became more open and accepting towards the hardships that come with life.

Positive disintegration is a theory about the domain of the self, focusing as it does on emotional development and inner transformation. But that's not all it is. In his paper *How Well Do We Understand Dabrowski's Theory?*, Dąbrowski's collaborator Dr. Michael M. Piechowski notes that "[t]he inner self cannot be healthy without empathic connection with one's fellow human beings and a sense of responsibility for one's place among them."[5] This means that, more than a theory about the self, the theory of positive disintegration is equally a theory about how the self relates to others and to the community on a larger scale—in other words, it is a theory of moral development. Both emotional and moral development happen through disintegrative growth. And these forms of disintegration, as Dąbrowski elaborates, can be *unilevel* or *multilevel*. Later on you'll learn how my disintegration process is connected to my voice, and what this process can mean for your voice.

The Unilevel Process

Unilevel disintegration is a process in which a person does not perceive a higher and a lower response to an inner conflict. If you are at this level, you have no hierarchy of values (which is why it is called "unilevel"). Therefore, you lack a sense of direction: today you do this, tomorrow you do that; today you feel this, tomorrow you feel that. This makes you especially susceptible to social opinion. When you do clash with others, you will worry about what they think of you. Because you haven't yet established your personal values, it is likely that you'll adjust to social norms—that is, those values you took from external sources like your parents, church, government, or other authority. But—unlike a person in an integrated state—you're not consistently so. You have, after all, begun a process of disintegration, so at times you also resist or rebel against those social norms and others' expectations. This leads to restlessness, increased inner conflict and consequently to an unstable voice that reveals that restlessness and inner conflict—like speaking too quickly, softly or monotonously.

In this developmental phase, people often experience their intense and sensitive traits—their overexcitabilities—as a vulnerability or burden. They could be a signal that some previously unknown part of you is coming to the surface, demanding to be acknowledged. If you're at the stage of unilevel disintegration, however, you are probably not yet ready to do this. Consequently, many people do not immediately respond to this call for development and attempt to turn away from the inner restlessness.

I now clearly see which episodes of my life represent the unilevel process: all those times when I was ignoring my vulnerability and sensitivity. Unsuccessfully trying to fit in with society as a "normal person." Searching for approval and recognition through music—first as a classical

---

5   M. M. Piechowski *How Well Do We Understand Dabrowski's Theory?* (2002) p. 177.

singer and later as a pop singer. Desiring control and my resulting frustration when control was impossible. The negative self-talk, stage fright, and blocked voice. My willpower and eagerness to succeed while always having conflicts at work. Lacking purpose. Feeling lost without having any sense of direction. The restlessness. And of course, being drawn to the fringes of society and acting rebellious.

The Multilevel Process

Multilevel disintegration is where the process becomes positive. In this stage, you have come to perceive a higher and a lower course. It's this realization that finally allows your inner conflicts to progress toward resolution, because you are now able to break down your old self and build a new one. This is a huge leap in your developmental process. Through self-reflection, emotional experience, and intense moral conflict, you gain insight into your personal values, along with a sense of what is "more yourself" and "less yourself." Now that part of you that was trying to make itself known can no longer be denied. I experienced this as I rediscovered myself as a songwriter and creative musician. This was clearly "more myself," whereas the classical performer was "less myself." I was ready to start a chapter in my life that was intrinsically motivated. As part of this multilevel process, your behavior comes to be guided by an autonomous hierarchy of values and aims, discovered through your emotions. Along the way, you may feel as if you are at a point of no return.

The inner conflict and intense emotion of multilevel development can be confusing. The reality is that, despite what's happening to you internally, it's still difficult to start living according to your own values. You develop increasing self-awareness and reject the social standards and expectations from your environment that are incompatible with your growing awareness and loyalty to higher values. This leads you to recognize the gap between your life as it is now and what it could be. But because you don't know how to reconcile this gap, you feel what Dąbrowski described as *inferior to yourself*—a very different experience than feeling inferior to others. It's the experience of understanding who you *could* be and recognizing that you're not living up to *that*. For instance, you can feel inferior towards your own voice. You have an idea of how you *could* sound as a speaker or a singer, but realize that you cannot currently live up to your own expectations. So you feel guilty and ashamed about yourself. And this, in turn, increases the intensity of your feelings and furthers the process of positive disintegration.

I too had struggled for years with the gap between my life as it *was* and how I knew it *could be*. Along the way, I discovered that I valued the creative process in itself more than the recognition and economic success I could gain from that creative process. I was following my own creative path and drifted further and further away from success and financial security. At the same time, however, I kept on fighting for my place in the music industry. I couldn't completely let go of the need for recognition and financial safety. I was trying to fit in and stand out at the same time. The fact that I still held on to these old desires made me feel ashamed and disappointed with myself. I knew I had more to contribute to the world than what I was doing back then, but I didn't have the faintest idea yet about what or how. It was necessary for me to reach rock bottom in order to enable a real transformation.

As you progress through multilevel disintegration, however, the inner conflicts decrease. They become less intense and less disruptive because you learn to deal with them in a self-aware and effective way. You come to value everything you encounter in life as a learning experience, even if it's difficult and involves inner conflict. At some point during the multilevel process, you become your own counselor, relying increasingly on your intuition. Others' opinions no longer direct you. To manage your remaining internal conflict, you practice something that Dąbrowski called *autopsychotherapy*. You also develop a process of critical self-evaluation where you are able to look at yourself from an observer's perspective. Moreover, you increasingly perceive others from their own subjective experience. You can imagine yourself in their situations. This process helps you develop a better understanding of yourself and others, so your exclusive bonds of love and friendship become deeper and more enduring.

As you shape your *personality ideal* (to use Dąbrowski's term), you finally manage to turn your values into actions. Purpose and meaning become increasingly important. You take responsibility for your actions and for the well-being of other people. You know what is really important to you. You might even decide to adjust to societal norms—if it is your own, conscious choice to follow them. What has vanished is any desire to conform for the sake of fitting in or out of fear of rejection. Now your values are leading.

3.7. Re-relating to Creativity and Voice

In the years following my positive disintegration, I gradually learned to recognize and value the person I became in this process. Consequently, I need less validation and recognition from others. I developed an inner sense that everything will go as it should if I act from a place of trust. I see the big picture—the context in which all things happen—and I am more willing to accept the hardships I'll encounter. My actions are based on personal values and motives, not on willpower or discipline. The things I do and the people I invite into my life are now a conscious choice. When something feels old and no longer suits me, I let it go.

I'm also less concerned with planning for the future. Sometimes I get an idea of what I want to do, what I want to work towards. But if there isn't anything going on, that's okay too. I experience emotions directly; they are not filtered or hidden away. That doesn't mean, however, that I always respond to them. I look at them and process them; then I move on. If something really touches me, I accept this and go all in on actively processing these emotions. The result of this new self-organization is that, for a couple of years now—and to my surprise—I've felt mostly tranquil, balanced and peaceful. I can be moved by many people, things and situations, but they don't devastate me the way they used to. Occasionally I get irritated, but I don't become angry. I sometimes feel restless or insecure about a situation, but it no longer rises to the level of fear or anxiousness. From a polyvagal theory perspective, I believe this means that my autonomic response modes are much more regulated now, and so is my voice. Except for particularly stressful and intense situations like the attempted robbery, I now generally know how to find my way back to ventral vagal response mode. Stage fright doesn't impact my voice anymore as it did before.

I have, however, experienced something that feels a bit like a trade-off in exchange for this tranquility. In this state of mind, my impulse to sing and create is not as strong as it used to be. I consider it a great achievement that I don't create to gain recognition anymore, but the absence of inner conflict has also caused that force that was driving me to create to dissipate. I don't feel the need to vent my emotions through making music because my emotions are no longer overwhelming. Singing, therefore, doesn't give me the feeling of satisfaction that it used to. Apparently, I now depend less on singing for regulating my nervous system. I don't even identify so much anymore with "being a performer" or "being a musician," and I can feel great for days without having to make music or create something.

At first, I was confused—even worried—by this development. After all, looked at from a certain angle, it feels like I have lost something. As I was trying to figure out about what had happened to my creativity, I came across this passage in Dąbrowski's work:

> The creative instinct, per se, does not usually contain hierarchical, evaluative elements. It is only the coupling of this instinct with other higher level dynamisms that links it with the need to develop an autonomous personality and its ideal. In such circumstances the creative instinct usually becomes "introverted," less "self-confident," less dramatically externalized, less manifested to impress other people. Instead it appears as a more hidden, more dependent, more "modest" factor subordinated to the forces of the growing personality and its ideal and the self-perfection instinct.[6]

Dąbrowski's insight made everything clear. When I reinvented myself as a creative musician, I got the chance to perform, travel, and meet wonderful people from all over the world—people who I would have never met if I wasn't into music. With them, I had profound, life-changing experiences. They made me realize that it's not making music so much as the connection with others that makes these experiences meaningful. It turned out that creativity was not the goal, but the vehicle. As a vehicle for meeting and connecting with others, my musical impulse led me to plenty of peak experiences and opportunities for growth.

I also relate strongly to Dąbrowski's description of the creative instinct becoming more introverted, as that's what happened with my voice. Today, I sing very differently from the way I did a couple of years ago. I've lost the urge to use powerful volume and resonance techniques, as I used to do in classical singing. Now I prefer to sing in a soft, subtle, and soothing fashion. I now see my creative instinct and my voice as tools for my development as a person. They gave rise to some of

---

6   K. Dąbrowski, A. Kawczak and J. Sochanska *The Dynamics of Concepts* (1973, Gryf Publications Ltd. London), p. 26.

my central values—things like connection, awareness, autonomy and compassion. Don't get me wrong: I still enjoy making music very much. But I don't feel a need to sing for self-expression anymore—to release my excess feelings into the Universe.

At this moment of writing, I'm still figuring out what this means. How do I express values like connection, awareness, autonomy, and compassion through music? How can I, through music and voice, contribute to a better world? If you're struggeling with similar questions, know that it is totally fine to not yet have ready-made answers. These things will unfold in time. In 2020, I took my first small steps in that direction. I wrote music for a series of non-conventional guided meditations. I also wrote and produced a song about how we are not taking good care of our Earth. I recorded the song remotely with my fellow musicians in Mexico to stay connected and inspired during the coronavirus lockdown. I decided to donate the proceeds of this song to the Dutch lawsuit against Shell Oil to hold them accountable for climate change. Alongside these musical projects, as a voice coach, I have equipped myself to be of service to others.

Looking back now, I would have never imagined that my voice could have been the canary in the coal mine—a barometer for my emotional state as well as the trigger for personal growth. Currently, my voice feels completely free and unconflicted. Earlier in life, my voice mirrored all my vulnerabilities and my need for recognition and safety. Later on, it developed into a tool to explore and express myself, and to find and shape my identity. By the time I had found that identity, it turned out to not be that important to me anymore. I now feel that my voice and creativity should serve my desire to address things that are larger than myself. I don't know exactly how yet, nor what my next vocal and creative phase will be. But I remain open and look forward to whatever the future brings.

3.8. What TPD Has to Offer for the Time We Live in Now

What sets the theory of positive disintegration (TPD) apart from many other personality theories is its central role for emotions in the process of personality development. In TPD, emotions are considered even more important than cognitive abilities.

In this respect, TPD was ahead of its time. From the 1950s through the 80s, psychologists generally believed that they could only study those observable actions known as behaviors. Thoughts and feelings, which cannot be objectively observed and studied, were therefore not an appropriate topic for scientific study, and emotion was not a popular field of study at the time. That was the era when Dąbrowski started to publish his work. As you might imagine, he didn't get as much recognition for his work as his behaviorist colleagues, which is one of the reasons why his personality theory is not as widely known as, for instance, Abraham Maslow's.[7]

Since the 1990s, the field of psychology has come to acknowledge the significant role emotions play in human behavior and personal development. This led, for example, to the introduction of the emotional quotient (EQ) as an important factor for success, alongside the intelligence quotient (IQ).

---

7   Maslow is best known for his theory of human motivation, in which he describes the hierarchy of needs and the process of self-actualization. He knew about and appreciated Dąbrowski's theory, and the two men were close friends.

Although EQ is not the same as emotional development, it was an important step in the emancipation of emotions in the field of psychology. Research on emotion is growing today, pointing psychological science on a different direction than the course it took in the twentieth century. As we will discuss in depth later, we now know that cognition is not superior to emotion. Rather, the processes of reasoning and decision-making depend on emotion to function.

Mirroring the developments in psychology, I believe that the influence of emotion on the voice was underestimated during the age of behaviorism. Consequently, mainstream methods for singing and public speaking that were taught at that time (and are still taught today) merely focused on techniques to change and train your vocal behavior. Although most people already agreed back then on the fact that the human voice is a powerful tool to channel emotions in singing, acting, or public speaking, this didn't lead to a broad understanding that these same emotions could also block the voice or cause vocal problems. The general attitude was—and often still is—that you either have a great voice or you don't. You either can sing, or you cannot. A beautiful voice is regarded as a unique talent, a special gift from nature or a higher power.

My work has shown me that these beliefs about the voice are not as black and white as some believe. The voice you have is not a given fact, but a dynamic feature of yourself that offers broad possibilities for development. Just as with the shaping of personality through positive disintegration, emotions play a central and significant role in the development of your voice. In return, the development of your voice will contribute to your development as a person. If indeed the majority of the vocal problems that medical doctor Brian W. Hands encounters in his practice are rooted in psychology and not physiology, then we should start to take a different approach to the voice. We need to understand it as much more than just a physical instrument in our throats.

In the next chapters, I'll take you through TPD's concepts of *developmental potential, overexcitabilities*, and *dynamisms*, and show you how they relate to all aspects of the voice.

4. Developmental Potential

The theory of positive disintegration outlines three developmental factors that play a role in your disintegrative process. In the unilevel process, you're ruled by the first and second factors, while the third factor surfaces when your development has become multilevel. Altogether, these three factors constitute what TPD calls your *developmental potential*.

This three-factor system is an inspiring way to assess the developmental potential of the voice as well. When people approach me for voice coaching, they often ask me to what extent it is possible to change the sound of their voice. The answer to that question is never straightforward. Some aspects of your voice are fixed and cannot be changed; other aspects are malleable. TPD's three developmental factors offer a great framework to make sense of which is which. In this chapter, I'll give you an overview of the most important aspects that shape your voice. I hope this will give you some insight into why you sound the way you do and how your voice is perceived by yourself and others. You will learn about the potential of your voice and which aspects can be changed or developed.

So what are these three factors of development?

The First Factor

Your hereditary, biological make-up and innate qualities like traits and talents. The overexcitabilities (more about them in chapter 5) are also part of this, as are your biological impulses.

The Second Factor

Your social environment, including your family, country, culture, education, friends and all the people you interact with during your life.

The Third Factor

A transformative inner force that develops as you sort out your values and make conscious choices on every level of your life. Instead of navigating with the autopilot of the first and second factors, you realize that you have a choice—in fact, you *must* choose, in accordance with your values.

The third factor is what Kazimierz Dąbrowski called a *dynamism*, his term for inner forces of growth and development. When you develop a strong third factor, you become more self-aware—and, gradually, self-determined. While the first and second factors influence your developmental potential from the beginning, the third factor typically takes years to unfold (although some people do seem to have it from an early age). It only appears after your development through inner conflict has progressed far enough. As that process unfolds, you gradually begin to recognize the third factor as a voice from within. According to Dąbrowski,

> *The third factor rarely appears in a "ready-made" form. We work it out slowly and gradually through inner struggles, through difficulties of affirmation and negation, until the time when our decisions are controlled by the synthetic "inner voice" and the growing role of the inner psychic milieu in the direction of the ideal of personality.*[8]

In my own life, there have been moments when I clearly felt the third factor at work. Take my decision to no longer fight for my place in the music industry, going independent instead. Commercially, it was not a great choice. But my inner voice was clear: *This is exactly what you have to do now. You don't know yet where this path will take you. But this is the only way. Going back is no longer an option.* Ultimately, it was the right choice for me. My third factor did not steer me wrong.

It's not easy to pinpoint the origin of the third factor, but scientific developments that came well after Dąbrowski's death in 1980 give us some food for thought here. TPD says that the third factor is a result of the interplay between the first and the second factors, but it becomes far more than the sum of its parts. According to the new science of epigenetics, personal experiences and environmental factors change the activity and expression of your genes. This means that the traits you develop are not wholly predetermined. You can even develop new traits. Your development as a human being—biologically, emotionally, psychologically, and behaviorally—is a complex interaction of gene activity, experience and environment.

Consider the development of the third factor in light of these epigenetic principles. Many different outcomes are possible within one person during one lifetime. Therefore, the course of your life is not *just* determined by your genes and environment. Yes, nature and nurture define a great part of who you are and who you can become. But your developmental potential is not merely a static sum of nature and nurture. When you're developing your third factor, you grow beyond saying things like "I was just born that way," or "I'm like this because of what happened in my youth, and there's nothing I can do about it." You start to take responsibility for yourself.

We can apply all of this to your voice. Allow me to show you how.

---

8   K. Dąbrowski, A. Kawczak and J. Sochanska *The Dynamics of Concepts* (1973, Gryf Publications LTD London) p. 79.

4.1. Nature | The First Factor

When it comes to your voice, the first factor is of course your body. But which parts of your body? The most obvious part, of course, is your voice box. Vocal folds vary in length and thickness: Women's vocal folds are usually 3.3-4.5 mm wide and 11-15 mm long. Men's vocal folds are about 4.7-6.2 mm wide and 17-21 mm long. Men speak at a pitch of roughly 122 Hz, women at 212 Hz. But the rest of your body affects your voice too. This includes the shape and size of your lips, tongue, mouth, throat, soft palate, and larynx; it even includes the shape and size of your bones and cavities in the chest, throat, nose, and mouth. These areas define your tone of voice, and how you are able to resonate sound throughout your own body. Even that isn't all. Other physical aspects like bone structure, hormones, and breathing pattern play a role too in the sound of your voice.

Altogether, these physical aspects define the distinctive sound of your voice. No two voices are alike, because no two bodies are alike. This is the reason why some features of your voice are a given fact and cannot be changed. With few exceptions, women are not able to create the deep voice-overs we often hear in movie trailers, and men are not able to sing the role of Queen of the Night from Mozart's *The Magic Flute*. You can compare their voices with string instruments: Women's shorter and thinner vocal folds are like violins (soprano voices) and violas (alto voices). Men's longer and thicker folds are like cellos (tenor voices) and double basses (bass voices). Like string instruments, human voices have limits in range. Depending on your voice type, your pitch has an upper and lower limit. Within that range, there is a pitch that's most powerful and feels most comfortable for speaking or singing.

Using the Full Potential of the First Factor

Modifying your voice is a little like learning to play a string instrument. Although you can't change the raw material of your instrument—whether voice or violin—you can learn to make better use of it. With voice techniques, you can alter elements of your voice that you did not learn to "play" to their maximum potential. Most of these techniques, however, are not for your vocal folds. Rather, you control your voice through other parts of your body, such as your lips, tongue, mouth, and other cavities. We call these techniques resonance, articulation, volume, and prosody. I will explain them here.

Resonance

When you speak or sing, your vocal folds produce sound waves that vibrate through your body cavities and your bones. The more space there is for these sound waves to vibrate, the better you resonate. High notes resonate better in the head, and low notes resonate better in the chest. A properly resonating voice sounds louder, stronger, and can handle more activity. This is why we tend to find resonating voices more attractive.

Moreover, we perceive resonating voices as lower than they actually are. With my clients, I always demonstrate the difference between a resonating vocalization and a non-resonating vocalization on the same pitch. Most of them think they hear that the resonating sound is lower in pitch than the non-resonating sound, even though both sounds have the same pitch. Because deep voices are in fashion and perceived as more authoritative, many men and women force the pitch of their voice down to a level that is below their optimal range. As a result, they lack volume and strength. They sound flat because they use a limited range. Sometimes they even sound fake. If you think your voice is too high, please don't try to speak lower. The deeper quality of your voice will reveal itself if you open up your resonance.

Try it Yourself: **Resonate**

You can optimize the resonance of your voice by simply allowing more space in your throat while you speak. To find this space, make a fake yawn while you open your mouth and drop your jaw. Now close your lips, but keep your jaw low and relaxed. There should now be an empty space in the mouth, the size of a ping-pong ball. Keep this open space while you speak, and your voice will sound more open and rounder. You may need to drop your jaw more than you're used to. You should also keep in mind that, whatever other benefits it offers, smiling is not an effective mouth position for resonance. Only two vowels show an advantage in smiling position: A as in *today* and E/Y/I as in *me*. For the rest of the vowels, avoid smiling and lower your jaw. You can smile again after you speak.

Articulation

Articulation is the act of vocal expression. Do people understand every single word you say, or are you asked to repeat something frequently? If it's the latter, then you'll want to work on articulation—on speaking clearly and intelligibly. It's quite easy to practice.

Try it Yourself: **Articulate**

You can improve your articulation by doing the following:
1. Become aware of every single word you say. Don't be sloppy when you speak.
2. Slow down. Take extra time to speak emphatically.
3. Become aware of the different positions of your mouth, lips and jaw while producing a sound. You make vowels with your jaw; you make consonants with your teeth, lips, and tongue at the front of your mouth. Here are some examples:

- For T, D, and L, you touch the tip of your tongue to your palate, right behind your upper teeth. Say "tatata," "dadada," "lalala," repeating each a couple times.

- For *P* and *B*, you make the sound at the front of your mouth with your lips. Say "papapa," "bababa," repeating each a couple times.
- For *K* and *G*, you touch the back of your tongue to your soft palate. Say "kakaka," "gagaga," repeating each a couple times.

The most common articulation exercises are tongue twisters. Each focuses on either a single letter or a combination of letters. As well as being fun, tongue twisters are extremely effective at this task. They strengthen and stretch the muscles involved in speech and bring your habitual speech patterns—which may be less than perfect—to your attention. Here's one example:

Peter Piper picked a peck of pickled peppers. If Peter Piper picked a peck of pickled peppers, where's the peck of pickled peppers Peter Piper picked?

Volume

When they want to speak louder, many people put pressure on their throat and vocal folds. This makes them sound strained, but not louder. The trick is to add more volume without wearing out your voice. Here's how you can do this:

- Using breath-voice connection and breath support (you'll find exercises for this in Chapter 8, *Breathe*)
- Using resonance
- Articulating well
- Projecting your sound
- Avoiding your pitch going too high

Prosody

This refers to linguistic functions such as rhythm, stress, speed, and intonation. It communicates so much more nuance than grammar and vocabulary alone: These features reveal your emotional state, and you use them—consciously or unconsciously—to express irony, sarcasm, emphasis, contrast, or focus. The lack of prosody is the reason why conversations in text messages and chats are more likely to cause misunderstandings. The use of emojis can compensate to some extent, but they can never replace the countless subtleties that come with spoken language.

Rhythm is the pattern of the sounds you produce. It's defined by changes in pitch and pace—and it's what brings your voice to life. Voices without proper rhythm sound dull, monotonous, or even robotic.

With **word stress** and **sentence stress** you can work expression into your voice. By stressing different syllables and words, you change the context of a sentence.

Try it Yourself: **Sentence Stress**

Say this sentence out loud three times, with each time, stressing a different word:

<u>I'll</u> be leaving tomorrow.
I'll be <u>leaving</u> tomorrow.
I'll be leaving <u>tomorrow</u>.

There are several ways to stress words or syllables:

- Changing your pitch
- Using loudness
- Pausing before or after the accentuated word
- Speaking slower or articulating very precisely

Speed, of course, is the pace of your speech. Speaking too quickly is a common speech problem. Most people speed up their speech when they are stressed or excited. When you speak too quickly, however, your ongoing stream of words won't give the listener a chance to digest what you've just said. Consequently, your words will not have the impact you'd like them to have. Here are some tips to help you slow down your speech:

- Focus on articulating very precisely
- Take a good breath after completing a sentence before you start another
- Pause more frequently
- Allow the listener to respond to what you say; create space for dialogue

Intonation is the variety of pitch within a word or sentence. By playing with pitch, you can completely change the meaning of a sentence or make dramatic changes in the emotion you are expressing.

Try it Yourself: **Intonate**

You probably already often use the right intonation to make something clear. You can, for instance, say "mmmm" in various ways:

- "Mmmmmmm?" if you react to something questioning
- "Mmmmmmm!" as an exclamation
- "Mmmm-(h)mmm." if you agree with something
- "(H)Mmmm....." If you're thinking about something

Do you hear the differences?

Train with a Specialist

I've quickly introduced you to voice techniques and a few exercises to improve them, but I haven't delved very deep into them. While there are online tutorials and courses available for voice techniques, you'll get the most out of these exercises if you work face to face with a speech therapist, voice coach, singing teacher, or other vocal professional. Together with a professional, you can effectively and safely practice techniques.

Without accurate direct feedback, you might practice techniques incorrectly or apply them inappropriately, leading to ineffective results or even harm. Moreover, even after you have developed self-awareness and located the problem with your voice, it can be tough to make changes without a reliable source of feedback. That's what a voice coach or speech therapist can offer you. Unlike a speech therapist who is trained in identifying and treating speech disorders, a voice coach is someone who works with generally healthy people to improve various aspects of their voices. Ideally, this professional would have some knowledge of psychology and understand how the voice is connected to your body, thoughts, emotions, and behavior.

4.2. Nurture | The Second Factor

The second factor of development is our social environment, like family and friends. In this section, we'll explore the impact other people have on your voice.

Family and Friends

Let's start with the most obvious environmental influence on your voice: your family. Your sensitivity to others' voices begins in the womb and guides you from the day you're born. Touch and sound are the most important means of communication between newborns and their caregivers, which makes infants especially sensitive to rhythm and pitch. Caregivers intuitively use vocal qualities to regulate their baby's nervous system, from encouraging joy to lulling them to sleep.

As soon as they begin baby talk, babies gain practice attuning their voices to those of their caregivers; as they learn to speak properly, they continue to copy them. Pitch comes first, as they quickly learn that men have lower voices than women. Then, around the age of seven, children begin to note qualities like articulation, pace, rhythm, and intonation and copy these from their parents, especially the parent of the same sex. This means that if you're a girl and your mother speaks in a soft, high voice with highly variable intonation, you're likely to grow up doing the same. If you're a boy and your father generally mumbles in a low and monotonous manner, you might develop a similar type of voice. As you can see, many aspects of your voice are copied from your environment and are not necessarily a reflection of anything innate about you.

Consider Eric, a client of mine who spoke with a flat, quiet, restrained voice. He rarely varied his rhythm or altered his intonation, making him sound robotic and emotionally flat. I understood from what he told me that Eric could clearly experience intense emotions, but his voice would never lead you to guess that. When he reviewed his recorded voice during a session, Eric's own judgment was that he sounded dull—even duller, in fact, than he had expected. He then told me that his parents both speak very quietly and monotonously. He was also an only child, and in his youth, not much was said at the dinner table.

During Eric's training, we worked on techniques for rhythm and intonation. I also invited him to consciously express emotions like anger, sadness, and joy. After exploring his voice for a while, it appeared that he had no problems connecting to these emotions in order to sound more expressive. This suggests that his flat, monotonous voice was mostly a result of copying his parents' behavior.

Of course, while family is the foundational part of the second factor, it's not the only one that matters. As you grow up and become a teenager, you probably engage more with your peers and less with family. This new phase opens you up to being influenced by other people's vocal and linguistic features. If everyone in your group of friends speaks very fast, for instance, you will most likely speed up your voice. Similar things can happen later in life when you go to college or start a new job. As a general rule, however, the younger you are, the more likely you are to copy behaviors and vocal styles from others.

Culture and Language

In the realm of the second factor, we can zoom out further and still find influences that we need to consider. Your native language influences the way you use your voice and how you use language in general. Country and culture matter too, as English is spoken differently in all the countries where it's the leading language, and even varies by region within those countries.

Languages are so much more than grammar and vocabulary: They are worlds that come with distinct cognitive, social, and emotional reference frameworks, shaped by the cultures they come from. Pronunciation and prosody are expressions of that reference framework, too. People usually only become aware of the vocal qualities that are typical for their cultures and native languages when they spend a long time abroad, speaking languages that are not native to them.

Consider the Netherlands. Dutch is the official language, but nowadays English is an additional lingua franca in business and higher education. Amsterdam, where I was born and work as a voice coach, has become one of the most culturally diverse cities I know. We've welcomed lots of permanent migrants, and—especially in the last decade—a lot of people on temporary working visas. As a voice coach with a bilingual website (Dutch and English), I get approached by people from around the world. I love that I have the chance to interact with so many different cultures and work with people who speak so many different languages.

The international clients who come to see me for voice coaching have a very high level of understanding of the English language—at least in terms of grammar and vocabulary. But they are often unaware of the differences in prosody, phonology (*i.e.*, how sounds are organized), and pronunciation between their first language and English. Most people unconsciously apply the prosody rules of their native language to any other languages they learn. As a result, Russians speak English with their typical Russian intonation, while the English of French and Spanish speakers is usually without the typical English use of word stress. All these non-native pronunciations of English can cause misunderstandings or even communication problems in the workplace, where more often than not, a colorful bunch of people from many different countries have to find a common understanding in a universal language that's not native to the majority of them.

Stéphanie is one of the many French speakers I've worked with. Through exercises for word and sentence stress in English, she realized how differently stress and intonation are used in French and English. She had never before used pitch and rhythm to emphasize certain words in sentences. Suddenly, it became clear to her where all the misunderstandings with her boyfriend—who was not French—were coming from. To train pitch and rhythm, Stéphanie started to copy the speech of a very expressive American vlogger. This allowed her to experience the major differences between French and English prosody. Once she was aware of this, she could then change her own prosody, making it sound more like English while also suiting her own style.

Prosody, phonology, and pronunciation vary in different languages, as I will discuss next.

Stress-Timed vs. Syllable-Timed

A stress-timed language is a language where long, stressed syllables are combined with short, unstressed syllables to fit in a particular rhythm. Such languages use these rhythmic patterns to make clear and distinct accents in words as well as sentences. Typical examples of stress-timed languages are English, Dutch, German, Russian, Arabic, Swedish, Danish, and Norwegian.

A syllable-timed language is a language where each syllable takes roughly the same amount of time to pronounce. Typical examples of syllable-timed languages are French, Spanish, Italian, Greek, Cantonese, and Mandarin.

Vowel Length

In English, Dutch, and German, vowel length varies significantly. They have short as well as long vowels. In contrast, in Italian and Russian, vowels are always roughly the same length.

Voice in Foreign Languages

Judging from my clients, native speakers of some languages can apply the pronunciation rules of their first language to English without giving it too much thought. Speakers of other languages, however, need to note that English has different pronunciation rules. Here are some examples:

English is a highly melodic language; its intonation patterns make use of a wide range of pitches. English, like German and Dutch, is stress-timed, so speakers use both long and short vowels and apply heavy word stress. Dutch and Germans can consequently apply their native pronunciation rules to speaking English. Italian, French, and Spanish, however, are syllable-timed. If you apply the rhythm from a syllable-timed language to English, you'll sound boring, unexpressive, overly cautious, and robotic. The same will happen if you don't differentiate between short and long vowels.

Among these Romance languages, however, there are some differences. In Italian, a statement and a question may have exactly the same words in the same order; if you are asking a question, you must add the interrogative tone and the question mark. Italian vowels are long and open, whereas Spanish vowels are closed and short in length. French varies more in length and openness of vowels than other Romance languages; it also uses more consonants. French and Spanish consonants are pronounced with many plosives and fricatives—that is, with activity from the teeth, tongue, and lips. Because they use these consonants combined with short and closed vowels, I notice that Spanish, and especially French speakers, make less use of the oral cavities that are needed to create a resonating voice. It's easier to resonate in English, Dutch, or German.

You should also be aware of the intonation patterns that are used in your language. English has four patterns, while Russian has seven. If you apply Russian intonation to an English sentence, an English-speaking audience will not pick up what you're trying to convey with that intention.

Culture also influences the volume and intensity of the voice. Dutch and Americans are infamous for their loud voices in public spaces, while most East Asians would never use their voices in such an expressive way. They avoid speaking loudly as they don't want to come across as rude. In Arab cultures, on the other hand, speakers can be so intense and expressive that regular chitchat between a shop owner and client might sound like they are caught up in a fight.

Try it Yourself: Get Inspired by Other Voices

If you speak a foreign language but are still applying the pronunciation and prosody rules from your native one, search for a vocal role model in your target language. You can learn a lot by consciously listening to and analyzing voices. What are they doing in terms of rhythm and pitch that makes them sound different from speakers of your native language? Do they use long or short vowels, or a combination of both? Try to copy their speech, taking note of how different this sounds from what you're used to doing yourself. What prosodic elements would you like to use more frequently? You can also try singing along with songs in your target language. This will give you plenty of opportunities to imitate how the language is spoken.

As we noted earlier, there are major variations in pronunciation and prosody even within a single language. Consider India. English is an official language there, but Indian English is quite different from the English spoken elsewhere. Studies of Indian English phonology illustrate its differences; so do the many Indians living in the Netherlands who struggle to sound intelligible to their coworkers. Stresses, accents, and intonations differ between British and Indian English, causing misunderstandings. While British English clearly stresses and destresses syllables and words, Indian English gives every syllable the same weight. Its rhythm and intonation also differ, usually emphasizing the second to last word in a sentence. One of my Indian clients told me that it was an eye-opener for him that he could stress particular syllables and words within one sentence and choose to lengthen or shorten certain vowels.

The cultural and linguistic variations in prosody described above are an oft-neglected challenge that comes with globalization. In her book *The Culture Map*, Erin Meyer writes that there are millions of people working in international settings who only see things from their own cultural perspective. They assume that all differences, controversies, and misunderstandings stem from personality, so they don't consider cultural difference. That's a mistake. We should be aware that patterns in thinking, behavior, and speech that stem from culture do influence our perceptions, cognitions, and actions. In a working environment where everyone speaks English, it's easy to forget about this.

Gender

Consider this: many people—mainly women—approach me with the following questions: *Why am I not being heard? Why do people interrupt me? Why does my message not seem to persuade? Why am I not taken seriously? Why does it happen that when I suggest something during a meeting, nobody reacts to it, but when my male co-worker later says the exact same thing, everybody thinks he is brilliant?* Usually these women work in a male-dominated corporate environment, and they wonder how they should present themselves at work. Should they act more like the men, or stay true to their authentic selves?

By now, you have a sense of how the second factor, *i.e.*, your environment, plays an important role in how your voice develops. Although your sex obviously belongs to the first factor, *i.e.*, your biological make-up, it affects the second factor as well. As children, we model our voices on our parent of the same sex. We also have unconscious beliefs about how male and female voices should sound, and we shape ours accordingly. Therefore, something you see as a behavior emanating from your authentic self could actually be learned behavior that you based on the cultural and gender norms in your environment. With this in mind, you may wish to look at your vocal behaviors and assess whether you truly are choosing to behave that way or if the second factor is at work here.

A good example of this is Fabiënne, a consultant who approached me because she felt she was not being heard. She always visited her clients together with a male coworker, but they were equal in their roles as consultants. Fabiënne was supposed to take the lead in the conversation fifty percent of the time, but even when she did, she noticed that the client still focused on her coworker.

She assumed that her voice must lack authority, but when I listened to her speak, I couldn't see why she thought so. I offered her some voice techniques and she performed them with excellence.

During the second session we had, however, Fabiënne realized that her struggle could have something to do with how she behaved. When she and her colleague entered a client's space, Fabiënne always went in second. She would then offer to pour everyone coffee or tea and to take notes. These actions might seem insignificant, but they're not. They are the behaviors of an assistant, not a partner, and by doing them, she presented herself as lower in the hierarchy. This positioned her colleague as the expert who had more important things to do than pour drinks and take notes. No wonder people paid attention to him over Fabiënne.

When we met for the third time, to my surprise, Fabiënne told me that her problems were gone. When she became aware of the role that her submissive behavior played in how others perceived her, she managed to change the behavior—and that made a huge difference. While she still sometimes felt she wasn't being heard, it happened much less than before. Rather than the female voice, the issue is the modest, caring behavior many women display because older women modeled it for them. Neither Fabiënne nor her co-worker were conscious of how their behaviors were reinforcing their traditional gender roles.

Discovering the deeper cause behind your voice problem is extremely valuable. Just like Maya from Chapter one, who spoke to her students as if she were proving herself to her father, Fabiënne was able to make huge steps in her progress because she knew where her behavior was coming from.

Double Standards

In our daily lives, we're not always aware of the expectations we have towards ourselves and others based on gender. Just because you are a man or a woman, you're expected to behave in a certain way. And you, in return, expect the same of others. This became clear to me when one of my best friends decided to transition from being a woman into a man. During his transition, I caught myself and my social circle acting out our unconscious beliefs about how men and women should behave. When my friend browsed through his phone for a long time at the dinner table as a woman, we considered this behavior rude; when he did the same thing as a man, we thought it completely normal. As a woman, others criticized him for never smiling. As a man, nobody expects him to smile all the time.

Let's zoom in a bit more on this smiling double standard. In order to come across as sympathetic, women are expected to smile. Just look at this example, from an article in *The Hill*: "A top surrogate for Hillary Clinton said that the Democratic presidential nominee needs to 'smile more' in the upcoming presidential debates against Donald Trump." We generally judge non-smiling women as strict or severe, while non-smiling men seem professional or mysterious. As a result, a lot of women plaster permanent smiles on their faces. Unfortunately, if there's one thing that will ruin the credibility, authority, and decisiveness of your voice, it's a smile. As we discussed earlier, for almost all vowels, the mouth position of a smile is the worst one for resonance. It makes you sound thinner, higher, and more nasally—think of how the stereotypical American woman says "oh my god!"—or how actress Fran Drescher performs in *The Nanny*. People who speak with this nasally, non-resonating sound are often taken less seriously, regardless of the content of their message.

A resonating voice fills a space with vibrating sound waves of many different frequencies, making a powerful impact on the organisms and objects that receive them. When you say that something "resonates with you", figuratively speaking, it means that it makes just such an impact on you. I have come across many women who want to develop leadership skills but feel conflicted if I tell them to ditch their smile while they speak. They are all afraid of losing their likability. Ladies, you can always put the smile back on your face after you're done talking or during pauses between sentences, if you really want to. Just don't smile *at the same time* as you speak. Learn to drop your jaw downwards for making vowels instead of curling up the corners of your mouth. Try this for a while and you'll be surprised what this does for your voice.

Of course, it's not only women who struggle because they believe they must conform to behavioral standards. Many men believe that their voice sounds too high. I have worked with gay men who, already in their youth, tried hard to lower their voices because they were afraid of being seen as gay stereotypes. Instead of developing lower voices, however, they just ended up speaking in a flat, monotonous style, which doesn't sound more masculine at all. As we discussed earlier in this chapter, your comfortable speaking range is a given fact—something you have to accept. To sound interesting, expressive, and engaging, you need to apply intonation. That requires higher pitches as well as lower ones. No matter your vocal range, every voice, from soprano to bass, will sound so much better—and more masculine, if that's important to you—if you apply the amazing vocal technique of resonance.

Transcending the Cultural Context of Gender

It goes without saying that men and women are different on many levels. They have different bodies and hormonal systems. However, I don't believe that any person is one hundred percent masculine or one hundred percent feminine. Women can connect to their masculine energy; men can connect to their feminine energy. Both sexes display strengths and vulnerabilities. Men can develop traditionally female strengths such as intuition, collaboration, free-spiritedness, empathy, creativity, or expressiveness. Women can develop traditionally male strengths such as confidence, ambition, focus, activity, firmness, or reason. Unfortunately, we are still living in a society that values the stereotypically masculine qualities over the feminine. This is one reason why so many women struggle to fit in the male-dominated corporate environment. It is my hope that the corporate world will come to value feminine strengths and realize that they need these qualities as well to be successful and sustainable. Instead of trying to adapt fully to the male-dominated environment, I hope that women will be given opportunity to use their feminine qualities at work while simultaneously exploring masculine qualities in themselves.

When you grow and develop as a person, it's inevitable that you will discover qualities associated with the opposite sex in yourself. Dąbrowski said that emotional development leads to the transcendence of your psychological type and of your biological life cycle. I interpret this statement to mean that you transcend the second factor's gendered expectations as well, coming to identify less with the cultural prescriptions for people of your sex. Dąbrowski said that all of us can develop a *personality ideal* toward which we aim our development. Personally, I picture that ideal as flexible and fluent in gender. In the process of developing a personality ideal, the feminine and masculine traits cease to appear as opposites; instead, they are two indispensable forces that are fully integrated within a single person. The feminine and the masculine keep each other in balance, like yin and yang.

To give you an idea of what gender flexibility might look and sound like in voice and communication, imagine the following:

- You stop worrying about sounding too high or too low
- You communicate competence and warmth at the same time
- You are centered and present in your own body, with open, empathetic attention to your surroundings
- You show authority and credibility by being calm and grounded; you're not afraid of silences
- You communicate your message clearly and concisely, in an engaging and expressive way
- You take up space yourself and allow others to take up space as well

4.3. The Third Factor

While it can be challenging, it's possible to modify vocal traits that have come into being because of second factor influences like family, friends, schools, gender norms, or linguistic and cultural norms. Vocal traits that are learned and copied from others are behaviors. And behaviors can be changed and unlearned—*if* you are prepared to devote time, effort, and patience.

You may be asking yourself some big questions at this point: What is my own voice? How do I find it? Out of all the vocal behaviors I've taken on from my environment, what do I want to keep, and what do I want to unlearn?

This is where the third factor of development comes in. And that is the name by which Dąbrowski referred to it—simply *the third factor*. It is the force by which individuals move beyond their nature and nurture to become more self-determined and self-aware, and thus able to change their behavior. It's not something you're born with, just as a nobody comes ready-made out of the womb as a fluent speaker. The way to be a calm, confident, engaging speaker is something that most people only figure out well into the course of their lives, after their thirties, forties, or fifties—if they ever do.

Third Factor and Voice: A Mutually Reinforcing Relationship

Third factor development is generally a gradual process, although sometimes people describe it as a sudden shift. Meredith Monk is a renowned performer and composer whose work is centered around exploration of the voice, in every possible texture and emotion. She describes in her biography the moment she first recognized the third factor through her voice:

> *Sometime in the mid-1960s, as I was vocalizing in my studio, I suddenly had a revelation that the voice could have the same flexibility and range of movement as a spine or a foot, and that I could find and build a personal vocabulary for my voice just as one makes movement based on a particular body. I realized then that within the voice are myriad characters, landscapes, colors, textures, ways of producing sound, wordless messages. I intuitively sensed the rich and ancient power of the first human instrument and by exploring its limitless possibilities I felt that I was coming home to my family and my blood. [....] There are events that change our lives irrevocably; that moment of discovery in the '60s changed mine. From that point on, exploring my voice and what it could evoke, delineate, uncover, and ultimately give to others became the core of my work. [....] When I began, my path seemed lonely. I was not aware of anyone working in this particular way. I had to trust my instincts. And yet, I was fortunate in that I had already built a body of work combining images, movement, objects, sound and film so that the discipline of daily work was essential to my life. Now I could use the same creative principles and apply them to my vocal exploration. It became immediately apparent that I had found what would be the soul of my work. What had been an urgent inner quest became the quiet certainty that this process would become my continuing and ultimate truth.[9]*

In front of her lay an unknown and lonely path, but Monk had a strong desire to follow her creative instinct. This inner conflict stimulated her to follow that path despite the uncertainties that came with it. In Monk's story, it was her voice that activated her third factor, which then triggered her again to explore and discover the possibilities of her voice.

But you don't have to be a vocal artist to experience a mutually reinforcing relationship like this. When their third factor is at work, people often look for books, therapists, coaches, and courses that support their curiosity for self-exploration. They sense that they can be more than the sum of their genes and upbringing. They question themselves: *Who am I? What do I want to contribute to the world? What is my authentic voice?* If you want to go beyond the vocal habits that you copied from your environment and want to find your own voice, start exploring. Go outside of your comfort zone. Learn voice or singing techniques that encourage you to go much higher, lower, softer, louder, slower, or faster than usual. Your comfortable speaking range is probably broader than you think, as many people use only a restricted part of their voice. If you use your voice in a technically safe way, you cannot go wrong here. Dare to experiment!

---

9   M. Monk *The Soul's Messenger* first published in Arcana V: Music, Magic and Mysticism, edited by John Zorn (Hips Road; New York, 2010)

When you start voice exercises for the first time, they will probably make you feel unnatural, uncomfortable, vulnerable, or inauthentic. You may feel like you're acting. This is normal. It just means that you have to get used to your new vocal possibilities. Can you get comfortable with feeling uncomfortable? Are you willing to accept unwelcome emotions? To do so, after all, can be incredibly liberating. Increasing your vocal repertoire means *increasing* your vocal comfort zone, not *leaving* your comfort zone. This is necessarily creative, and giving space to your creative instinct contributes to developing your personality.

Redouan, a client of mine with a strong third factor, experienced the shift from discomfort to liberation within a single session when we worked on volume. He wanted to avoid sounding stereotypically gay, so he used only the lower pitches from his natural range. This, as we have discussed, made him sound dull. When I challenged him to speak louder, he got uncomfortable. The added volume made his pitch rise. It also felt, to him, like he was screaming. To my ears, however, he was hardly speaking as loud as one would normally do among a small group of friends. When he listened to the recordings we made of his voice, he didn't think he sounded genuine.

Then we had an idea: Redouan should imagine he was an actor. In this role, he suddenly felt he had permission to do more extreme things with his voice. So he started to explore. This exercise let him drop the discomfort—and, gradually, he began to enjoy himself. Speaking loud and high, he said, was a liberating experience. Creative play can lead us to discover our complexities. If you're open to such discoveries, you may well astonish yourself. Redouan experienced what in the theory of positive disintegration is called *astonishment with oneself*. It's one of the forces for change that the theory calls dynamisms, as we'll discuss in Chapter 6.

It's important to note, however, that this sort of challenge doesn't always lead to feelings of liberation. The same exercise can make you feel so vulnerable that your voice becomes blocked.

This happened to Shelly, a woman from the United States who spoke, as many American women do, with her mouth always in smiling position. Her voice had no resonating frequencies and sounded thin, so she avoided higher pitches. In fact, she was trying so hard to avoid them that her voice became blocked during her intonation exercises. She grew uncomfortable and told me she found the exercises difficult. She began to speak softer and softer, looking like she wanted to disappear. At first I wasn't sure whether to challenge her to go outside of her comfort zone; after a while, it became clear that challenging her would be counterproductive.

I decided that we had to change tack. We stopped working on intonation and did an introspection exercise to find out where her uncomfortable feelings came from. She said she felt vulnerable; instead of being challenged, she needed to feel safe. At work earlier that week, she had been asked to do something that felt too overwhelming for her, but she had done it anyway.

Shelly told me that this happened a lot in her life. She had difficulties setting boundaries and saying "no." She joked that even the dog at her mom's house doesn't listen to her when she gives him commands. This pointed us toward the direction where Shelly could grow. Her voice triggered unwelcome emotions, which in turn prompted her to look deeper into herself and examine her habits, like unhealthy boundaries. Responding to these issues, Shelly realized that a more decisive voice could help her set clearer boundaries. We worked on that in the following sessions.

The Source of Your Motivation to Change

The third factor is the force that enables you to change your behavior. Which habits and behaviors do you want to develop, and which do you want to reject and unlearn? The most effective incentive for change comes from your own motivation and values. You don't do it because someone else tells you to, or because you think that you should adapt to societal norms. If you've ever learned to play an instrument, you probably know that you really only get good results if you *enjoy* playing. If your parents forced music on you when you would have preferred to play sports—or even if they picked the violin when you would rather have played the trumpet—you know there's not much chance this will lead to excellence. It's a waste of time for both teacher and child. So if you want to change your voice, ask yourself if your desire for change is self-driven—because it will ask a lot of you.

It's easier to change behavior when you are truly self-motivated. This means that in order to change your behavior, you must investigate what is *more yourself* and *less yourself*. Since you are not changing to conform, your new behavior will be in accordance with your values. However, this doesn't mean that changing behavior now is easy. You have been speaking with the same voice all your life; your speech habits are on autopilot. Changing this doesn't happen overnight. The commitment required to change your voice is similar to that required to learn to play an instrument. It can take a few weeks, or even months, before you're able to use the new techniques—and years before you perform them without thinking. Give the process time. It's two steps forward, one step back.

The way to do this is simple: *practice, practice, practice.* Every day.

Schedule a regular time for voice exercises as part of your daily routine. It's better to practice five minutes every day than half an hour per week. Even with just a couple of minutes per day, repetition builds the new skill into your muscle memory. Set an alarm on your phone for exercise time.

Start by practicing your voice techniques when reading text aloud from a book or magazine. The advantage of reading text aloud is that you don't have to simultaneously think about what you're saying. Instead, you can exclusively focus on the pronunciation of the words. When you've mastered this step, try out these techniques in everyday conversations with someone close to you. Keep conversation topics simple and light so you can focus on your voice. After you've mastered techniques in relaxed conversations, you can start to use them in challenging situations like meetings and presentations, where you need to focus on complex content as well. At some point, the new techniques become part of your vocal repertoire. You won't always have to think about using them consciously.

Your voice may have more potential than you imagine. Developing this potential—by unlearning unwanted habits and making the new techniques your own—is a process that takes time. The third factor is the force that enables you to consciously choose what's more yourself and less yourself. The process can give rise to vulnerability, as with Shelly, as well as astonishment, as with Redouan. These moments reflect not only on your voice, but also on the entirety of your personality.

5. Overexcitabilities

My friend Milo has a profound love of music. He is an insatiable collector of underground house music from the nineties, a genre he loves because it stirs deep emotions in him. This stands in contrast with most vocal music, which he can't bear to listen to. The way most contemporary pop singers use their voices is, to him, too intense—too *present*. Without even noting the lyrics, he perceives the singer's voice as a transmitter of her emotions, a process he finds intrusive. He has no desire to receive intimate emotions from strangers. You see, he's already so moved by the subtler emotions conveyed by instrumental music that, in his experience, the magnified emotions in the vocals are out of balance with the atmosphere of the song.

Luckily for me, Milo is not completely turned off by my vocal performances. We know each other well, which is probably why he's open to receive the emotions I transmit through my voice. Still, whenever I send him a new recording, he says something like, "I'm really digging this tune! Can you make an instrumental bounce for me?"

Along with his sensitivity to music, Milo has an incredible sense of smell, an abundance of physical energy, and an impressive sense for detail and creative expression in photography. He's also emotionally expressive and comfortable connecting deeply with other people.

Milo clearly exhibits what Kazimierz Dąbrowski called *overexcitability* (frequently shortened to OE). Dąbrowski noticed that many people—children as well as adults—consistently react intensely to both external and intrapsychic stimuli. They respond more strongly and more frequently to these stimuli; their response may last significantly longer than that of the average person; and they would respond to smaller stimuli than most people. All of this together makes up the experience of overexcitability.

5.1. What Is Overexcitability

Our nervous system processes everything we experience. As we discussed in Chapter 2, we can subdivide this complex system into the central nervous system and peripheral nervous system; subdividing further, the latter contains the autonomic nervous system.

People with overexcitability have a nervous system that responds more powerfully than average. They have thinner nerves, more sensitive endings, and faster synapses. That's why they process stimuli so intensively. If we have OE, it is part of our genetic make-up, the first factor of development.

Since we're born with this intensity, we can't "unlearn" it. The way we experience and express our OE, however, can change during unilevel and multilevel development through the influence of the second and third factors—that is, our environment and our conscious choices.

Being overexcitable means being more sensitive and, perhaps, more easily overwhelmed. As an overexcitable person, your experience of the world can be intensely joyful and positive—or intensely frustrating. Your involvement in life is different from that of most others, as you may already recognize to some degree. The emotions associated with OE supply a lot of energy and fuel talents like creativity and empathy, but they also come with a certain vulnerability. The more intense your OE is, the greater your chance of going through the disintegration process. You can reach the highest of the highs and the lowest of the lows; you have a tremendous capacity for nuance. Others might say that you are too intense, too present, too restless, or just simply too much. On the level of voice they say you are too quick or too dramatic. In that case, your OE is externally expressed. If your OE is expressed internally, however, others might describe you as too shy, too inhibited, or too enigmatic. They might say the same about your voice. Do you identify yourself with one of these profiles?

Dąbrowski identified and described five different domains of OE. You can possess any or all of these types of OE, or you may have none at all. The first two—and to some extent, the third—are most strongly correlated with multilevel development. First I'll discuss the five different domains of OE in general, later I'll explain to you what they specifically mean for the voice.

Emotional Overexcitability

You experience your feelings and emotions as intense, delicate, and complex. You are highly aware of your feelings and recognize how they develop over time. You are also often able to correctly sense the emotions of others, giving you the capacity to be especially considerate and even identify with them. In fact, empathy and compassion come naturally to you. Though the second factor may have taught you not to act on it, you are inclined to be highly affectionate towards others, developing strong attachments to people, animals, places, or objects. Because of this, you probably long for long-term, intimate relationships, or—if you don't feel safe—you withdraw from intimate relationships entirely, protecting yourself from the intense negative feelings they can generate. Though all people with emotional overexcitability have strong emotions, some have learned to regulate and control them. Others are more expressive of them, for better or for worse. Perhaps even more than for the average person, emotions play a powerful role in your connections with others as well as your process of personal development.

Intellectual Overexcitability

You are a thinker—independent, analytical, deep, and curious. In your quest for truth, you absorb all kinds of knowledge and like to immerse yourself in topics of interest. Your thoughts cover both the ethical and the conceptual, so you're likely concerned about worldwide issues that don't affect you directly. You want to know exactly how things work, and, you're probably an excellent observer. You have rapid streams of thought and a tendency to rationalize or intellectualize. Prolonged concentration is no big deal for you, and problem solving, detailed planning and organizing are among your talents. On the other hand, you may be overcritical and impatient with others. It's important to note that intellectual OE is not the same as intelligence. The former describes enhanced desire for knowledge and interest in theory; the latter is about cognitive ability.

Imaginational Overexcitability

You have a powerful capacity to visualize, whether a place you haven't ever been or a future you have not yet reached. As a child, you may even have mixed fantasy and reality. You probably have some talent for art, drama, music, poetry, or writing, and you likely enjoy fiction—perhaps especially fantasy. You may think in images and have a talent for associating—that is, for connecting one image or subject with another. Because of this, you probably have a penchant for metaphors, using them often when you speak. If a task does not offer an outlet for your creative energies, you can get bored easily.

Sensual Overexcitability

You have a heightened experience of sensory perception: sight, hearing, taste, smell, and touch. This intense sensual input means that you are able to enjoy music, sounds, language, images, sights, art, tastes, good food, smells, textures, and physical contact. On the other hand, you might also experience acute irritation towards certain sensory experiences, like labels in clothing or vocal music. You may experience this intense response to one, several, or all of your senses. Because you get overstimulated easily, you might actively search for sensual experiences. This, however, puts you at risk of addiction or similarly unhealthy behaviors, like overeating or seeking excessive sexual stimulation. Others with sensual overexcitability may do the opposite and withdraw from such things.

Psychomotor Overexcitability

You have an abundance of physical energy because your neuromuscular system is easily stimulated. You like movement, exercise, sports, and games. Action draws you in, perhaps especially when it involves a challenge or a competition. Others may have called you a workaholic or enthusiastic. You might also be restless, nervous, and impulsive, or have tics and talk quickly or continuously.

Overexcitability and Diagnoses

If you recognize similarities between Dąbrowski's overexcitabilities and the construct of the highly sensitive person (HSP) described by clinical research psychologist Dr. Elaine Aron, you're right. A study about the relationship between giftedness and sensitivity shows that HSPs do indeed significantly outscore non-HSPs on all OEs except psychomotor. Despite the overlap of these two constructs, however, high sensitivity and overexcitability are different models and use different criteria.

Moreover, unlike Dąbrowski, Aron didn't study the role of sensitivity on a person's development. This may be why her description of the HSP traits tends to focus on the vulnerabilities associated with OE. I have found the HSP framework especially applicable to people experiencing unilevel development—which, as you'll recall, is the phase of positive disintegration during which an individual has not yet perceived a higher path in line with his or her authentic values. You can compare this to multilevel development, in which, as Dąbrowski observes, sensitivity and intensity act as powerful and transformative traits.

There is also a link between OE and giftedness. Studies repeatedly showed that the most gifted individuals are significantly overexcitable in one or more of the five domains. These studies mostly included children, but some also studied adults. Many in the field of gifted education argue that being gifted is not just about high intelligence. Gifted people also show intense and complex sensitivity, emotional experience, creativity, curiosity, and autonomy.

It's also worth noting that there is some relationship between OE and the symptoms of ADHD, autism, and related conditions. However, the two constructs do not overlap perfectly, with OE allowing for higher levels of development and ADHD and autism describing a disability. According to psychologist William Tillier, this confusion between traits of giftedness and traits of disability often leads to misdiagnosis, missed diagnosis, and even missed giftedness in children who are *twice exceptional*: gifted along with a learning or developmental disability. For instance, it's possible for a person to have ADHD without psychomotor and imaginational OE, or to have psychomotor and imaginational OE without meriting an ADHD diagnosis. It is also possible to have both.

I suggest that you research for yourself whether and how you are fitting the profiles of OE, giftedness, disability, or a combination of them. Later on in this chapter I'll discuss a client case in relation to ADHD and OE, to give you an idea of how to relate yourself to this.

5.2. Your Voice as Vulnerability and as Strength

In Chapter 2, we explored how the autonomic nervous system controls our internal organs. It subconsciously detects cues of threats and safety, and as a result, activates either a defense response mode or the ventral vagal response mode. People with overexcitability process stimuli more intensely and more deeply—and those cues of threat and safety are stimuli. It seems reasonable, then, to expect that people with OE will find themselves in fight, flight, or freeze more often, more quickly, and for a longer period time than less excitable people.

By considering the framework of overexcitability and its five domains, we can focus on specific ways that our intense processing might be manifesting itself. That in turn can be useful when we look at how overexcitability can interact with the voice. As we discussed in Chapter 2, the vagus nerve controls the muscles around the voice box, linking our voice to our defense and social engagement systems. When we get nervous, the muscles in our throat tighten and our voice sounds strained. As a result, the voice expresses cues about whether we feel safe/comfortable or unsafe/

uncomfortable in a given situation or environment. This makes the voice one of the preeminent ways for overexcitability to manifest itself. It's obvious from this description how OE can reveal what bothers you—that is, your vulnerabilities. From a polyvagal theory perspective, this means that your nervous system functions as a sensitive security system with the purpose of protecting you. Sometimes these responses get dysregulated, shifting into overdrive. What may be less obvious is that you can also transform your OE, through multilevel development, into a strength—that is, a talent. On the level of the nervous system, this means that you can learn to regulate your defense systems so they function under the supervision of the ventral vagal response mode.

Let's explore what that would look like in each domain of overexcitability.

Emotional Overexcitability

Let me start by saying that emotional OE has many faces, and you cannot say much about someone's emotional capacities solely based on how they express themselves. When we meet someone for the first time, we generally don't yet know anything about what that person has had to put up with in the past. Therefore, I strive to stay open and non-judgmental during an initial meeting, and I advise you to do the same. The subtle cues we pick up from body language, facial expression, and voice say something about the person's behavior and the response of their nervous system *only* in the moment we interact with them. This is just one narrow slice of their character and may poorly represent what they have to offer the world.

If you are emotionally empowered, you use your voice in a creative and expressive way to show your emotions. You speak from the heart, and people are moved by your dynamic emotional perception. You always consider the feelings of others without ignoring yourself. You have a deep desire to show what you value through your voice. This is why we love to listen to people who have transformed their emotional OE into a strength, like poet Amanda Gorman. With her voice, she has the ability to communicate what she values. When she speaks, people hang on her every word.

In emotional vulnerability, however, you might have trouble regulating your emotions. You react to everything in overdrive, so if you are angry, sad, nervous, or uncomfortable, you struggle to mask this, and your voice always gives you away. On the somatic level, your autonomic nervous system is probably activating a sympathetic response: An angry, defensive voice indicates fight mode, while speaking faster, softer, with less diction and intonation indicates flight mode. We see this in climate activist Greta Thunberg. Her voice strongly expresses her frustration about how world leaders have failed to act on climate change.

We can also see this emotional vulnerability in the case of my client Joshua, who accurately described his struggles with emotional OE to me in our intake call. He told me that when he felt completely at ease, he could easily convey his emotional engagement. In professional meetings, however, he often said things in such a way that his emotions didn't come across as he wanted, especially when he felt out of place. At times, he would get too intense; then he would inevitably get nervous and speak much more than necessary, with his voice shrill and high. He could recognize when this was happening, but he didn't know how to get out of that state. Eventually, he would become exhausted from the strain on his own voice. Sometimes this would even happen in private situations. Though at times he was satisfied with how he conveyed his emotions, at others, he would become so flooded with emotion that he totally took over the conversation, leaving no room for the other person to speak. What he hoped to learn through voice coaching was how to speak in a more grounded way, regardless of who was in front of him. He knew his voice had the potential to show his strength; he only had to learn how to use it calmly and effectively. Awareness of his emotional OE was the first step for Joshua in achieving a sense of calmness.

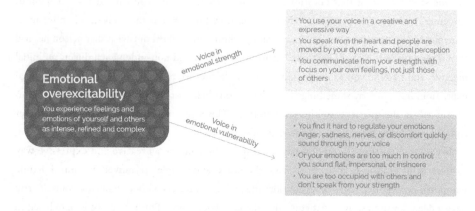

The vulnerable side of emotional OE doesn't only manifest in emotions getting out of control, however. It's also possible that you regulate your emotions quite well–maybe a little *too* well. Because of this, you give the impression that you're flat, cold, unempathetic, unfriendly, superficial, or insincere. If you're emotionally overexcitable, of course, you're anything *but* flat and cold! But you don't show the intensity of your inner world, as doing so makes you feel uncomfortable. I suspect that this is how the voice expresses freeze as a defense mode.

Through my coaching practice, I've met many people who struggle with this burying of emotions. Usually, they simply don't know how to express them. There are many reasons a person may learn to be emotionally unexpressive. Trauma is one, but there are less obvious causes, too. In many cases, this stoic façade used to serve as an effective coping mechanism for them. It protected them from being rejected, bullied, hurt, or laughed at when they were children. The physiological reaction to such incidents probably involved activating that state of immobilization and freeze.

Later in life, when these threats are no longer present, this coping mechanism becomes counter-productive. If your cognitive capacity is strong, there's a good chance that you'll develop a coping mechanism in which your mind takes the lead over your emotions. This enables you to suppress the physical expression of your emotions while explaining and reasoning about what you feel in a controlled way.

Emotional OE can also lead you to focus too much on others' emotions when you interact with them. *What are they thinking? Am I doing it right? Am I boring them? Am I offending anyone?* Because watching conversation partners and parsing their emotions like this draws all your energy to your mind, you end up less present in your body, not firmly grounded. This makes your voice lose strength and engagement.

Moreover—and contrary to what you might think—this anxiety about other people's judgments isn't always conscious. This was the case with Iris, a police officer who taught at the police academy. When she stood in front of her classroom, she struggled to speak with decisiveness and to deliver her lectures in a clear way. The main problem was that she used too many filler words like "um." During an introspection exercise about her lectures, she was able to connect with certain emotions she was not aware of earlier. Although she was hesitant to admit, it became clear that in front of the class she felt like a little girl: anxious, embarrassed, and afraid of being judged by those present. At first, she hadn't been conscious of those emotions, but they had affected her just the same.

Whether it's too intense or too inhibited, you can learn how to get a grip on your emotional OE. The first steps in this process are to breathe properly, increase body awareness, and make sense of what you feel. You'll read more about this in Chapter 8.

Imaginational Overexcitability

If you are imaginationally empowered, you can use your voice to bring others along and show them what you see with your mind's eye. You can clearly articulate a possible future or a concept you've visualized. You respond intuitively, finding the right words without getting caught up in your thoughts. We admire imaginational overexcitability in the voice as a strength in actors, singers, comedians, and other speakers. Consider comedian Trevor Noah, who uses different accents masterfully in his routines, playfully pretending to be someone entirely different.

In imaginational vulnerability, however, all those different thoughts are liable to carry you away. I suspect that this is due to dysregulated sympathetic energy in your autonomic nervous system. You are prone to big mental leaps and skipping from one subject to the other. To keep up with yourself, you start talking quickly and unclearly and may not even complete your sentences. Your listeners have a hard time following you, and you may even lose them entirely. You find it difficult to distinguish between the primary issue and things that are tangents. Perhaps even you no longer know exactly what you wanted to say—there goes your train of thought! Under this kind of tension, what comes out of your mouth might be unexpected or abrupt. To see an example of this, watch actor Roberto Benigni winning the Oscar for best actor. In his two minute speech he expresses his feelings of joy with a motormouth, talking about things like wanting to go to Jupiter and making love with everyone in the audience.

Imaginational overexcitability
You are creative and drawn to many ideas that catch your attention.
You may think in images

Voice in imaginational strength

- You are able to articulate clearly a future situation or new idea that you visualize
- You take people along with your enthusiasm without losing contact with them
- You react intuitively and find the right words naturally without getting caught up by your thoughts

Voice in imaginational vulnerability

- You talk quickly, unclearly, make abrupt statements, or don't complete your sentences
- Others may have a hard time following or understanding you. You're all over the place
- Sometimes you find it hard to distinguish primary and secondary issues in a presentation and lose your train of thought

My client Margot was the one who made me realize how imaginational OE is connected to the voice. She had the self-awareness to recognize that the way she spoke reflected her lifestyle. She has many ideas and plans, but starts many projects without finishing them. Her speech is the same: She speaks quickly, under her breath, and doesn't always finish her sentences properly. She doesn't always give her listener enough time to truly receive what she's saying. When she became a manager, her speech patterns threatened to derail her. When discussing important, complicated, or highly charged content, or when she had to present something ad hoc, she felt too much was going on in her head at the same time. Her mind was going much faster than her ability to speak, but she tried to make her words keep up with her thoughts. That will never work, since thoughts present themselves to us at a pace that our speech could never keep up with. As I listened to Margot talk, it was evident to me that she was thinking while she spoke—and that her mind had a tendency to take her in different directions than she had planned.

Margot was overburdened at work, and her team struggled to carry out her plans. Over the course of our work together, she understood that this was because she wasn't able to convey her ideas in a way that would resonate with the team. It was clear to her that she would have to improve her awareness of her own thought processes and behavioral patterns if she wanted to change this.

To manage this, she needed to slow down and choose an external focus for her attention, drawing it away from her busy mind. For Margot, key to this process was stepping back from her thoughts, and training in focused attention through meditation. In Chapters 11 and 12, I will give you exercises that will help you do that yourself.

Intellectual Overexcitability

If you are intellectually empowered, you use your voice to express your message in an engaged, inspired way. You know what you are talking about, so you speak with conviction and a sense of authority. Your self-awareness demands that you formulate your ideas precisely, calmly, and clearly, with respect and understanding for others, leaving space for dialogue. You won't easily jump to conclusions or raise your voice. Martin Luther King, Jr. is a powerful example of someone who was able to use this talent in his voice, making compelling arguments in ways that people with far less active intellects than his could still easily understand.

In vulnerability, intellectual overexcitability can manifest in a couple different ways. Because you are constantly analyzing everything, you may tend to doubt yourself. *Is what I'm claiming correct? Is it the absolute truth?* People in this vulnerable state will avoid answering with a plain "yes" or "no," even to obvious, closed questions. They always want to convey the nuance of how they perceive the situation. Although nuance is generally a good thing, too much of it will make you look indecisive and reluctant. I argue that this vulnerable form of intellectual OE is a *flight* response of the autonomic nervous system. It kicks in when you feel unsafe in the face of a rational argument.

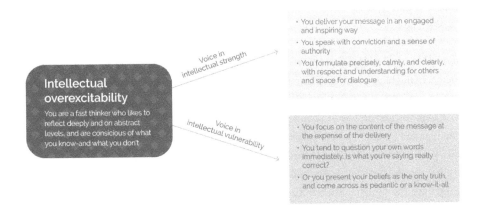

Intellectual overexcitability

You are a fast thinker who likes to reflect deeply and on abstract levels, and are conscious of what you know—and what you don't

Voice in intellectual strength

- You deliver your message in an engaged and inspiring way
- You speak with conviction and a sense of authority
- You formulate precisely, calmly, and clearly, with respect and understanding for others and space for dialogue

Voice in intellectual vulnerability

- You focus on the content of the message at the expense of the delivery
- You tend to question your own words immediately. Is what you're saying really correct?
- Or you present your beliefs as the only truth, and come across as pedantic or a know-it-all

Consider the example of defending a research thesis. The culmination of all your hard intellectual work, it can be an empowering, even joyful experience; at the same time, it's frightening and highly stressful. I get a lot of requests for voice coaching from academics who need to defend their PhD dissertations or apply for research grants. These people have worked for years on a particular subject in such a detailed scientific way that being factual and precise has long been their top concern. Besides, the more you know about a subject, the more you realize what you actually *don't* know. If you're a specialist in a field, you know that it's much more complicated than the amateur understands. When the time comes for you to speak about your project to those amateurs, however, this precision—which is a first factor trait for you if you have intellectual OE, reinforced by the second factor of academic tradition—can be a real burden. Suddenly, you have to transform the results of your research into an engaging talk that other people can comprehend. But here's the paradoxical truth of the matter: Intellectual OE in its vulnerable state will make you sound insecure and reluctant, obscuring your knowledge and experience.

Then there's another possible manifestation of intellectual OE in vulnerability—and that's when your autonomic nervous system activates *fight* mode. By that, I mean those times when your intellectual OE leads you to believe that your conviction is the whole truth, leaving no space for the views of others. Truth—or what you *believe* to be true—is more important to you than connecting with others. Moreover, when you're in intellectual fight mode, you throw intellectual humility out the window. You forget that there may be some important data in other people's views, and you give up on the difficult, messy, human work of bringing them around to your view. Instead, you come across as pedantic or a know-it-all. An example of this is Australian comedian Hannah Gadsby, who can come across as fierce and defensive, setting some people against her.

In both the fight and the flight manifestations of intellectual OE, you're concerned with the content of your message at the expense of its delivery and the connection with your audience. On the level of the autonomic nervous system, this means that you don't feel safe, so your social engagement system is not in the lead. Because of this, you're unable to move people. Once you reach that point, self-consciousness begins to inhibit your enthusiasm.

This is what my client George experienced while preparing his best man's speech for his friend's wedding. Being highly critical of himself, George didn't want to let anyone down. So he overprepared, going so far as to memorize what he had written. When he practiced it with me, we agreed that it sounded like he was presenting the annual numbers of his company. His intonation was monotone, and his inner critic went over everything he said with a fine-tooth comb. Memorizing a talk word for word doesn't necessarily lead to a good presentation. If you stay fixed on saying the exact words you rehearsed, you'll sacrifice your spontaneity. Your brain will work so hard to reproduce the content correctly that it will be impossible for you to convey its message in an engaging way.

To avoid overpreparing, focus on your delivery, not the content of your message. You do this by setting intentions about the feelings and values you want to convey. In Chapter 11, you'll learn how you can do that. It will also be helpful to know some ways to nurture your social engagement mode. Chapters 9 and 10 will help you with that.

Sensual Overexcitability

Development through positive disintegration mainly unfolds through emotional, intellectual, and imaginational overexcitability. During this process, the sensual and psychomotor OEs will gradually come to be channeled differently, supporting the other three domains of OE. Sensual OE, for instance, invites those who have it to express their voice in an aesthetic way. When sensually empowered, you desire artistic and emotional expression through your voice. For you, vocal expression is an enhanced experience, and it brings you intense joy to use it for singing, acting, giving speeches or voice-over work. In fact, among vocal artists who enjoy taking the stage, I suspect there are few individuals who *don't* have sensual OE. When this OE is expressed in vulnerability, however, the result is a desire to be admired for your voice, chasing attention, recognition, or fame. Such a person can also be overly theatrical or dramatic in vocal expression.

I identify with sensual overexcitability a lot myself, and certainly not only in the field of the voice. I invite you to reflect on the possibilities of sensual OE within yourself, because understanding your relationship with your sense perception will teach you a lot about yourself and how you experience the world. Which of your five senses are the most intense? Is there one that clearly stands out, or are all of them strong? Do you think your sensual perception is stronger or weaker than others'? Are you explicitly drawn to certain stimuli, or do you avoid them?

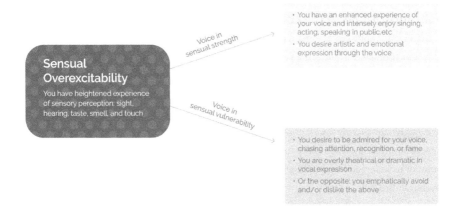

It's always tricky to compare the intensity of your own sense perceptions to those of others because your own senses are the only ones you can perceive directly. Moreover, many people enjoy music, art, good food, scents, and touching without being sensually overexcitable. Nevertheless, I have come to suspect that my responses to sensations of sight, smell, and touch are stronger than average because they quickly overwhelm me. For example, the smells coming from the garbage bin evoke my gag reflex. I love touching animals: Whenever I meet a cat or dog, I get intense enjoyment out of stroking their fur and feeling their warmth. Thanks to a boost from my overexcitable imagination, even watching animals on TV has this effect on me, leading me to imagine how the fur of a tiger or a bear would feel under my hands. When it comes to performing concerts, I struggle with my sensitivity to visual stimuli. Rather than an open hall where people are walking around, I prefer to perform in a theater, where everybody sits in seats. It distracts me when people are moving around in front of me, walking in and out, which means there's a good chance I'll forget the lyrics or play a wrong note. You might think that this is something an artist would just have to get used to, but after years of performing, I've only noticed a minor improvement. I actually perform best with my eyes closed. I'm also much more comfortable as a studio musician than as a performer. Live performance will always be challenging for me.

When it comes to hearing, however, I think my sense perception is normal. I can listen to music non-stop without feeling overwhelmed. This could be one of the reasons why I was drawn to music as a profession instead of, say, graphic design. I'm perfectly capable of energetically rehearsing, recording, and mixing music for hours, whereas working at a screen all day wears me out. I try to avoid too much screen time. I also enjoy being in the spotlight as I perform. Is it possible that sensual OE directed me into the career of a singer and musician? Is my sense of hearing in the sweet spot to intensely enjoy and create sound aesthetics, without getting overwhelmed too easily? These are the sort of interesting questions you might also ask yourself about your experiences with intensity.

Psychomotor Overexcitability

The mobilized, impulsive, energetic people who have psychomotor overexcitability tend to talk quickly and abundantly. This is the sympathetic response mode of the autonomic nervous system in its purest form. Its strengths and vulnerabilities on the level of the voice overlap somewhat with those of imaginational OE, and in my experience, the two domains often go hand in hand. When your psychomotor OE is balanced, you are an energetic, inspiring speaker. In conversations, you reply quickly and sharply and you often take the lead. In vulnerability, this goes into overdrive. You speak too quickly, don't allow space for others in conversations, and reply too impulsively. It is common to have vocal tics, and I also believe that stammering can be an emergent phenomenon of psychomotor OE.

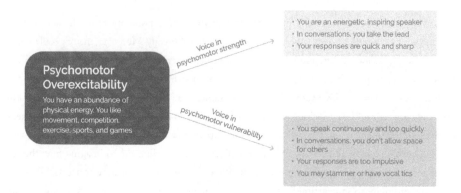

It's worth noting that the psychomotor is the only domain in which I myself am not overexcitable, so my analysis here is based on working with others who do have this trait.

I want to share one particular case with you on this subject. Though I base this only on my observations and not on formal research, it offers an alternative take for people who fit this overexcitable profile and aren't satisfied with the limited understanding offered by speech pathologists.

Jamie was in his twenties when he contacted me. His problem was stammering. He'd tried several therapies, none of which had been successful. It was clear to me that Jamie had several domains of overexcitability, but psychomotor OE stood out in particular. This seemed, in fact, the origin of many of his strengths and vulnerabilities. He was brimming over with so much energy that he was always on the move, whether going somewhere or engaging in sports. He was constantly searching for new challenges and activities in his daily life. He told me that he used movement to ground himself and to calm his active mind. His overload of energy also translated into tics such as drumming on objects with his hands or feet. Being a real doer, he was always on the lookout for solutions and next steps.

He needed significant variety in his daily activities so as not to get bored and lose focus. He found it difficult to sit still and could only focus his attention when something truly interested him—at which point he went into hyper focus. This focus on an activity or subject could be quite strong for a couple weeks, after which he got bored quickly and lost interest. This made it challenging for Jamie to commit to a three- or four-year course of higher education. Instead, he worked at a deli shop. On top of all this, Jamie was extremely sensitive to sensory information from his environment. When too much was going on around him, or when he was among too many people in a compact space, he got overwhelmed by all the different energies and lost his sense of grounding and contact with his body. His nervous system couldn't process all that information and began, as he described, to short-circuit.

Then there was his speech—way too fast. I suspect this was related to the high processing speed of his nervous system. The pace of his speech made him trip over his words. When this mechanism went into overdrive, it turned into stammering. In these moments, he said, it was as if his head was overflowing with thoughts and emotions, and he wasn't able to regulate them. As with most people who stammer, this only happens when they have to relate to other people. When Jamie sings, he doesn't stammer. Nor does he when he reads my voice exercises from the sheet. He also told me he stammers in different ways with different people. Another client who overcame stammering told me that, for him, the issue had to do with whether he felt that he had permission from his environment to speak. All of this leads me to suspect that stammering can be a symptom of heightened sensitivity or an overstimulated nervous system.

Jamie was aware that speech was not only his vulnerability, but also his strength. Because of his sensitivity, he was extremely good at observing his environment and spotting details; consequently, he had a unique and original view of the world that he believed was worth sharing with others. But speech was also Jamie's preferred coping strategy: Whenever he wanted to avoid unwelcome feelings, he started talking nonstop in order not to feel what he felt.

Here's something to note as well: The things that are most important and valuable to you are generally the ones that will make you feel most vulnerable.

Jamie's main challenge each day was how to regulate his energy. He was afraid to try new things because he thought he wouldn't be able to channel his energy properly. He therefore didn't play music, try his hand at making films, or sign up for further education—all projects that he would really have liked to pursue, but thought his excess energy would doom him to failure. This led him to feel further restlessness, as he was not doing the things he wanted to do in life, nor living according his values. It was a vicious circle.

I mentioned earlier that gifted people sometimes get (mis)diagnosed with ADHD. Given that Jamie's story may look to some eyes like a textbook case of ADHD, you might ask why I argue that Jamie's abundance of energy, sensitivity, and restlessness is better described as psychomotor, emotional, and imaginational OE and not ADHD? As he and I both understand it, his story is not one of an innate, primary deficit of attention. Rather, it's about the challenges that come with living with intensity, when this intensity is mainly expressed in vulnerability.

If you have psychomotor OE, there are ways to regulate this and avoid ending up in overdrive. In order to do so, you need to know your body very well and listen to its signals. In Chapter 9, you will find exercises to train body awareness. Generally, when you feel an overload of energy in your body, mobilize: exercise, play games, dance, go for a walk, or do whatever you like to do to release energy. At the same time however, be aware that after intense activity, your body needs to restore. So after this outburst of energy, see if you can slow down and relax for a while, listening to music, reading a book, or watching a movie. Understand that it might take a while for your body to adjust to this calming activity, so don't give up immediately if you still feel restless in the beginning.

As my friend and medical doctor Caroline van Oene—who identifies with the abundance of energy that comes with psychomotor OE—says, "The faster you go, the longer it takes to slow down." Allow your nervous system some time to regulate your state. Moreover, if you find it hard to focus, and quickly lose your attention, it's essential for you to practice focused attention meditation, as described in Chapter 12. The best time for you to do this is after you've engaged in an activity to release energy. There's still a good chance that you won't like this type of meditation because you'll feel you're extremely bad at it. This emphatically means that it is the right exercise for you!

In my clients' experiences, I've seen evidence that a person's overload of physical energy can—if regulated in the right way—eventually come to serve his imaginational talents and creative output. This is also what I advised to Jamie, to channel his energy into activities that would make use of his creative talents. This would help him to find a new direction for his excess energy and to develop the strengths of his imaginational OE. So ask yourself, what's your preferred creative outlet? Instead of always going for the physical release of energy, try channeling this energy through activities such as painting, writing, making music, making videos, or building something.

5.3. Taking a Closer Look at the Sensitive Nervous System

"In the end it is not vulnerability but sensitivity that defines the orchid, and when given the right support, that sensitivity can blossom into lives of great joy, success and beauty."
- W. Thomas Boyce, MD

The people I describe in this chapter seem to have extremely sensitive nervous systems which are at the root of the problems they experience with their voice. But maybe you want to know what it actually means, to have a sensitive nervous system? And where does it come from? In the last part of this chapter we'll dive deeper into this matter.

When the concept of the highly sensitive person (HSP) was introduced by Elaine Aron in 1996, many who recognized themselves in what she described embraced the framework. They didn't need to toughen up; they were actually wired differently than most others, not just weak, whining, or overemotional. The scientific community—and the general public—remained skeptical for many years, questioning whether high sensitivity was a real phenomenon. Nowadays, however, the fact that sensitivity is not equally distributed over the population is increasingly backed up by research.

One especially insightful addition to this evidence is *The Orchid and The Dandelion*, a book by medical doctor W. Thomas Boyce detailing his career's work studying high sensitivity. During pediatric research on the effects of stress on the physical health of children, Boyce discovered that children differed in their reactivity to stress. In one experiment, he had children execute challenging tasks in a controlled laboratory setting, then measured their cortisol, blood pressure, heart rate, and heart rate variability. His findings suggested that neurobiological reactivity—including markers of fight-or-flight activity like cortisol production—varies enormously within populations of children. The variation in stress response follows a standard bell curve: about 60-70% of the children show average stress reactivity, 15-20% show low stress reactivity, and 15-20% of the children show high stress reactivity.

Image source: W. Thomas Boyce, MD *The Orchid And The Danelion - Why Sensitive People Struggle And How All Can Thrive* (2019, Penguin Radndom House LLC, New York)

Through her own research, Aron also found that 15-20% of the human population is more sensitive than the rest—the individuals she called highly sensitive people. Boyce, who executed his research in the same decade as Aron, gave his 15-20% a different name: *orchids*. Orchids are fragile flowers that need special care and nurturing to blossom. If you neglect their special needs, they will quickly wither. But if you take care of them properly, they blossom with an exquisite beauty. On the other side of this metaphor, he called children who were less reactive to stress *dandelions*, after the sturdy flowers that thrive virtually anywhere. Like these flowers, children with lower stress reactivity are much more likely to overcome neglect and difficulties.

Based on that, you might think anyone would prefer to be a dandelion. But, as Boyce found, it's a bit more complicated than that. When he researched the rates of respiratory illnesses in relation to stress exposure for children, he made another remarkable discovery. Children with highly sensitive nervous systems *had* both the highest *and* the lowest rates of respiratory illnesses, depending upon their levels of exposure to stress. The dandelions, with their low to average levels of stress reactivity, had modest levels of illness under both low- and high-stress circumstances. Children with a more sensitive nervous system, however, actually got sick less than average *if they were in a supportive environment;* otherwise, they got sick *more* than average.

After years of research on this subject, Boyce has concluded that it would be a mistake to see orchid children as weaker. Rather, his findings mean only that they are more susceptible to the conditions of their environment. As he writes, "They were more open, more permeable, more tender to the powerful influences, both bad and good, of the context in which they were living and growing."[10] Imagine what this means for the second developmental factor from Chapter 4, your environment. For orchids, this factor should be more influential in the shaping of their voices than for dandelions.

The Origin of Sensitivity

So, does this mean that you are born either an orchid or a dandelion, and that this is written in stone? The answer is not simple, since both genes and environment decide where you are on the sensitivity spectrum. Boyce tells us that sensitivity probably develops from interactions between genes and external influences. A genotype plus its environment creates a phenotype.

So why would a trait like sensitivity be distributed so unevenly in the human population? The current theory points to evolution. Highly reactive, super-sensitive phenotypes have probably been favored by natural selection in humans (and animals)—to a point, that is. Having some individuals with enhanced vigilance would have been beneficial to the protection of a group. They are more alert to their surroundings and better able to detect danger cues. However, this sensitivity comes with a cost. When the environment is not safe, orchid types suffer intensely from the consequences of stress, to the extent that they don't function well anymore. So after danger is detected by the orchids, it is up to the more sturdy dandelions in a group to mobilize, fight, and protect the herd from intruders.

Currently there is no therapy to make the nervous system less reactive, nor is there treatment for

---

10   W.T. Boyce, MD *The Orchid and The Dandelion – Why Sensitive People Struggle And How All Can Thrive* (2019, Penguin Random House LLC, New York) p. 48.

those whose fight-or-flight responses stay activated for too long. You can take tranquilizers and beta-blockers, but these treat merely the symptom, not the cause. Psychiatric researchers are working to find a treatment to "reset" the nervous system, as youth trauma affects more people than you might expect (approximately 1 out of 6). It can, however, help to get to know your nervous system and identify what triggers your defenses. If you listen to your body, follow up on its signs, and learn to regulate your nervous system, sensitivity becomes less of a burden.

Orchids and Overexcitability

What I find most striking about Boyce's findings is the orchid's capacity to reach the lowest of the low as well as the highest of the high. This offers a scientific basis for understanding why overexcitability can manifest as vulnerability, as well as strength. Moreover, it reinforces Dąbrowski's theory that the more sensitive and overexcitable among us are more likely to have inner conflict and possibly undergo a developmental process through disintegration.

Recall the second factor of development. If, as Boyce has shown, it has an outsized influence on these sensitive souls, then that helps explain why they are likely to have at least a unilevel disintegration—a process in which, according to Dąbrowski's work, the second factor plays an outsized part. For one child, getting bullied at school is a nasty experience, but it doesn't affect the course of his life. For another child, bullying is a traumatic experience that will cause problems with self-confidence, trust, and anxiety as an adult—and lead to the sort of internal and external conflict that is the gateway to positive disintegration. And it was the overexcitability of a sensitive nervous system that made this happen.

But there's a difference between Boyce and Dąbrowski—and that is with the possibility of *multilevel* disintegration and development. Whereas Boyce claims that orchids will only thrive in a good environment, Dąbrowski's theory argues that conflict is a *condition* for personal growth. You could say that Boyce's theory only looks at the first and second factors of development in the theory of positive disintegration—the process we would call "normal development." Dąbrowski defines this as

> a type of development which is most common and which entails the least amount of inner conflict and of psychological transformation. Development is limited to the maturational stages of human life and to the innate psychological type of the individual. In developmental terms normality means an undistorted, i.e., free from accident, expression of developmental potential.[11]

Dąbrowski takes this process one step further and says that *those with a great developmental potential can still thrive when the environment is not good.* And Dąbrowskian potential consists of more than genetic make-up and the environment: It also includes the third factor, the impact of your conscious choices, and autonomously selected values. Recall that this is the process where you increase your vocal comfort zone, and consciously choose what type of voice is *more yourself* and *less yourself.*

---

11   K. Dąbrowski *Multilevelness of Emotional and Instinctive Functions* (1996 Towarzystwo Naukowe, Lublin 1996) p. 20–21.

The stronger a person's third factor is, the more resistant to environmental pressures her development will become. It pushes development beyond unilevel to multilevel development, proceeding from conflict with, to opposition of, first and second factors. The medical research Boyce did on stress reactivity, sensitivity, and susceptibility to the environment nevertheless gives the theory of positive disintegration a solid grounding, offering valuable information for those who identify with Dąbrowki's overexcitabilities or Boyce's orchid metaphor.

6. Transformative Inner Forces

Mainstream mental health providers do not typically seem to recognize the potential dynamic power of experiences like intense feelings, nervousness, or depression. Our society generally sees these things as disorders that need to be fixed. If you tell a therapist that you're feeling overexcited, dissatisfied with yourself, or maladjusted to your surroundings, he might give you a diagnosis that suggests something is wrong with you, from ADHD or autism, to burnout or borderline personality disorder. If you have ever received such a diagnosis this may gave you a sense of reconciliation, or maybe not at all. From a polyvagal theory perspective, all mental disorders are dysregulations of the nervous system. And it's true that when you experience these things that we call mental disorders, you are most likely in an ongoing, unregulated sympathetic or dorsal vagal state of response. It makes you feel like you're in a crisis that needs resolution. And of course, as you know by now, your voice will reflect such a crisis.

Kazimierz Dąbrowski's insight, however, takes it even one step further. He says that not every psychological disturbance is a mental illness. He saw the developmental potential contained within certain painful experiences like dissatisfaction with oneself, positive maladjustment, and even guilt and shame. He called these things *dynamisms*. A dynamism is an inner force that ignites or accelerates the process of positive disintegration.

In Dąbrowski's theory of positive disintegration, dynamisms are processes of personal growth—and therefore a positive thing. Some dynamisms—especially those in the early stages of multilevel growth—have disintegrating qualities, while others serve to reintegrate. Each dynamism develops during the course of personal growth; some will resolve as part of that process, while others will sustain themselves going forward.

The creative instinct is itself a dynamism, and one of the ones that sustains itself through the process of development—but it does change as you develop. My own development as a singer is an example of this process. As you may recall from Chapter 3, I experienced classical singing as a form of musical craftsmanship, aiming to achieve aesthetic perfection. It adheres to established patterns, allowing only a modest space for unique, personal expression. Therefore I experienced this as a poor environment for developing my creative instinct as Dąbrowski defines it: a dynamism that pushes you to discover and mold new forms of reality.

When the creative instinct developed within me, I no longer saw a path forward through classical singing. But that experience—which originally felt like a failure—was an example of the dynamism of *positive maladjustment*. It motivated me to find other ways to express creativity through my voice, including vocal improvisation and composing my own music.

These dynamisms are often present in people who experience voice problems with no direct physical cause. Instead of trying to fix the voice itself, I encourage people to look at what's behind their perceived problem. What events and situations in your life might have caused it? Is your wish to change your voice intrinsically motivated, founded in a desire for personal growth? Or is it motivated by social pressures like fitting in at work? Maybe your vocal problem stems from a part of yourself that you're turning down. Can it be an invitation to identify your own values?

6.1. Unilevel vs. Multilevel Dynamisms

Each dynamism in TPD is linked to a developmental level. For our purposes, the most important distinction is between the dynamisms of *unilevel* and *multilevel* development, which we discussed in Chapter 3.[12] The unilevel development process has two characteristic, disintegrative dynamisms: *ambivalences* and *ambitendencies*. *Ambivalence* is going back and forth between opposing feelings or opinions, or the simultaneous experience of conflicting feelings and opinions. This can manifest as mood swings or fickleness. *Ambitendency* is the experience of wanting to follow conflicting courses of action; it stems from holding desires that are incompatible with one another. This typically leads to indecisiveness.

In **unilevel development**, though the creative instinct may be present in the form of a vague striving for artistic (vocal) expression, it's not yet connected to emotional and cognitive growth. When a creative person experiences ambivalances and ambitendencies, her aesthetic experiences lack the search for the "higher", which makes them unilevel. Instead, she creates to obtain approval and recognition.

Nevertheless, for many artists, the unilevel process does give rise to inspiration. Ambivalence and ambitendency are major causes of human suffering. In fact, they have inspired our most iconic works of art, music, literature, film and theatre. Virtually everyone can relate to unilevel suffering.

In **multilevel development**, however, the artist begins to perceive higher and lower paths—and begins to strive to take the higher. Here, the creative instinct combines with dynamisms that reflect this search for the "higher", and the challenges you'll encounter on this path. Examples of these dynamisms are *astonishment with yourself, dissatisfaction with yourself,* and *positive maladjustment*. In multilevel development, the creative instinct is also associated with nervousness, disquietude, depression, and anxiety. Creative expression—such as singing, acting and spoken word—is therefore one way to deal with these states of mind that are part and parcel of personality development through

---

12   In the theory of positive disintegration, Dąbrowski developed five levels, with each dynamism linked to a level. Level II is unilevel disintegration, while Levels III and IV are stages of multilevel disintegration. Level I is defined by the absence of dynamisms, while the dynamism of Level V is something Dąbrowski called the personality ideal.

inner conflict. For a long time, singing was my most important strategy for regulating my emotions. Singing a few songs was the best way for me to deal with nervousness, disquietude, depression, and anxiety. I always felt so much better afterward. If you like to sing as well, can you relate to this?

When I started to compose music and write lyrics myself, my singing became even more powerful, because I used it to reflect on myself and the world. By then, my creative instinct was strongly intertwined with my own developmental process. My songs were mirrors in which I could see myself. By playing them over and over, I integrated their messages into my system. I couldn't ignore what I was saying to myself anymore, and that gave them a therapeutic function.

Besides that, performing my songs before an audience required me to confront my own vulnerability. I was no longer dealing with my emotions privately; I was sharing them with the world. This was *painful*—certainly not something I'm naturally inclined to do! I'll never forget the first time I performed two of my songs at an open mic. I felt so uncomfortable—like I was practically naked. Although that performance went much better than the Billie Holiday song I performed in high school twenty years earlier, I had the same overwhelming emotional reaction after the open mic performance as I had back then: a combination of relief, ecstasy, failure, shame, exposure, and vulnerability. Over the years, I grew more accustomed to sharing my inner world with strangers while in the spotlight; nevertheless, I'm still much more comfortable composing and recording than I am performing.

Besides the creative instinct, there are other dynamisms in TPD that are connected to vocal expression. Because of the strong emotional charge of certain disintegrating dynamisms, these show themselves powerfully through the voice. This is where your voice functions as a barometer—an indication that something is out of balance in your life. In my personal experience, my voice has been the canary in the coal mine, signaling when change in other areas was necessary or even inevitable. When I had resolved those problems, my voice gave me further signals that things had fallen into place.

In this chapter, I'll review some dynamisms that are typical for multilevel development, using stories from my clients to illustrate how they reveal themselves through the voice. I will finish this chapter with a review of these dynamisms in the life and voice of a vocal artist who is close to my heart.

Astonishment with Oneself and Feelings of Inferiority Towards Oneself

A woman named Kim sent me the following email:

> *I want to be able to present more powerfully and use my voice more confidently in presentations, during meetings, and in groups when telling a story. When all eyes are on me, all tension goes to my throat and neck and I want to overcome this. I want to feel relaxed and at ease when telling a story.*

When we started working together, it became clear that the tension in Kim's voice stemmed from her tendency to put others first, constantly seeking their approval. Through the course of her sessions, Kim went through an intense period of change. Suddenly, she began to experience intense emotions that took her by surprise and overwhelmed her.

The dynamism *astonishment with oneself* is the beginning of the desire to change. By now, you know that I've experienced plenty of this myself. It is also the central motive for people like Kim to come to me to work on their voice. Their desire to change is activated by thoughts along the lines of "Something is not quite right with me." They want to find out what that is, so they can make it what it "ought to be." When this dynamism is at work, you develop a critical attitude towards yourself. You might be surprised by your own talents or mental and emotional abilities—or by the world and how other people behave.

During our sessions, Kim revealed that she didn't really find work important at all. She would have preferred to live a creative life in the countryside with her family, contributing to society in a more meaningful way. But though she had a clear view of the type of life she wanted, she was unsure of the path she would have to walk to get there. She had a desire to inspire others and therefore wanted to become a speaker—but to do that, she would first have to find out what she stood for. Together we noticed that her voice could be powerful and inspiring when she spoke from her intuition, with her attention in the present moment. But whenever she started to doubt herself, her voice would immediately reveal this. When she openly expressed her values, she felt vulnerable and insecure, worrying about what others would think. This fear of judgment was a blockage that kept her from expressing what was important to her. When we first recognized this, she interpreted it as fear that others wouldn't think she was good enough. The truth, however, was that *she herself* didn't think she was good enough.

In your disintegration process, astonishment with yourself can evolve into *inferiority toward yourself*. This happens when you become aware of what you could be—but also of the fact that you're not there yet. Inferiority toward yourself is about the disparity between "what is" and "what ought to be." It's the stage in your development where you are consciously incompetent, striving to become consciously competent. This can be on the level of voice technique, communication, singing, public speaking, or any other aspect of your life. You're also increasingly aware of your pitfalls, vulnerabilities, potential, and strength. You get more insight into your essence and your personal values—the person you would like to be. You get a sense of what is "more yourself" and "less yourself". And you recognize that there's a lot of work ahead.

At the end of our time together, Kim realized what was holding her back from speaking up, and expressing what she stood for. She learned that she doesn't always have to put the needs of others first. Her own developmental process is important too, and she now allows herself to devote time and energy to it. Granted, it's an intense and tiring process, and her emotional roller coaster has accelerated in recent months. This, however, is a sign that dynamisms are at work and that she's on the right track. She's now fully willing to feel everything she feels—without suppressing or avoiding it. That's already a major achievement. In the long run, Kim will learn how to make sense of these strong emotions and develop skills in regulating them.

Disquietude and Dissatisfaction with Oneself

Victoria came to my practice looking for voice coaching because of conflicts at work. In our first session, I immediately noticed that she talked to me in a high-pitched, artificial voice. When I confronted her with that, she told me that this always happens when she's in a new situation or when she doesn't feel confident. She explained that she often avoided giving honest opinions or saying what was really going on in her mind because she was worried about what others might think of her. That artificial high voice is a mask that she put on in an effort to sound sweet and endearing—but that actually made people find her inauthentic and annoying.

Victoria feared disappointing others, not being taken seriously and coming across as stupid. She also feared showing that she was easily moved emotionally and was ashamed of her looks. (As a child, she was bullied because she was heavier than others.) Moreover, she was still ashamed of the things she experienced as child, and she wanted to get over it. In order to do so, she thought she needed to toughen up. The fact that she hadn't been able to do so just deepened her disappointment in herself.

She was conscious of all of these feelings, but her disappointment led her to fight against them. So I asked her to allow those feelings to unfold instead of pushing them away. By actively practicing this awareness, she was able to feel how they affected her body. This goes to show how much such feelings can affect the voice—as well as the rest of the body.

These feelings also spilled over to cause the problems she was having at work. Victoria had many talents, but she kept herself small and downplayed her potential. She feared that showing her potential would offend or threaten her colleagues. But those colleagues already sensed that she was acting inauthentically, picking up on something insincere in her communication. Moreover, Victoria also had a strong sense of justice. This caused conflict because her colleagues played manipulative games with each other, and she found it hard to adapt to this culture. I asked her what would happen if she started to share her opinions at work—to open up and show who she really is. Her colleagues could either appreciate her directness or condemn her opinions. But either way, she would have retained her integrity.

In Victoria, I recognized the dynamisms *disquietude* and *dissatisfaction with oneself*. Disquietude with yourself gives rise to a vocal inner critic, spouting negative attitudes and feelings of dislike or disapproval toward yourself. In Victoria's case, she also disapproved of the fact that her emotional overexcitability revealed itself through her voice. She kept on running away from these parts of herself because she felt she ought to overcome rather than accept them.

A strong emotional charge is a burden when you are in the spotlight. Speaking up at a meeting at work can overwhelm your already-burdened nervous system. Disquietude can be a sign that you are gradually becoming open to inner psychic transformation. It shows that you have a strong desire to understand yourself, your thoughts, emotions, and actions. This often leads people to search for professional guidance.

When a feeling of disquietude develops a particularly negative slant, it becomes dissatisfaction. The dynamism of dissatisfaction with oneself is an expression of a critical, condemning attitude towards yourself (and maybe, if you're reading this book, your voice). You may experience anxiety, depression and a strong desire to escape or eliminate the things you don't like about yourself. As you think about who you really want to be, you gradually become aware what is "more yourself" and "less yourself."

During our sessions together, it became clear that when Victoria expressed what she really thought and felt, her voice sounded honest and sincere. She became aware of how she came across when she puts on the mask, and of why people reacted to her the way they did. We also established that the high-pitched, artificial voice is Victoria's coping mechanism to bypass emotions she doesn't want to show. She was ashamed of being so emotionally moved and didn't want others to notice. Without her protective mask, she often got a lump in her throat and teared up. Consequently, she felt she could never be herself in the work environment and speak up about what was really on her mind. It was a big step for her to acknowledge all of this. However, she now knew that, in order to grow as a person, she needed to be more aware of her emotions. The next step for Victoria was to accept her emotional overexcitability by truly coming to understand how it could be a strength—that it was part of the potential she offered the world.

Feelings of Shame and Guilt

Khadija came to me for coaching because she found it difficult to speak up in groups. She had a sense that she wasn't being heard by others. It was clear to me that there was a lot inside her to be heard: She described an intense inner world, and her emotional overexcitability became clear when I encouraged her to try speaking with a louder voice. The loudness of her voice took her by such surprise that she got overwhelmed, her eyes welling up with tears.

Khadija had always been self-conscious and critical of her own performance. This led her to double down on her focus regarding the content of her message. The problem was that this came at the expense of her delivery, which was where her weakness truly lay. Whenever she was in a situation where she wanted to contribute to a discussion, she feared others' judgment. Her mind would go blank and she didn't know what to say. While it's not uncommon to experience fight-or-flight reactions in uncomfortable social situations, they don't always go as far as Khadija's, whose autonomic nervous system took her all the way into freeze. While in such a state, it can be hard even to recognize what's happening, let alone articulate it. But when she recalled one of these experiences afterward through an introspection exercise, her feelings of vulnerability, sadness, uncertainty, uneasiness, and fear came clearly to the surface.

Although Khadija didn't explicitly mention feelings of *shame*, her experience is an example of this dynamism. Shame is a powerful feeling of embarrassment and dissatisfaction with yourself. When it comes to the realm of the voice, a lot of people feel shame over the quality of their public speaking or singing, with stage fright as a result. They get nervous and want to get the situation over with as quickly as possible. I remember these feelings all too well from my first solo performance in high school. When you are in the spotlight, feelings of shame can cause fight, flight, or even freeze responses. Khadija aspired to perfection, which made her extremely critical of her own performance. She was highly concerned with what others might say and think about her. Not only was she afraid to disappoint others, she also didn't want to disappoint herself. Whenever her nervous system immobilized her—which it did automatically to protect her—she would judge herself afterward for overreacting to the situation. This is a feeling of *guilt* over letting someone (namely herself) down.

When you feel this sort of guilt, which is a dynamism, you're aware of your own imperfections. You recognize that your self-improvement in certain areas, for instance, public speaking and self-development, are going slower than you'd like. It's self-oriented perfectionism: You are intrinsically motivated to reach high personal standards and extremely self-critical when you fail to do so. You can observe your own behavior, think about it, and evaluate. You tend to think thoughts like, "I should have done or said this instead of that," or "If only I could go back to that situation and act differently." It's the experience of feeling embarrassed, not only in front of others, but also about yourself and your own ideal of personality.

After we were finished with our sessions, Khadija emailed me about her progress. The fact that now she was willing to accept uncomfortable emotions, actually gave her more opportunity to express herself:

> I notice now that there is a pattern: if I have to get through my first uncomfortable feeling of being on the spot, I often can't get my words out. But now I manage to keep on talking at moments like this, and from there I can get myself back together and things are improving. I think acceptance of the discomfort has played an important role here. When it comes to using my voice now, I notice that I have more control, and that I am no longer uncomfortable when I think that others cannot understand me. I know what I can do to make myself heard, and I am able to do that.

Positive Maladjustment

Thomas was a highly intelligent young man who came to see me because he wanted to learn how to express more emotion and enthusiasm with his voice. He had had a tough childhood, going through some traumatic events that might have caused him to speak, as he did, in a flat voice, with all syllables short and little intonation.

Like so many of my clients, Thomas was concerned with what others thought of him. He didn't like to show too much emotion because it made him feel vulnerable. When he got nervous, he would begin to talk faster, more monotonously, and under his breath.

Thomas was perfectionistic, analytical, and thought a lot, which led him to formulate his sentences carefully—except in those occasional instances when he'd surprise himself by letting something intuitive pop out. He felt he must always perform at his best and never give up. To get any rest at all, he had to justify it to himself by reminding himself that it would help him continue later with what he needed to do. But he didn't enjoy his rest; nor did he pause to enjoy his achievements much, always going straight to his next goal. When he failed to meet his own requirements, he felt like he was not good enough.

During our work together, Thomas discovered that what he sought was to become less judgmental and more compassionate towards himself. Although he experienced emotions like self-judgment, Thomas reported that he didn't experience strong emotions of joy. He told me that, at the moment, he was quite satisfied with having a job and a relationship, and that he was planning to undertake an acting course. After his turbulent childhood, he was content to experience some peace and tranquility—even if it came with a certain emotional flat-line. This, however, didn't make it easy for us to work on expressing emotion and enthusiasm through his voice.

Thomas's case presented a key question for us to explore: Did he truly *want* the things he set out to achieve, or was he driven by the fact that he never felt good enough? Was voice coaching something he wished to pursue for himself or to better fit in with his work environment?

In addition to voice techniques, Thomas and I worked on awareness of his thoughts and feelings. We discussed the process of accepting difficult emotions and dealing with unhelpful thoughts through the practices of mindfulness and of actively identifying his values. In the end, he realized that for now, it's okay that he doesn't express many emotions. Moreover, if he doesn't feel certain emotions, he doesn't need to pretend that he does. He realized that society may see this differently, expecting him to be more emotionally expressive—but he doesn't feel an obligation anymore to meet this expectation.

These realizations helped Thomas accept himself, allowing him to feel more peace and less chaos in his mind. And once he developed that self-acceptance, he realized that *that* was what he was really here for: at this moment in his life, he didn't really need to learn vocal expression at all. Thomas now trusts that he can live according to his own values and he is prepared to accept whatever consequences come with that.

Thomas's acceptance of the fact that he's out of step with his environment—but in step with his own values—is an example of *positive maladjustment*. This dynamism is the attitude of rejection of the primitive requirements of a social group. This can be a certain social norm, like the expectation that you will communicate emotions via your voice. It can also be a rejection of violations of your own ethical principles. At some point in your development, you might feel the need to step away from how everyone else is doing things and figure out who you are, independent of your social group and its norms. Such a process will ultimately require you to determine your own authentic hierarchy of values—and to live your life by them. As your awareness of higher values grows, you drift away from the status quo, reject the standards of your social environment, and walk your own path. Ultimately, however, you are able to develop a healthy attitude toward your environment instead of rebelling against it. You understand others' needs and motives, and you even tolerate their imperfections and distortions (as long as they are not harmful to anyone). Thomas understood that being accepting and compassionate toward himself was more important than adapting to a social norm about how he should use his voice.

6.2. The Unilevel and Multilevel Development of Marvin Gaye

The process towards inner transformation is never easy. While some survive this period relatively safely, others experience serious despair, the diagnosis of mental disorder, addiction, and even self-destruction.

Those who are public figures face additional challenges. Despite their fame and fortune, many respected creative artists struggled their whole life to combine their desire for creative expression with the expectations of their families, their industries, and their audiences. Sometimes they were also haunted by traumatic experiences from their youth. It's no coincidence that pop stars like Amy Winehouse, Kurt Cobain, Avicii, Jimi Hendrix, Jim Morrison, Michael Jackson, and Whitney Houston died young.

Marvin Gaye is another musical artist who died before his time. I discovered his work in my early teens. I had just subscribed to *OOR*, a Dutch music magazine; as a welcome present, they sent me a CD called *The Very Best Of Marvin Gaye*. Though I only had a faint idea of who this man was, I was curious, so I put the disc in my CD player. What I heard blew me away. The first two songs on the CD were indeed two of his very best: *I Heard It Through The Grapevine* and *What's Going On*. These Motown classics were a far cry from the grunge bands like Nirvana, Pearl Jam, and Soundgarden that were popular at that time, in the early nineties. These bands had little to offer a teenager who aspired to become a trained, lyrical singer. Gaye's music, however, was honey to my ears. His voice—with its light timbre and multi-track vocal arrangements—inspired me to develop my voice in a similar way, ultimately creating my own vocal harmonic arrangements.

Woven together with the quality of his sound was the content of his lyrics. Gaye shared his confusion, struggles, and inner conflicts in a raw, unfiltered way, inviting his listeners to see their own struggles reflected in his. And this extremely intense, hypersensitive man had a mountain of struggles to share.

Overexcitabilities and Growing Up in an Unsafe Environment

The son of a church minister at a Hebrew Pentecostal church in Washington, D.C., Marvin Gaye (born Marvin Pentz Gay Jr.) had a strict religious upbringing. He was close to his mother—the ideal woman against whom no other woman would ever measure up. His father, however, who was probably an extremely damaged man, held a grudge against him, beginning when he was very young. Gaye struggled to meet his father's unrealistic expectations:

> *Living with Father was something like living with a king, [...] a very peculiar, changeable, cruel, and all-powerful king. You were supposed to tip toe around his moods. You were supposed to do anything to win his favor. I never did. Even though winning his love was the ultimate goal of my childhood, I defied him. I hated his attitude. I thought I could win his love through singing, so I sang my heart out. But the better I became, the greater his demands. I could never please him, and if it wasn't for Mother, who was always there to console me and praise my singing, I think I would have been one of those child suicide cases you read about in the papers.[13]*

At his father's hand, young Marvin underwent emotional abuse and brutal beatings. Such a childhood leaves a mark, tainting love and affection with violence through his adult life.

He grew up with many insecurities. He felt inferior towards others as well as inferior towards himself—the latter of which, as you will recall, is a dynamism. He was especially insecure about his voice, as explained by author David Ritz in his biography of Gaye, *Divided Soul*:

> *I was always afraid that I had no style. Compared to the other fellas on the street, my voice sounded small. It took me a long time just to open my mouth, and when I did, I was sure to be slapped down by the singer next to me. Besides, the kind of vocalist I wanted to be—pure pop—was almost always a baritone. All the famous ones, like Tony Bennett and Nat Cole, had deeper voices than mine.[14]*

Gaye clearly had overexcitability. Sensual, emotional, and imaginational OE stand out in particular. A girl from his music group at school described him like this:

> *He was different. You sensed that right away. Extremely sensitive and very lonely. Marvin was definitely a loner. No girlfriends, and not the kind of fella who'd hit on girls either. He had fine manners, and you could tell he had real breeding. He used to wear his pants real baggy—I remember that—and he was always neat and well-groomed. He was a gentleman. Fact is all the time he was in our group I didn't know he could sing, 'cause he was strictly playing piano. Marvin had a perfect ear and played just beautifully. I suppose he was too shy to sing.[15]*

One of his best friends painted a similar picture:

> *He had such a relaxed and breezy sense of humor that you'd think that he didn't have a care in the world. Then the next day he might start telling you about his problems, and it seemed he was carrying the world on his shoulders.[16]*

---

13   D. Ritz *Divided Soul: The Life of Marvin Gaye* (1991, Omnibus Press, London) p. 28.
14   Ibid. p. 48.
15   Ibid. p. 45.
16   Ibid. p. 148.

Gaye's sensitivity probably contributed to his confusion about manhood and sexuality, which would remain a source of tension and even conflict throughout his life. His music might give you the impression that he was a slick seducer and confident lover. But in reality, he was convinced that his elegant, flexible tenor voice was not masculine enough, and he felt sexually inadequate throughout his life. Being the son of a preacher, sex was an inner conflict—a dangerous force that was incompatible with peace of mind and a virtuous life. While in his musical career he found himself playing the role of Dionysus, god of indiscriminate sex, he longed to be Apollo, god of song. We see this in his ambivalence toward his female fans, whom he feared and hated for turning him into a sex symbol—but whom he needed for the recognition he desperately sought.

Adding to this inner conflict was the fact that his father was sexually ambiguous and liked to dress up like a woman. Gaye admitted to his biographer that he had similar feelings: "[T]o tell you the truth, I have the same fascination with women's clothes. In my case, that has nothing to do with any attraction for men. Sexually, men don't interest me. But seeing myself as a woman is something that intrigues me. It's also something I fear. I indulge myself only at the most discrete and intimate moments. Afterwards, I must bear the guilt and shame for weeks."[17] By the time Gaye was signed by Motown, he had added the letter 'e' to his surname. In no way did he want to be associated with a word like "gay."

Ritz believed that it was precisely these feminine qualities that made Gaye so successful with a female audience. He used his voice to express his most intimate feelings. By exposing his vulnerability and emotional sensitivity, he drove women crazy:

> It was a power that frightened me. [...] My singing covered up for the action I was not getting. It always has. I'm a sexy singer, though, I think it has to do with something deeper than sex. I saw that I was reaching these girls on a mystical level. Almost like I was one of them.[18]

Gaye however, never accepted that his feminine qualities were part of his talent. This inner conflict continued throughout his life.

It was in his youth that we begin to see Gaye's unilevel dynamisms, emerging from the tension between his sensitivities and his desires. He longed for recognition and attention from girls while at the same time aspiring for his music to be part of a greater cause. As an adolescent, he joined a doo-wop group—his first venture singing outside of church—but even with his talent on display, Marvin was too shy to approach girls—too afraid of rejection. Instead of risking it, he opted to fantasize about love. The sensitive doo-wop songs turned out to be a perfect outlet to vent his emotions of loneliness and unrequited love. At the same time, this quiet, sensitive boy had megalomaniacal fantasies. He aspired to be the next Frank Sinatra, admiring not only Sinatra's music, but also his glamorous Hollywood lifestyle. He dreamed of sleeping with as many women as Sinatra.

Simultaneously—and despite this less than holy ambition—Gaye took a spiritual perspective on his life. He felt driven to spread the message of God through musical ministry, and he wanted to

---

17   Ibid. p. 33.
18   Ibid. p. 55.

use music to make the world a better place. His role model in this respect was Bob Marley, who he thought came closest to his ideal of using song to raise people's consciousness and improve their lot in life.

The Early Motown Years: Negative Adjustment

Gaye's fantasies became reality when, in 1961, he got signed by Motown. In those early years, he sang uncomplicated, happy love songs that reflected his love for Anna Gordy, the sister of Motown founder Berry Gordy. Gaye married Anna Gordy in 1963, on the way to becoming Motown's best-selling male artist. He was especially successful as a duet singer with Diana Ross, Kim Weston, and Tammi Terrell.

As he adjusted to Motown's social norms—a type of adjustment that in TPD is called *negative adjustment*—inner conflict lingered. He never believed that his success was a result of his talent; rather, he credited it to external influences like his marriage to Anna Gordy, who was seventeen years his senior and had inside knowledge of the music industry. The fact was, such tremendous success was not easy for someone with as complex an inner world as Gaye. Suddenly, he had access to the fame and fortune he'd dreamed of, but he felt that he wasn't suited to play the role of the slickly produced Motown entertainer. Troubled that he was not spreading the Lord's message and raising people's consciousness, he was feeling inferior toward himself. As he saw it, there was a huge gap between how things were and how things ought to be. Being a man of integrity prone to self-criticism, he was also dissatisfied with himself. He hated himself for being a sellout and betraying his own artistry. He got easily bored by routine methods of succeeding and needed adversity to stay sharp and challenged. As his biographer quotes:

> I remember I was listening to a tune of mine playing on the radio, "Pretty Little Baby," when the announcer interrupted with news about the Watts riot. My stomach got real tight and my heart started beating like crazy. I wanted to throw the radio down and burn all the bullshit songs I'd been singing and get out there and kick ass with the rest of the brothers. I knew they were going about it wrong, I knew they weren't thinking, but I understood anger that builds up over years—shit, over centuries—and I felt myself exploding. Why didn't our music have anything to do with this? Wasn't music supposed to express feelings? No, according to BG [Berry Gordy], music's supposed to sell. That's his trip. And it was mine.[19]

Music that expressed his true feelings—that, for Gaye, was *more himself*, whereas music that would sell was *less himself*. This attitude led him to rebel against the system, Anna and Berry Gordy, and everyone else in the music business. But Gaye was not yet ready to walk his own higher path. He kept on coming back to the Gordy family. As he recalled:

---

19   Ibid. p. 121.

I'd gripe, I'd walk out of the meetings, I'd miss recording sessions, I'd complain about how Berry had everything locked up—the publishing, the tours, the personal management. I'd bitch about being slaves to the system and stir up all kinds of shit. But finally, like everyone else, I'd fall in line. Somewhere along in here—don't ask me the time or date—I lost my self-respect.[20]

His attempt to fit in and to stand out at the same time drove him toward extreme indulgence in all forms of sensual pleasure—especially drugs and women.

To make matters worse, Gaye suffered from extreme stage fright. While he loved composing and recording in the studio, his fear of singing live on stage was so bad that sometimes he couldn't make himself get on the plane, and his concerts had to be canceled. He thought performance was inferior to creation: "I was tired of going out and getting the women to scream. I had to be more than a sex symbol. I had to be an artist, and artists work in the privacy of their own imaginations."[21] At the same time, he knew that his female admirers were the key to his success. If he wanted to become a star, he had to sing concerts. So he was trapped in unilevel disintegration and its ambivalence: Live performances continued to make him feel guilty and self-scorned, as if he was prostituting himself. In fact, prostitutes would fascinate him throughout his life.

What's Going On: Positive Maladjustment

During a concert in 1967, Gaye's most beloved duet partner and close friend Tammi Terrell suddenly collapsed in his arms. They found she had a brain tumor. After a number of operations spanning three years, Terrell died, aged only 25 years. Gaye was devastated by her death. With his marriage to Anna Gordy on the rocks, he was finally done with Motown's happy love songs. Now he was only capable of expressing disappointment, sadness, and anger. In the following years, he refused to perform, going through a period of retreat, withdrawal, and reflection. He longed to escape life and committed the first in a series of suicide attempts.

But his agony also ignited his creative instinct. As he withdrew from Motown, he continued to grow creatively, developing skills as a producer. "I was also writing—really writing—for the first time in years," he recalled. "I could feel my juices flowing again and began realizing that there was really only one person who could design my music: me."[22] His suffering became the most powerful source of musical inspiration for his next album—and all the albums to come. Through creative expression, Gaye transformed his depression and his writer's blocks into a record that would not only change his career, but soul music as a whole: *What's Going On*. This album, in the words of Ritz, is a socioreligious work of astounding originality.

In his first self-produced album, Gaye combined his spiritual beliefs with his increasing concern about poverty and political corruption in the United States. The seeds of *What's Going On* were planted early—he had started to question society and its values in the 1950s. As he became increasingly aware of racial inequality and discrimination, he came to regard the government as the enemy, giving him an anti-authoritarian attitude. The death of Malcolm X made a deep impression

20 Ibid. p. 119.
21 Ibid. p. 146.
22 Ibid. p. 154.

on him when he was in his twenties. Gaye identified with the explosive anger of Malcom X, even as he aspired to the peaceful idealism and courage of Jesus Christ and Martin Luther King. Feeling that an age of terrible violence and suffering was just beginning, he aspired to political involvement. But in the years before Terrell's death, he wasn't prepared to ruffle the feathers of his mainstream, middle class audience. Terrell's death stirred up something inside him that made him ready to make this leap. He could no longer look at his music as a product—from that point on, it would be a creative and personal expression. His greatest power lay in his own emotions, and he could tap into it by singing directly from his own life.

What's Going On is Gaye's personal benchmark of positive maladjustment. As he created it, he was clearly in touch with his personal values about music and creative expression:

> *I understood that musically I'd have to go on a path of my own. The Motown corporate attitude didn't give me much room to breathe, but I was starting to feel strong enough to start down my own path. When my brother Frankie came home from Vietnam and began telling me stories, my blood started to boil. I knew I had something—an anger, an energy, an artistic point of view. It was time to stop playing games.* [23]

As he became aware of a higher path—a path of multilevel development—Gaye moved beyond personal issues and addressed the universal. As he would later tell *Rolling Stone*:

> *In 1969 or 1970, I began to reevaluate my whole concept of what I wanted my music to say. [...] I was very much affected by letters my brother was sending me from Vietnam, as well as the social situation here at home. I realized that I had to put my own fantasies behind me if I wanted to write songs that would reach the souls of people. I wanted them to take a look at what was happening in the world.* [24]

This new artistic path went together with a change in style. He got rid of the suits and ties that Motown artists were expected to wear, replacing them with baggy clothes, sneakers, and caps. He also grew a beard.

Multilevel Growth and Breaking with Traditions

What's Going On is positively maladjusted in a musical sense as well. Most of its songs segue into the one that follows, making it a conceptual song cycle—something highly uncommon in popular music of the time. The songs are not shaped with the usual structure of pop hits: a couple of verses, alternated with catchy choruses. Instead, most are rather formless. They seem to follow complex varieties of the strophic form, in which only one section functions as a building block that's repeated a few times throughout the song. It's also the first album where Gaye made multi-track recordings of his voice, singing duets and trios with himself and creating vocal arrangements that sound like

---

23 Ibid. p. 157.
24 This quote is taken from a secondary source, not the actual Rolling Stone Article: Sound on Sound *Marvin Gaye 'What's Going On?* (2011)

harmonic tapestries of contrasting shapes and colors. The multi-track vocals were newly-explored territory in soul music and would continue to be a characteristic feature in his later work. For the first time, Gaye said he that he had found his voice. He felt like he'd finally learned how to sing.

The lyrics were also a break with tradition. No longer focused on romantic love, Ritz describes the lyrics of *What's Going On* as thought-provoking inner dialogues. After listening to the experiences of his brother Frankie, a Vietnam veteran, Gaye created the narrative of a vet returning to his home country to witness injustice, hatred, and suffering. Other lyrics explored topics like poverty, ecological issues, and his growing concern for the state of the world and the future of mankind. The more personal lyrics on this album are about the inner conflicts he had with living a wealthy, privileged life, his addiction to cocaine, and his propensity for self-destruction. In his more spiritual songs, he addresses God and Jesus, offering hope and proclaiming that only love can save us.

Initially, Motown refused to release *What's Going On*. But Gaye was ready to stand up to them:

> They didn't like it, didn't understand it, and didn't trust it. Management said the songs were too long, too formless, and would get lost on a public looking for easy three-minute stories. My attitude had to be firm. Basically I said, "Put it out or I'll never record for you again." That was my ace in the hole, and I had to play it.[25]

Motown eventually gave in and released the record—and it quickly earned both commercial success and critical acclaim. It is still regarded as one of the most important records of the 1970s. This not only gave Gaye the freedom to work on more serious and creative work, it also drastically changed the direction of Motown. His departure from traditions paved the way for other talents like Stevie Wonder and Michael Jackson to gain more control over their careers and determine the direction of their own creative development.

With the success of *What's Going On*, Gaye found himself at the top. He had gained some equilibrium between his life and his art. But despite his accomplishments, he still felt troubled. Though he'd managed to create and, to some extent, live by an authentic hierarchy of values, he couldn't manage to spread it beyond his artistic life. In the years after *What's Going On*, his ambivalence and ambitendency grew stronger as he swung between extremes: seeking and rejecting love, accomplishing success and then destroying it, and being tempted by wealth and sensual pleasure, while scorning such a lifestyle. Gaye's ensuing albums reflected his ongoing inner conflicts. Musically, he continued to develop richness, complexity, depth, and originality. His lyrics, however, became darker. They were extremely intimate and self-focused. His love for Anna Gordy was long gone, and he publicly expressed his anger and frustration about their divorce on the record *Here, My Dear*. Meanwhile, he had found a new muse in Janis Hunter, seventeen years his junior, who became his second wife. He worshipped her, completely losing himself in his obsession—something that is characteristic of unilevel disintegration. Albums like *Let's Get It On* and *I Want You* are vulnerable expressions of the raw, intense desire he felt for her. Hunter, of course, was unable to live up to the idealized

---

25   D. Ritz *Divided Soul: The Life of Marvin Gaye* (1991, Omnibus Press, London) p. 160.

version he had of her, leading to a stormy and occasionally violent relationship that ended in divorce six years after they met. Gaye, However, never got over her completely. Even after they broke up, he sang exclusively for her.

Back to Unilevel Disintegration

His life was becoming darker and more complicated by the day. He was disappointed with America and governments in general. Above all, he was disappointed in himself, calling himself selfish and spoiled. He had buried his conflicts too deep inside of himself to resolve them. He felt that he was split in half—that he had an angel and a devil living inside of him. Instead of integrating his dark side into his personality in a healthy way, he kept on fighting against his dark side, which only made things worse. This resulted in obsessions with prostitutes, sadomasochism, and pornography, freebasing cocaine, tax problems, paranoia, continued rebellion against Motown, the Gordy family, and Hunter, and several suicide attempts.

Despite all of this, Gaye kept composing and recording music. It was the one thing that kept him going while his personal life fell apart. In the years before his death, he managed to release a couple more albums. *In Our Lifetime* expressed Gaye's fears that nuclear power would destroy the world. Convinced that the world was coming to an end, he saw mankind as hopeless, just like he saw himself. As Ritz writes, "In his mind, the fate of the world and his own life were inseparable. They were both overdue for a disaster which at times, Gaye deeply desired and, in his own life, provoked." On the other hand, the album expressed his spiritual belief in gratitude as a way of coping with a worrisome world. We can hear this complex conflict in his voice. Where despair and grief are mixed with hope, he sounds extraordinary. Though it wasn't a huge commercial success, *In Our Lifetime* is regarded as one of his best albums from the late-Motown period—although he angrily claimed the label had re-edited the album without his permission.

With his relationship with Motown at an all-time low, Gaye stayed in Belgium for an extended period. Drug abuse and performance stress had exhausted him, making him unable to sing concerts. A man named Freddy Cousaert offered to help and invited him to live with his family in Oostende. This was the best thing that had happened to Gaye in years. With the Cousaerts, he could recover from the stress, eat well, and play sports. He quit cocaine. He and Hunter were talking about getting back together. He ended his twenty-year relationship with Motown. Creatively, he was now a free man, ready for a new start. But he also needed money. Cousaert took on the role of concert promoter and organized *The Heavy Love Affair Tour*, his comeback tour in Europe—a tour that felt different to Gaye than the ones Motown had run. For the first time, he was able to take control of his life and career. He put his shows together based on how *he* felt—not someone else's standards.

The tour marked the interlude between *In Our Lifetime* and his final record, *Midnight Love*. The latter album was a massive commercial success, containing the hit *Sexual Healing*. Personally, it was a new step forward, away from the extreme introspection of his previous albums. Gaye told a reporter:

On one level, it's a party record. It's a record you can dance to and even freak to. But if you listen closely and go beneath your surface, you'll hear my heart speaking. You'll hear my heart saying, "It's time to put the madness behind and let love lead the way." You'll hear me testify that I still believe in Jesus, I still believe in God's miraculous grace, I still believe that the Lord forgives even when—and especially when—we cannot forgive ourselves. [26]

Looking back now, it's clear that the second factor, his environment, had a huge influence on the course of his life. Living in Europe did him a world of good. He planned to stay there permanently, far away from everything in the States that seduced him to his dark side. But then Gaye's mother fell ill, and everything changed. When he heard that she would need surgery, he decided to return to the US. Back home again, he jumped into the honors that *Midnight Love*'s success had won him, including another tour. It seemed like he was making a comeback.

Underneath the public façade, however, his disintegration continued—this time negatively. In March 1984, even though the relationship with his father was more troubled than ever before, Gaye moved in again with his parents. This environment could not have been worse for him and he deteriorated extremely fast. Within the course of a few weeks, he lost himself in unhealthy substance use, and his psychological and emotional condition worsened. His paranoia increased; he became more and more unpredictable. Dwelling in his bedroom for days, high on cocaine, he was withdrawn from society, losing his grip on reality. These are indications of full-fledged negative disintegration and what in TPD is called *negative maladjustment*.

We will never know if Gaye would have been capable of rebounding from this rock bottom. Maybe he would have been capable of another episode of multilevel growth, as he experienced after Terrell's death. On the first of April, the day before his forty-fifth birthday, he got into a heated argument with his father—the man he had feared his whole life—and his father shot him dead.

The blend of musical talent and forthright emotion brought Gaye worldwide recognition as one of the best soul singers that ever lived. It's also fertile ground for the sort of development that shows through the voice. Gaye's voice is a direct expression of his personal development process, and his later work is overflowing with dynamisms. Ambivalence and ambitendency are reoccurring themes in his personal life, and they're distilled in his music and voice. In his early years, music and vocal expression was predominantly a tool for him to obtain recognition and entertainment. Even in those early years, however, there are signs that he had the potential for inner transformation. His album *What's Going On* represents a leap from unilevel towards multilevel development, and in this leap, his style changed dramatically. From then on, Gaye pushed his entertainer persona to the background and his voice and music became introspective: direct expressions of his emotions, self-reflections, and reflections on the world. Unfortunately, he ended up in a unilevel existential crisis in which his despair rendered him unable to disintegrate positively, and the end of his story is one of negative disintegration.

---

26 Janis Gaye *After The Dance: My Life With Marvin Gaye* (2015)

The Voice as Your Counselor

Gaye's life story shows that even if you have great developmental potential, this is no guarantee of a disintegration process with a positive outcome. But I didn't tell his story to discourage you. Rather, it is an invitation to take a different path and look for the counselor in your voice.

Let's recall the four people I described earlier in this chapter. They were clearly in the midst of transformative processes at the moment I met them. I worked with each of them for five to eight sessions, after which they felt empowered to continue their development process by themselves. If anything became clear during these sessions, it was that the development of their voices would go hand in hand with the development of their personality. Their voices, being only the tip of an iceberg, pointed to some part of them that was vulnerable but nevertheless had to come to the surface, leading to tension and conflict. By recognizing the internal and external conflicts these people experienced in this process as dynamisms, their voices ceased to be problems and became instead counselors in their development processes. They pointed in the direction where their disintegrative transformations would unfold: accepting certain parts of themselves, coming to terms with their emotions, expressing their values, and walking their own paths in this world.

7. Emotions

Some years ago, I found myself caught up in an emotional thunderstorm. Someone who is very dear to me unexpectedly cut off all communication, without any warning or explanation. The effect that had on me was beyond anything I could have imagined. It felt like a stab in my soul—a real physical pain. It also left me feeling confused, rejected, wronged, ignored, dumped, and indignant. At times I was desperate, craving an explanation. While I grappled with this reality, I learned a lot about myself and my emotions, including where they were coming from and how I could deal with them. Through this process, I came to recognize my emotions as fuel for my personal development. In this chapter, I'll explain how I came to that profound realization. In the end, this thunderstorm turned out to be one of the most transformational experiences I've ever had.

Since they are so tightly connected to the voice, I'm dedicating a chapter of this book to the roles that emotions play in our lives and how we can make good use of them. But before we can parse those, we should define what emotions are.

Although all of us experience them, this question—"What are emotions?"—turns out to be difficult to answer. The easiest way to describe them is on the level of experience, because that's how we notice them in the first place. Scientist and therapist Krystyna C. Laycraft describes emotional experiences in her book *The Courage to Decide* as dynamic entities that depend on our perception and evaluation of our situation. As she goes on to explain:

> *They signal to us that we need to make changes. Emotional experiences change constantly. They usually appear as the interactive patterns of emotional states rather than single entities. Ultimately, emotional experiences depend on how we perceive and evaluate our situation and surrounding environment.*[27]

There are two ways in which we can become aware of these emotional experiences: One is through physical sensations in our bodies, and the other is when we identify them in our minds as feelings. Sometimes we ignore the messages from our bodies because we're not ready or willing to confront them. Allowing those emotions to unfold may hurt, or it may conflict with what we consider rational or reasonable. This process is central to human life, but it is demanding. With too much emotion, life is overwhelming. With too little emotion, life lacks meaning. Finding equanimity can be challenging.

---

27   K.C. Laycraft Ph.D., *The Courage to Decide* (2015, AwareNow Publishing, Victoria, BC, Canada) p. 4.

We can also answer the question, "What are emotions?" from a subjective perspective. Nobody knows how it feels to be you. You can give an extremely detailed description of how you feel to someone else, but this other person, no matter how empathic, can never experience your specific emotional states. Nor can you ever know exactly how someone else feels. We rely on cues from others' social engagement systems, such as voice and facial expression, to get information about their subjective emotional experiences. Our own empathic skills come into play by helping us assemble these cues into a reasonable estimation of that experience that we can't know directly.

If the gap between what you feel and what others understand of your feelings is too wide, you feel lonely. When we recognize that others share our emotions, we connect and forge emotional bonds with them. Such shared emotions are among the most meaningful life experiences. We can even have strong emotional experiences with complete strangers—just think of the emotions that arise during concerts, spiritual events, sporting events, festivals, and the like. In this way, emotions are simultaneously deeply personal and universal experiences.

We can also answer the question, "What are emotions?" from a physiological perspective. Neuroscience tells us how emotions come into existence and how they work in the brain. Thanks to recent insights like the polyvagal theory, we now know why our voices reflect our emotional and bodily state. To truly understand what emotions are—and how we are most likely to misunderstand them—here's a brief overview of the theories that have shaped our scientific understanding.

7.1. Our Evolving Understanding of Emotion

In Chapter 3, I noted that twentieth-century personality theories focused mainly on cognition and assumed that emotions play only a marginal role in personal development, with the theory of positive disintegration as a notable exception. It wasn't until the 1990s that emotions became a serious research subject in psychology and neurology. Since then, the discourse has taken some surprising turns.

For a long time, emotions were regarded as lower, instinctive impulses. The narrative was as follows: We humans inherited emotion from our great great grandparents, the reptiles, whose brains are dominated by the autonomic nervous system. This gave them their basic instincts. As we evolved into mammals, we developed the limbic brain, which produces the primary emotions of anger, joy, disgust, sadness, and fear. These emotions enhanced the social nature of these animals by completely ruling their behavior, or so the narrative went. Fortunately, as we evolved into human beings—*i.e.*, the pinnacle of evolution—we were supposedly blessed with reason. This came from the neocortex, the latest development in our brain structure.

Dualism, Descartes, Darwin

We see the seeds of this narrative in the seventeenth century, when philosopher René Descartes concluded that only reason and rational thought can lead to knowledge and truth with his famous claim, *I think, therefore I am.* With this declaration, he established the strict separation between body and mind that has come to be known as dualism—and that influences our society to this day. Dualism posits the body as the mechanical source for instinct and emotion, and the mind as the source for rational thought. It tends to encourage us to value rational thought as the only strategy to make factual, evidence-based claims, while emotions are seen as mere obstacles to the decision-making process. In the battle between these opposing forces, highly evolved humans should always aim for reason to prevail over emotion.

Fast forward two centuries to the time of Charles Darwin. The father of the theory of evolution endorsed Descartes' dualism when he wrote in *The Expression of the Emotions in Man and Animals* that we inherited emotions from our animal ancestors. Casting them as universally-shared essences that are hard wired in the most ancient part of our nervous system, Darwin said that each emotion has a distinct fingerprint in how it expresses itself. Take joy, for instance: in Darwin's view, whether in the form of a mild happiness or a triumphant exhilaration, it had a core essence that emerged from a different location in the brain than the essences of anger or sadness—or so people thought at the time.

Damasio's Break: Emotions Are the Basis for Rationality

The ideas of dualism and of emotions as hard-wired essences in our brain would hold up more or less unscathed for another hundred years. Then, in 1994, neuroscientist Antonio Damasio made a breakthrough. In his book *Descartes' Error*, he describes a patient called Elliot who suffered from a brain tumor. Doctors decided to remove it, along with a part of his frontal lobe that was affected. The doctors expected that his cognitive abilities would remain completely intact. What they didn't anticipate was that Elliott would lose his capacity to experience emotions. Before, Elliot had been a good husband, father, and employee—even a role model for his younger siblings and colleagues. After the surgery, Elliot was still intelligent, skilled, and coherent. He clearly knew what was occurring in the world around him. But in other ways, his behavior had changed significantly. He couldn't manage his time properly, and began making highly questionable business and financial decisions. One thing led to the other, and Elliott lost his job as well as his family. The problem was that, without emotions, he utterly failed to apply his cognitive abilities in his daily life. Instead, he became impulsive, struggled dramatically with decision-making and future planning. Damasio's research suggests that reason *requires* emotion for decision-making:

> *The apparatus of rationality, traditionally presumed to be neocortical, does not seem to work without that of biological regulation, but also from it and with it. The mechanics for behavior beyond drives and instincts use, I believe, both the upstairs and the downstairs: the neocortex becomes engaged along with the older brain core, and rationality results from their concerted activity.* [28]

---

28   A. Damasio *Descartes' Error* (2006 Vintage, London) p. 128 (Original work published 1994)

In this way, mind and body are not separate entities, nor can we strictly divide the brain's functions between the reptile brain, limbic system, and neocortex. The biology of human beings is far more complex than that. In fact, reason and emotion are tightly linked in everything we feel, think, say and do.

So what does this imply for our understanding of what emotions are? Damasio defines emotions as physical experiences that are triggered by sense perception (external stimuli) or mental images (internal stimuli). He distinguishes between primary emotions, secondary emotions, and feelings. Primary emotions such as fear, anger, joy, sadness, and disgust are instincts that get triggered by events. Imagine how disgust can overtake you when you drink a glass of milk and the milk has turned sour. Your body reacts immediately to the perception of your senses; the emotion of disgust is a reaction that changes your bodily state.

Secondary emotions, however, can be learned through experience. These get triggered not by actual, events, but by mental images and language. Take stage fright, for example, and all the vocal symptoms it stirs up in you—like speeding up, or a trembling, high-pitched, monotonous voice. There is no direct threat to your body, but you have a mental image of the fact that performing on stage is risky and that you can fail. Before you even consciously know or think, *I'm nervous,* your body has already detected that you're in a threatening situation and activated an autonomic defense state: Your chest tightens, your voice shakes, and your palms sweat.

Finally, a feeling is what happens when an individual consciously experiences an emotion. We can define it as a subjective self-perception of a specific emotion that we label with language: *I feel irritated, happy, insecure, lonely, satisfied,* etcetera. To feel an emotion, you need your mind. Moreover, a feeling can emanate from an emotion, but it can also emanate from a thought. Imagine that the person you're dating is not responding to your texts. This can generate all kinds of thoughts: *I'm being ghosted. I must have said something wrong. I'm not fun to hang out with.* These types of thoughts can cause you to feel sad, lonely, or disappointed. Unlike emotions, which are expressed by the body, feelings are expressed by the mind. In my personal story at the start of this chapter, the physical pain I experienced because of abandonment is an emotion. All the other things I described are feelings: confused, rejected, wronged, ignored, dumped, indignant. Some of these feelings came from the thoughts I had about the situation. Feelings have the same effect on the voice as secondary emotions.

Damasio developed a hypothesis about emotional functioning that he dubbed the somatic marker hypothesis. Somatic markers are emotional responses emanating from the body. They may be negative, leading to the rejection of options, or positive, leading to the acceptance of other options. These responses mark a specific, personal, mental representation, like a memory from a performance when you forgot your lines. Somatic markers provide our brain with valuable information for decision-making: We use them to compare our mental representations. For example, based on your previous experiences with performing, you decide whether you will perform again. If the somatic marker of that ill-fated performance rules in your mind, you'll choose not to—even though you won't necessarily forget your lines again. In this way, our decision-making process is based not on pure reasoning, but rather, on our previous interactions with the world around us. Gut feeling thereby plays a bigger role in decision-making than we might think. And while listening to your gut feeling might seem the wise thing to do, it's not infallible. After all, your gut may tell you to not perform again because of the risk of embarrassment. In the end, avoiding unwelcome feelings at all cost prevents us from working to achieve the things we want in life.

How We Construct Our Own Emotions

In explaining what emotions truly are, psychologist and neuroscientist Lisa Feldman Barrett goes even further than Damasio. According to her research, primary emotions are not universal instincts that are hard wired in the brain, and they're not even triggered by other people and events. Instead, they're culturally dependent—and we construct them ourselves.

Your Predictive Brain

Feldman Barrett's research demands a paradigm shift on how we think about emotions. To understand how she came to her conclusions, we have to look at the physiological origins of feelings and emotions, starting with how we perceive the world around us. What we perceive as reality is in fact our brain *making predictions* about reality, which it then uses to construct a simulation of the world that will make sense to us. The basis for these predictions is information from our sense organs—what we see, hear, smell, taste, and touch. But to animate what the sense organs tell it, the brain relies on information it has stored from past experiences. When I look outside my window, for instance, I see all kinds of rectangular, colorful tin boxes on wheels. Based on previous experience, my brain tells me that these are cars. When I hear a repeated pattern of short, high-pitched, rhythmical sounds, my brain again relies on previous experience to tell me that this is the neighborhood blackbird.

When we were born, we entered this world without concepts and predictions. To make sense of the world around us, we had to pay close attention to the information our senses were giving us. What do we feel, see, hear, taste, and smell? Imagine you're a toddler. You're in a garden, mesmerized by a bunch of green stems coming from the soil. On the stems are small, green leaves that you can touch. These stems also have smaller, nasty green prickles that hurt if you touch them. On top of the stems are these bundles of deep, red petals, folded closely together. When you put your nose above such a bundle of petals, it smells fantastic. Someone will tell you that this is a rosebush; somewhere else you will pick up that roses are flowers. But your first meeting with this rosebush is based above all on sense perception, not prediction.

That will change in the future. As you come across more roses in your life, your mind will increasingly rely on prediction. Based on your experiences, you will create a mental image of a rosebush. If your dad talks to you about roses, you can imagine those roses without them needing to be present because you have a *concept* of a rose bush in your mind. When you do see a real rose bush, your brain now simulates the bush before it has even received all the data. It efficiently filters out just enough sensory input to be consistent with the concept of a rosebush in your brain—that is, the prediction. We rely on prediction to move through life successfully because the process of predicting is much faster than interpreting sensory experience. Constantly constructing the world around us based on sense perceptions would take too much time and energy. We would be completely absorbed by it, unable to focus on other tasks. So our brain predicts what's about to happen and prepares to act on it.

Now imagine that you're in the same garden again. You think that, out of the corner of your eye, you still see that same rosebush. But after you've come closer, you notice that the roses are gone, replaced by a hibiscus bush. This time, your mental prediction of the rosebush was not correct; it was a prediction error based on your previous experience, which your brain then adjusted based on visual information. But if you had not paid close attention to the bush, your brain might instead stick with the original prediction, filtering the sensory input in such a way that it matched the rosebush. In that case, the prediction error would not be corrected, and the simulation in your brain would not correspond to reality.

In our lives, we come across many situations where our prediction errors are not being corrected. It happens more often than you might think—perhaps even daily. Can you think of any examples from your own life? One typical prediction error is a typo in a text. You can read the text many times over and over, and still not see the typo. Your predictive brain will automatically correct this for you. In general, whenever we're caught up in thoughts, we focus less on sense perception. And the less sensory information we perceive, the more we depend on predictions. In this way, our brains are constantly predicting, simulating, comparing, resolving errors, and starting the prediction loop again. We perceive this process as reality, while in fact we only see whatever our brain has simulated for us. That's what Feldman Barrett means when she says we create our own reality.

Affect, Interoception, and Emotion Concepts

What does this process have to do with emotions? Your predictive brain not only makes sense of the world around you, it also has to figure out what's going on inside your body. For this purpose, your organs, muscles, and joints have receptors that send information about their state to your brain. These receptors function in the same way as your senses do in relation to the outside world, allowing your brain to make predictions about what's going on inside. With the help of these receptors, our brain predicts and simulates in such a way that we can recognize our heartbeat, breathing pattern, being cold or warm, pain, nausea, hunger, thirst, if we need to go to the bathroom, and so on. This process, *interoception*, is related to neuroception, the process by which our autonomic nervous system detects cues of threats and safety from our environment, other people, and our own bodies without our conscious awareness (see Chapter 2). This way we can react to the needs of our body and keep it alive, safe, and healthy. Interoception is detection without awareness from our own bodies. From the information we retrieve from our bodies, we first detect if we are comfortable (safe) or uncomfortable (unsafe), and then if we are calm, agitated, or somewhere in between. This general experience of physical sensations throughout the day is called *affect*. From the information offered by physical sensations, our brain tries to make sense of what's going on inside us.

As newborn babies, we were only able to experience our bodily state along these two spectra, calm/agitated and comfortable/uncomfortable. By the way we expressed ourselves to our caregivers, they labeled our expressions as hungry, tired, satisfied, cold, warm, etcetera; they interpreted our affective expressions. This way, our caregivers knew how to make us feel comfortable again. They also taught us how to interpret our affect by talking to us, teaching us emotional concepts like happy, sad, and angry in the same way they taught us the concept of the rosebush.

In fact, according to Feldman Barrett, you need to have been taught a specific *emotion concept* in order to experience the associated emotion. Without the concept "fear," you cannot experience fear. Instead, you would experience highly uncomfortable and highly agitated physical sensations. With emotions and feelings, we give meaning to these physical sensations through language. And just as our brain simulates the outside world through predictions and resolving errors, it does the same with our inside world, predicting and simulating our emotions and feelings based on previous experiences. You might think that your emotional state is influenced by what you see and hear, but it's mostly the other way around: your emotional state alters your sight and hearing.

This means that when we experience uncomfortable physical sensations without knowing their cause, we tend to think that something in the outside world triggered them. But what's actually happening is that we're interpreting the world in a particular way *because* we experienced uncomfortable physical sensations! When we feel bad, we often blame others or the state of the world, acting as though they are responsible for how we feel. I know that when I'm tired, I get irritated and gloomy more quickly than when I'm well-rested. Similarly, after twelve years together, I know that when my partner gets cranky with me out of the blue, this means he needs to eat something ASAP. Strikingly, he doesn't always recognize his physical sensations as hunger himself; he just feels irritated by something I say or do. Feldman Barrett sheds light on why this happens, and the implications are huge. Consider this: Judges are more likely to deny parole to a prisoner if the hearing is just before lunchtime.

The Difference Between Pain and Suffering

Though we create our own emotional reality based on physical sensations, that doesn't mean the outside world plays no role in the process. Our physical discomfort doesn't stem only from the inner workings of our body like fatigue or hunger. The outside world does play a role in our physical sensations. Most people feel more joyful and energetic on sunny days, to the point that interviewers even tend to rate applicants more negatively when it's rainy. Rainy weather impacts your bodily state, producing unpleasant physical sensations. And weather is just one example of an environmental influence on our feelings.

Another big one is other people. Do you recall from Chapter 2 how we co-regulate each other's nervous system through social engagement? Imagine that someone you love disappears from your life. A loss like that hurts. On the level of physical sensation, a person you co-regulate with—who makes you feel safe and comfortable—is no longer there. Your body goes into a state of distress, feeling agitated and uncomfortable. This is the stab in the soul I described at the beginning of this chapter as a result of losing my friend.

For those who are emotionally reactive, it's valuable to understand intellectually how we create our own emotions, since it really puts what you feel into perspective. Those who tend to ignore their emotions, however, should be careful not to downplay what they feel. Your feelings may be self-created, but they still give you valuable information about what you need and what actions you should take. The most valuable lesson we can learn from the theory of constructed emotions is that we have the power to *change* our emotional reality. To do this, however, we still need to recognize and discern primary emotions, from secondary emotions, from feelings. Even though they don't exist as such in the brain, for clinical purposes and your own experience, this differentiation is helpful.

In Laycraft's book *Acceptance: The Key to a Meaningful Life*, I learned about Emotion-Focused Therapy (EFT). This form of therapy, developed by Leslie S. Greenberg, uses awareness, acceptance and understanding of emotions to make sense of our lives. Later on, in Chapter 10, I'll explain why this process is essential for regulating vocal symptoms of emotional overexcitability. In her book, Laycraft gives the following definition of emotions:

> *They are important factors in motivating perception, thought and action, and give richness and meaning to individual life and relationship. If we don't have access to our emotions, we're missing a very important source of information and then we're not oriented well in the world.*[29]

Greenberg distinguishes between primary and secondary emotions, but in a different way than Damasio does. Damasio's "primary emotions" are called *primary adaptive emotions* in Greenberg's framework. They help us take appropriate action, such as fleeing when we find ourselves in a situation that triggers fear. Damasio's "feelings" are *secondary reactive emotions* for Greenberg, when we blend emotional experience with thinking. Going forward, I will use Greenberg's language.

The sadness and the physical pain I experienced because of the loss of my friend were primary adaptive emotions. The physical experience was painful enough, but to add insult to injury, I experienced many *emotion concepts* that made the situation even worse. I felt confused, rejected, wronged, ignored, dumped, and indignant. These were my secondary reactive emotions, and only expressed how I *thought* my friend was behaving towards me. However, I didn't *really* know his actual motivations; I was only interpreting his behavior from my point of view. These feelings caused me extra suffering on top of the pain, making me feel even worse than I already did. While processing all of this, I gradually became aware of the fact that these feelings did not just happen to me. Instead, I was creating a mental narrative to give meaning to my dysregulated nervous system and uncomfortable physical sensations. I was blending my emotions with beliefs I had about the situation.

---

29 K.C. Laycraft & B. Gierus *Acceptance: The Key to a Meaningful Life* (2019, Calgary, AB, Canada: Nucleus Learning) p. 206.

There is a Buddhist saying: If you get struck by an arrow, you will feel pain. But you'll also have a reaction to the arrow. And for most of us, that's going to be negative. You might get angry or scared of the blood you're losing; maybe you'll want revenge on the person who shot you. Those reactions are *a second arrow*. According to Buddhism, pain and suffering are two different things, represented by the first and the second arrows—and you inflict the second arrow on yourself.

Acceptance and Commitment Therapy (ACT), a therapeutic model I work with, makes the same distinction between pain and suffering. Pain is direct, in the present moment, caused by outer circumstances, and uncontrollable. Examples of pain are disease, physical pain, the death of a loved one, divorce, problems at work, etcetera. Suffering is how you relate to the experience of pain. For most of us, that takes the form of resistance. Examples of suffering are worrying about the past or future and fearing things that may or may not happen. Suffering is indirect and caused by the mind, typically as a blend of memory with thoughts and language. When my friend ghosted me, my pain was real, but I built my suffering myself out of thoughts, beliefs, and memories.

But there were more pieces to the puzzle. Negative somatic markers also contributed to the intensity of my emotional experience. These somatic markers—known in Greenberg's framework as *maladaptive primary emotions*—are direct reactions to situations that no longer help us deal constructively with the situations that caused them. Taking forms such as loneliness, abandonment, worthlessness, and stage fright, they are based on previous experiences, often traumatic ones, and cause us to make negative judgements about ourselves—even when we can no longer rely on these emotions. Greenberg's work echoes Damasio's secondary emotions, which are learned through experience and come into being through mental concepts and language. All of these researchers are pointing to emotions that originate in past discomfort, when needs such as safety and belonging were not met.

The problem with maladaptive primary emotions is that your brain uses that past experience to keep making predictions about similar events in the future *even if circumstances have changed*. In a sense, your emotions have not caught up to your present reality.

Transforming Emotions

Fortunately, Greenberg says it's possible to transform these emotions. When we experience negative feelings and emotions, we should explore them through self-inquiry exercises. This makes it easier to access and accept the primary emotions in which they're rooted. Moreover, negative feelings and emotions also point in the direction of unmet needs. If we know what our needs are and what we value, we know what we can undertake in order to relieve our suffering. EFT describes six fundamental principles of emotional change—and my experience overcoming the pain of my friend's rejection lines up with them quite well.

1. Awareness

As I began to perceive what I felt in my body, I became aware of the primary adaptive emotions at the core of my feelings. Instead of trying to control or eliminate these feelings, I welcomed them wholeheartedly. I realized that they were all rooted in sadness.

2. Expression

Fully accepting my core sadness meant allowing myself to be sad—and allowing an emotion means expressing it. That's why crying—and I cried a lot—was an act of compassion to myself. What I had to do was grieve until the pain began to abate.

3. Regulation

During this period, I took up a variety of activities that helped me regulate my emotions—listening to and composing music, going for long walks, and baking cakes. I also adopted a practice tailor-made for this purpose: For about fifteen minutes every day, I sat down and closed my eyes. Taking a couple of deep breaths, I directed my attention away from my thoughts, into the present moment, and asked myself, *at this very moment, am I doing OK? If I'm not entangled in my thoughts about the past and the future, am I in pain right now? Or am I safe, comfortable and in peace between the four walls of my living room? Do I have caring people around me, values and purposes to live for?* Every time I did this exercise, the answer to the question whether I was in pain at that moment was *no*. Without those thoughts and memories, I was feeling peaceful and doing perfectly fine. By recognizing this for at least fifteen minutes per day, I became aware of a deep, solid strength inside of me.

4. Reflection

Somewhere in the process, I realized something: How was it possible that my emotional well-being could depend so completely on this one person? When I thought about it that way, it was really ridiculous. By browsing through old diaries, I started to reflect on similar experiences of abandonment in my past that were connected to these feelings. I vividly re-experienced these situations in my mind, and this time, I consciously felt the emotions that I had suppressed back then. Suddenly I recognized that my friend's choice to cut me off was not the cause of *everything* I felt. Rather, it was a trigger, activating an old reaction pattern related to abandonment. It wasn't just that this particular situation bothered me; it was that it made me relive painful emotions from experiences of abandonment I'd had in the past. This was the first time I had allowed myself to feel what I had avoided feeling before. By doing this, I gave rise to the healing process. If you don't heal your wounds, the outside world will keep on causing what are essentially emotional inflammations. It's only after your wound has turned into scar tissue that it becomes resilient.

5. Transformation

Through my reflection, I came to realize that feeling rejected, wronged, ignored, dumped, and indignant meant that I was in need of honesty, safety, acknowledgment, communication and understanding. Moreover, my emotional response to this situation was so strong because it touched on one of my core values: namely, the importance of human connection. So I spent time with the people in my life who were able to provide those things, thereby transforming my feeling of abandonment.

This was when I also recognized that I couldn't change my circumstances, only my attitude toward them. The fact that someone I loved was not there for me anymore—that hurt. I couldn't change that and would have to accept it. But the only thing responsible for my emotional misery was my thoughts about the past and future. As it turned out, my mind wasn't particularly useful in dealing with pain—and was in fact the *cause* of suffering.

And then I realized something else. Because I myself had constructed my feelings about the situation, I had a choice in how to deal with my suffering. At some point, I found myself willing to accept that I had lost my friend. Gradually, I could expand those fifteen minutes of practiced peace to fill the rest of my day. Peace became a familiar state of mind.

The Myth of Rationality

Let's recap where we find ourselves in the history of our understanding of emotions: After centuries building our culture around the purely rational mind, we have only recently developed the science to recognize why humans are not and cannot be purely rational beings. Not only is our thinking always blended with emotion, the process that creates emotion, physical sensation, is the foundation of our behavior and every decision we make. As a result, it's a challenge—and sometimes an insurmountable one—to influence our emotions with rational thinking. The best we can do is identify which of our thoughts and beliefs are caused by emotions and defuse them so that they don't contribute additional suffering.

The bodily origin of emotion explains why people can have such different experiences of the same environment. As Feldman Barrett explains:

> You might think about your environment as existing in the outside world, separate from yourself, but that's a myth. You (and other creatures) do not simply find yourself in an environment and either adapt or die. You construct your environment—your reality—by virtue of what sensory input from the physical environment your brain selects.[30]

It follows that the dichotomy that Descartes imagined between the cognitive mind and the emotional body is a myth as well. Our society and economic system, however, is built on this myth: We are all *homo economicus*, capable of perfect rationality. We always act in a way that maximizes utility as a consumer and profit as a producer (or at least, we're supposed to, and it's our fault if we don't). Economics textbooks encourage us to believe that we are capable of thinking through all possible outcomes, choosing that course of action that will result in the best possible result for our individual selves.

Unfortunately, this myth couldn't be further from the truth, as science is gradually coming to recognize. In his book *The Righteous Mind*, social psychologist Jonathan Haidt says that the worship of reason is a delusion—an example of faith in something that does not exist. Based on his research, he developed what he calls the social intuitionist model. According to the social intuitionists, when

---

30   L. Feldmann Barrett *How Emotions Are Made* (2017, Houghton Mifflin Harcourt, New York) p. 83.

we make arguments, we think we've defined them through reason. This, however, is not the case. When we make rapid judgments, we base them on moral intuitions—that is, on our values. Strategic reasoning only comes second, serving to justify our intuitions. Our reasoning is ruled by morality. When we stay open to different arguments, however, we create the possibility of triggering new intuitions and values in ourselves, making it possible for us to change our minds.

According to Haidt, people respond to the world in different ways because they have different values. Generally speaking, left-wing voters have a hierarchy of values in which values of care and fairness figure much more prominently than those based in loyalty, authority, and sanctity. Right-wing voters, meanwhile, feature all five of these basic moral foundations in their value hierarchies, though loyalty, authority, and sanctity sometimes figure more prominently than care and fairness.

Haidt's work further undermines the concept of reason as a mental activity completely separate from emotion. Damasio says that reason is a result of a somatic marker rooted in an emotional response. Feldman Barrett adds that we ourselves construct this emotional response. And according to Haidt, reason is the result of a moral intuition. It's therefore striking that our society doesn't have any way of formally teaching us to become aware of our emotions and values. Education, after all, is heavily oriented toward cognitive abilities, and in many families and social circles, emotions are not talked about or even repressed. Although we all have values, few of us are aware that they influence our judgment and decision-making process to the degree they do. Most people, moreover, will never reflect on whether the values we espouse are our own personal values, or simply the ones prevailing within society—let alone have a conscious conversation about the subject. That means there's a lot we can learn to make our lives better, by actually having these conversations—even if only with ourselves.

7.2. Emotions as the Source for Values

Let's dig a little deeper into the connection between emotions and values, starting with defining what values are. In chapter two, I briefly described them as intuitive principles that guide how we live and act. Knowing what's important to us allows us to define what we want to do with our lives and make choices based on what we personally believe we ought to do.

Early in our lives, we learn and generally adopt values from external sources like our parents, teachers, churches, governments, and other authority figures. Unless our family is very unusual, these tend to be the source of prevailing values in society. As we develop our personality, especially if we go through positive disintegration, we discover our own authentic values. These are truly ours, not imposed by others, so it's possible that they will turn out to be different from those of our family, company, or society.

Some values will be more important to you than others. In the theory of positive disintegration, the process of sorting out which values are higher and which are lower is considered a dynamism, known as *hierarchization* (for more on dynamisms, see Chapter 6). Your most important values should have the greatest impact on how you use your time and how you decide the course of your life. Your hierarchy of values thereby serves as a guide for your decision-making—which is why you want to make sure you've given it proper thought, with attention to the emotional reactions you feel as you consider them.[31]

Here are some questions for you: When you think about what you value, do you notice any physical sensations? Perhaps a slightly higher heartbeat or a flow of energy? What do your emotions tell you? I hope that after reading this chapter, you recognize that emotions play a tremendous role in this choice, even if some of us have learned to ignore them. But the fact is that our values grow from our emotions.

Laycraft explains this connection, detailing several theories about emotions, values, and personal development. Dr. Arnold Modell, MD, calls feelings and emotions somatic markers of value, stating that "[f]eelings assign value to what is meaningful and the absence of meaning is excruciatingly painful. To find life meaningful is to be attached to life."[32] Can you relate to what Dr. Modell says? I know I can. When something or someone is meaningful to me, I can feel an energy charging through my body. In other words, it resonates with me. Because connection is extremely important to me, it is extremely painful when I lose it.

A rich emotional life is a meaningful life. But this doesn't mean it will be an easy life. Living from our values is not easy. It takes courage. Our values reveal where we are vulnerable—where we can be hurt. Experiencing negative emotions is therefore part of the deal. As we navigate through life, we'll be confronted with opposing values that stem from complex, conflicted emotions—that is, inner conflict.

To function smoothly in society, many of us have learned to avoid inner emotional conflict. We are encouraged to distract ourselves from negativity, improve our capabilities, and learn to think positively to bypass anger, fear, and sadness. What we fail to see is that inner conflict is the driving force in our development. Laycraft describes why:

> *Negative emotions play a significant role in our decision-making and subsequent actions. They mobilize our cognitive resources, increase our awareness, signalize approaches to our problems, and make us more perceptive and sensitive to the external world. Finally, negative emotions help us figure out what is the most important to us and which values are essential to our lives. Subsequently, we are able to look at our problems more realistically and become more aware of the outside world.[33]*

Fortunately, when we identify our personal hierarchy of values, we can use it to resolve these conflicts. We decide what is higher and lower, more ourselves and less ourselves. When our higher values motivate our decisions and guide our actions, we get a clear and strong sense of the direction our life should take. This makes it possible for us to grow and develop our personality. Values and emotions are fundamental to this process.

---

31 Dąbrowski even argued that the hierarchy of values of those who rise to high levels of development, is objective. He sees similarities in the values of, for instance Christ, Socrates and Ghandi. Their sensitivity to what is truly worthwhile, and the way they organize their lives around it, is indicative of an objective hierarchy of values for which others may strive (William J. Hague, 1976).

32 K.C. Laycraft Ph.D., *The Courage to Decide* (2015, AwareNow Publishing, Victoria, BC, Canada) p. 6-7.

33 Ibid. p. 25-26.

Before we wrap up, let me tell you how my personal story ended. After I'd dealt with my suffering and fully accepted the loss of my friend, something unexpected happened: He decided he wanted to restore our relationship. Because I had processed my pain, I didn't feel any need to make him do penance, as I might have before. I decided to open up my heart without any strings attached. After all, compassion and forgiveness are high on my personal hierarchy of values. Our bond now is better than ever: We're less needy, more stable and emotionally mature. It turns out that separation can be a way to learn from each other and contribute to each other's development. By cutting off all contact with me and disrupting my emotions, my friend inadvertently gave me a precious gift. The way I learned to deal with the situation radically changed my attitude toward life. It was truly transformative. Not only did I learn to distinguish pain from suffering, I also realized how I create my own emotional reality and how this linked to my values. Looking back, I'm grateful that I had to go through it.

Voice and emotion are inevitably intertwined. Clients often tell me they would like to gain more control over their voice. In practice, what this usually means is that they want to have control over the emotions that influence their voice. Controlling your emotions, however, isn't really possible. At first it may seem that you've got them under control, but eventually it turns out that you're only suppressing them. Suppressed emotions pile up in a dark closet that you try to keep closed at all times and this costs you a lot of energy. When the closet gets too full, you can't keep it closed anymore. The door will ultimately buckle and your emotions will tumble out in a messy heap, less controlled than ever before.

The good news is that, if you give up thinking about *control*, you *can* develop *agency* over your emotions if you become fully aware of them, what they're telling you, and how they're made. Note that I'm not saying that you should always act on your emotions. *Acting* on what you feel is not the same as *identifying*, *processing*, and *responding* to what you feel. In the following chapters you will learn how to do that.

Part 2
Work with Your Voice on a Deeper Level

8. Breathe

Have you ever heard a baby with a hoarse voice? Infants and small children can cry, and we know how good at it they are. It's impressive enough that these small bodies can produce such volume, but on top of that, they virtually never lose their voices because of it. Apparently, their vocal folds facilitate this type of voice use. As adults, we still have the same vocal folds we were born with. So why do some of our voices get hoarse so easily? Or feel tired after a day filled with meetings and presentations? Why do some people struggle to speak loudly when, as an infant, their crying kept the whole neighborhood awake?

The answer to these questions is *breathing*. You can only speak as well as you breathe. My first session with a new client is almost always centered around breathing. This way, we immediately tackle the basics of a healthy voice, including breath-voice connection, calming the nervous system, and developing awareness.

8.1. How Voice and Breath Are Connected

Contrary to what most people think, the vocal folds are not where you want to focus your attention when trying to speak well. The best way to explain how this works, as I learned from my singing teacher Lyda van Tol, is with the metaphor of a violin. A violin's sound comes from its strings. Imagine your vocal folds are the strings on a violin. They can't produce sound on their own; they need to be activated. You get the best sound out of a violin when you gently bow the strings. Imagine this bow is your breath. The strings are lying passively on the violin and only produce sound if they are touched by the bow, which is creating all the action. It's only then that the sound waves resonate in the body of the violin, which has the same feature as your oral cavities.

There's one important way that our voices differ from a violin, though. While a violin can produce only one sound texture from the bow, humans can make a broad spectrum of different sound textures. We do this by changing the position of our jaw and the muscles in our face—lips, tongue, and teeth. These are called articulators.

To summarize, your vocal instrument consists of the following elements:

- The vocal folds (strings on a violin)
- The breath (the bow)
- Oral cavities (sound body of the violin)
- Articulators of your face

Now let's dive a bit further into the anatomy. Your voice is produced by your vocal folds, which manipulate pitch and volume while you speak. This voice production is officially called *phonation*. Your vocal folds are two tiny muscle strings. They're situated in the cartilage of the larynx, the voice box, at the top of your throat. When they're in default position, there's an opening between them that allows you to breathe. When you want to talk or sing, you use the breath that flows out of your lungs to create a change in air pressure, which makes your vocal folds hit each other rapidly. The amount of air pressure needed depends on your activity. Speaking needs more air pressure than breathing silently, and singing needs more than speaking. As these vocal folds hit each other, they create sound waves, which are just vibrations in the air that our ears receive as sound. These sound waves then spread out, resonating in your oral cavities. They leave your body through your mouth (or, if you are humming, your nose). The position of the face—the articulators—determines what type of sound it will be: which vowels and consonants you will produce.

> *Try it Yourself:* **Feel Your Vocal Folds**
>
> Although you can't directly examine the function of your vocal folds and the process of phonation without an actual camera in the larynx, you can monitor the process indirectly. Here's how:
>
> - Gently placing a hand on your throat, make a prolonged sound like "ssss" of "pfffff." The articulators in your face are at work, but you won't feel resonating activity in your larynx. You are making these sounds without your voice.
> - Now gently make a prolonged sound like "zzzzz" or "wwww." On top of the activity in your articulators, do you now feel a vibrating sensation in the larynx as well? That's your vocal folds in action.
> - With your hand still on your throat, gently say prepositions—*in, out, up, under, above*. These short words will also show you the activity in your vocal folds.

When my clients experience hoarseness, voice loss, or pain in the throat after speaking, the first things I check are their breathing, breath-voice connection, and articulators. More often than not, these voice problems are the result of pushing from the throat with too much pressure or not supporting the voice with sufficient air. If, on top of that, the articulators are lazy, it's no wonder they're exhausted after a day filled with meetings.

Breath-voice connection is the awareness of the outbreath while we speak. When we have good breath-voice connection, we use the right amount of breath and the right air pressure to enable us to vocalize with ease. Later on in this chapter you'll learn more about it.

Try it Yourself: **Speak Without Breath-Voice Connection**

The following is emphatically *not* an exercise to train your voice. Try this only once to experience what happens when you speak without the support of your breath.

- Blow all the air out of your lungs, until you have nothing left.
- Now try to say a full sentence.

How did it feel, and how did it sound? Probably not very nice. Did feel your throat muscles contract and get tensed?

Why Most People Don't Breathe the Way They Should

Breathing is a continuous movement that never stops. You go from expansion to contraction—an instance of ebb and flow, of yin and yang. An inhalation is a sympathetic activation of the autonomic nervous system, and an exhalation is a parasympathetic activation. In breathing, you constantly balance these two systems.

If you are one of those people who are under continuous stress and never feel quite relaxed, you might want to pay some attention to the way you breathe. Here are some signs that your breathing or breath-voice connection are less than optimal:

- You breathe through your mouth
- You never exhale fully
- After an exhale, you immediately breathe in again, without taking a pause
- You often hold your breath
- You take fast, short breaths in the chest, not the belly
- You hold your breath while you speak
- You breathe out before you speak

Looking at the list above, take notes for yourself. Do you breathe through your nose or your mouth? Where does the air go in your body—only to your chest, or all the way to your midriff or lower belly? Do you breathe slowly or rapidly?

There is a variety of reasons why people might breathe wrongly. Here are two examples: Sometimes I meet people who speak using what in yoga is called the ujjayi breath, in which you contract your throat muscles as you breathe. Ujjayi breathing is very effective while practicing yoga, but you shouldn't take this technique with you off the mat. Contracting your throat muscles is anything but helpful when you want to use your voice in a healthy way. Speaking and singing require a different approach to breathing than yoga.

I've even talked to people who are afraid to breathe into their belly because they think an inflated belly would make them look fat. They always keep their belly pulled in, resulting in continuously constrained muscles. I can assure you, however, that a healthy breathing pattern offers you many more advantages in life than an apparently slightly slender figure.

Now that we know how these types of vocal problems begin, let's explore why some of us develop them. After all, when we were infants, we all knew how to use our voices correctly.

A baby enters the world with automatic breathing skills. From the moment she leaves the womb, her lungs are activated to breathe and her voice is activated to make sound. No mental processes are yet involved; the autonomic nervous system regulates her breathing. As a newborn, her breath may be fast and irregular. But between the age of two and five years old, her lungs develop fully, and she will have a normal, healthy breathing pattern. If she's like most people, however, she will not keep this regular, healthy pattern throughout her life.

As we grow older, breathing remains regulated by the autonomic nervous system. You read in Chapter 2 that this system also regulates functions like body temperature, heart rate, and blood pressure, and that these bodily functions change when we are exposed to stress. By stress, I don't mean only trauma and tension, but any situation that we experience as emotional, including the exciting or thrilling, from learning to ride a bike to having a party for your birthday to being bullied by classmates. Basically, everyday life as you grow up is stressful enough to have an impact on your autonomic nervous system. In your journey from infancy into adulthood, you'll be confronted with plenty of situations that disrupt your natural, healthy breathing pattern. Here are some questions for you: Can you describe your breathing pattern? Do you know what happens to your breathing under stress? Were there any significant life events that influenced the way you breathe?

In my case, for example, I was diagnosed with asthma at the age of five, which caused me to breathe short and fast in the chest. My asthma is a byproduct of multiple allergies to pollen, animal fur, and dust mites. My airways are extremely sensitive to these allergens; they contract when I'm exposed to them, making it harder for me to breathe. When I couldn't breathe properly as a child, I would intuitively start gasping for more air. I didn't know at the time that I should have breathed less instead of more. That's how I ended up a fast, shallow breather with a high heart rate who could never quite get enough air. I became a chronic hyperventilator, which contributed to my sympathetic response mode always being on. Based on what I've since learned about the way breathing works, I suspect that my bad breathing habits reinforced my exercise-induced asthma on top of the allergic asthma, and it all became a downward spiral. As a child, I could never participate in high-impact sports, and they remain challenging for me today.

Though my medical caretakers gave me all kinds of inhalers to relieve my symptoms, they never monitored my breathing. With the knowledge I have now, I see this as a huge missed opportunity. What saved me from my downward spiral of poor breathing were the saxophone and singing lessons I began as a teenager. Those lessons taught me to support my breathing. For the first time in my life,

I was able to experience the calming breathing style that activates the ventral vagal response mode. Maybe it's not a coincidence that my allergic and asthmatic symptoms gradually lessened during my teenage years. Luckily for me—and everyone else—it's never too late to change your breathing habits.

Healthy breathing not only supports your voice, it offers plenty of other health benefits, too. These other improvements in your health can then further improve your voice. You'll read more about that later on, but first, let's find out what *healthy* breathing really looks like.

8.2. The Right Way to Breathe

Because breathing is regulated by the brain stem, it's not something you actively have to do. It even continues without any problems while you are unconscious. In its default, optimal state, your breath should enter slowly through the nose, moving into the belly and lower lungs before ultimately leaving again through the nose.

Breathe Through Your Nose

Your default breathing should be through the nose. It filters, humidifies, and warms (or cools) the air you inhale, allowing your lungs to receive cleaner air with a constant temperature. You should breathe with your nose as much as you possibly can. You can even try it during workouts, if you're in good enough shape! It may be harder in the beginning, but eventually you'll get used to it. The only time you should breathe through the mouth is when you engage in an activity that requires you to open your mouth: speaking, singing, or specific breathing exercises.

If your nose is congested and it is difficult for you to breathe through it, then my advice would be to just make a start with nose breathing, however difficult or uncomfortable it may be in the beginning. Your airways need to get used to this change of use, and they will. Just be patient and don't give up. It will become easier with each day.

As I learned from James Nestor's book *Breath: The New Science of a Lost Art*, mouth breathing is bad for your health in several ways. It transforms your airways so that it's increasingly difficult for you to breathe through your nose, making your throat's soft palate weak and limp. When your soft palate is flabby, it closes the airways when you lie down to sleep, causing snoring and sleep apnea. Inhaling through the nose, on the other hand, trains the soft palate, keeping the airways wider. According to Nestor, mouth breathing also dehydrates. It dries out your throat, leading to a 40% increase in water loss each day compared to what you'd lose breathing through your nose. Besides that, mouth breathing is associated with diminished cognitive abilities, chronic insomnia, bad breath, fatigue, hoarseness, and dental problems. Is this enough to persuade you to ditch mouth breathing?

There's one other issue with mouth breathing: When you breathe through the mouth, you also take more breaths per minute than when you breathe through your nose. That's bad, because we generally want to breathe less instead of more.

Breathe into the Belly and Slow Down the Breath

When people tell you to "breathe from the belly," they mean that you should actively use your diaphragm when you breathe. While your lungs are the central organ responsible for breathing, they can't inflate and deflate without the help of the diaphragm. It's an umbrella-shaped sheet of skeletal muscle situated just below the lungs and the heart. When you inhale air, your diaphragm contracts and moves down in your body. This enables your lungs to fill up and expand. Because of its downward movement, your lower body needs to make room for organs like the bowel system. Your belly therefore expands when you inhale with the diaphragm, which is why it's called belly breathing. When you breathe out again, your diaphragm relaxes and lifts, which causes the air to leave your lungs again. Your bowel system gets back into place and your belly flattens.

Though it might seem counterintuitive, taking breaths too frequently means your body's cells won't get enough oxygen. At the rate most people breathe—an average of twelve breaths per minute—they absorb only about a quarter of the available oxygen, exhaling the rest back out because they don't have sufficient carbon dioxide. This is because our body only transports more oxygen to our cells, carried by a protein called hemoglobin, when the concentration of carbon dioxide increases. Hemoglobin also carries away the waste product carbon dioxide. So when we breathe rapidly, inhaling a lot of oxygen, the hemoglobin transport slows down. Consequently, the carbon dioxide doesn't get carried away and the hemoglobin doesn't go on to pick up more oxygen, disrupting the distribution of this life-giving substance to our organs. This process can start a vicious circle, as the body can respond to oxygen deficiency by hyperventilating.

A healthy breathing pattern provides your body with the right amounts of oxygen and carbon dioxide. If you take longer, slower breaths, your cells will actually receive more oxygen in fewer breaths. Though it's thanks to recent science that we understand why, we've long known this to be the case in practice. Many ancient teachings place the ideal breathing frequency at around five to six breaths per minute, from Ave Marias spoken in rosary prayers to the chanting of yogic mantras. Perhaps there was more than met the eye in those religious rituals, given that they incorporated a restorative breathing pattern that could send people into a relaxed but focused state of mind.

Try it Yourself: This Is How You Get Low and Slow Down

You can do the following exercise sitting, standing, or lying down. Ideally you want to breathe through your nose, but if you find that difficult, start with breathing through your mouth.

Instead of focusing on your inhalation, shift your attention to your exhalation when you take a breath. Slowly and deliberately, let go of all the air in your lungs, until there's nothing left. You might notice your midriff muscle contract a bit. This is because during an exhalation, your diaphragm lifts and your lungs shrink. The lifting diaphragm opens space for your organs, so your belly becomes flatter. You can monitor that by putting a hand on your belly throughout the breathing exercise, following the movement.

After a thorough exhalation, you probably want to take a deeper breath than usual into the lower lungs. But please note that breathing deeper is not the same as inhaling more air! You are simply sending the air lower in your lungs. It can help to visualize this as breathing into the belly. You should also make sure you don't suck in the air quickly and with force. Your lungs will take in air because they are a vacuum; you don't have to force anything. Your abdominal muscles should feel relaxed but slightly active. As you inhale, your diaphragm will descend, filling your lungs with air and pushing your organs down to make space. This is why your midriff and lower belly should expand when you inhale. As you practice, make sure your upper chest doesn't move much. It's always possible to make space for your lungs to expand into the lower part of your chest. You should expand not only to the belly, but also to the back and the sides.

By breathing this way, you should be able to breathe ten times a minute or less—aiming for fewer if you can. To get to the sweet spot of five or six breaths per minute, try inhaling for a count of five, then exhaling for a count of five. You might feel a desire to breathe more rapidly, but it should soon disappear if you can manage to resist it. Your body just needs to get used to this new breathing pattern.

Sometimes, people who experiment with breathing differently experience dizziness or tingling fingers. These are symptoms of hyperventilation, and they mean that you're taking in too much air. It usually helps to take gentler breaths, recognizing that you don't have to inhale a lot of air. You can also make sure that your outbreaths are longer than your inbreaths: inhale for a count of four and exhale for a count of six.

If you're used to breathing fast and find it difficult to slow down, you might find it useful to exhale through a tiny opening in your mouth, as if you are blowing out candles, or imitating the hiss of a tire leaking through a tiny puncture. You can't let go of all the air at once because of the tiny opening in your mouth. This will also help you feel the activity in your abdominal muscles when you exhale. During the exhalation, you gradually contract your abdominal muscles in a regulated and controlled way. It is important to practice this supported breathing separately, without any vocalization; you can add vocalization into this practice later. You'll have succeeded in belly breathing when your abdominal muscles can properly regulate the air pressure needed for talking or singing.

Speak with Breath-Voice Connection

Breath-voice connection is the secret to using your voice in a healthy way—you focus on the breath and the articulators instead of your throat or larynx. But how do you do that, exactly?

You establish breath-voice connection by breathing into your belly and speaking on the exhalation with the right amount of air pressure. You actively use your articulators and don't push from the throat. When your diaphragm isn't engaged enough to enable belly breathing, you're not creating sufficient air pressure to support your voice. As a result, you're likely to contract your throat muscles while you speak as an alternative to air pressure. This creates tension in that area, making you feel like you're running out of air and tiring you quickly when you speak.

When you support your voice with your breath, we can say that you are embodying your voice. You realize that speaking or singing is not an isolated function, but rather, the result of mutual efforts of so many simultaneous functions of the body, from your lungs and diaphragm to your articulator muscles and oral cavities. This embodiment will make your voice stronger, enabling you to talk or sing for hours without feeling strain or fatigue. You won't lose your voice or get hoarse easily. Moreover, the movement of your diaphragm when you breathe provides an internal massage that assists your heart. This means that, on top of breath-voice connection, you're also establishing heart-voice connection. It's this connection we feel in ourselves or sense in others when we talk about "speaking from the heart." Emotions have their origin in physical sensations, mostly in the torso. Breathing into your belly helps you become aware of these physical sensations. When your voice is embodied, you can connect to your emotions and express them with language while you speak or sing.

Try it Yourself: **Speak With Breath-Voice Connection**

See what happens when you speak in a supported, embodied manner. Be sure that you speak only on the outbreath.

- Take a small inhale into the belly.
- As you gradually let go of the air from your lungs, say a full sentence.
- Monitor the movement of your belly by keeping one hand on it. It should deflate gradually.
- Pause to relax your muscles and let go of any surplus air.
- Take another small inhalation, noting the feeling as your belly inflates slightly.
- Say another sentence while you let go of the air.
- Repeat this a couple of times.

Though most people do this correctly, they aren't usually aware that they speak on the exhalation, since it's an unconscious habit. For others, however, breath-voice connection gets out of sync. Some people inhale and then immediately exhale, speaking only after the exhalation without any support from the breath. Others hold their breath, speaking without letting go of any air. Both of these create tension in the larynx and place extra pressure on the delicate vocal folds, making the voice sound weak or tense. This is a frequent cause of hoarseness, pain, and fatigue in the throat.

Remember that changing your breathing pattern permanently is not quick or easy. Any behavior is hard to change, especially something we do 24/7, usually without thinking, like breathing. You will get the best results if you practice your new breathing patterns a couple of times each day, for several months. This will give your body time to reprogram your muscle memory. With time, as these exercises turn into new habits, it will be easier to actively draw upon them to support your breath-voice connection when speaking or singing.

8.3. Other Benefits of Healthy Breathing

So far, I've explained how your breath helps you to embody your voice, enabling you to talk for hours without damaging your vocal folds. This is the first reason why breathing is so important for the voice. But it helps in other areas, too: You can use breath techniques to regulate your emotions, deal with stress, strengthen your immune system, and grow your awareness.

By now you know that emotions are connected to your voice—the way you speak reveals how you feel. To regulate emotions, breathing should be your first intervention. To understand how this works, we have to look again at the autonomic nervous system (ANS).

Breathing As a Tool to Relax and Regulate Emotions

Ideally, you navigate through the different response modes of the ANS—dorsal, sympathetic and ventral—in a regulated way: You go from socially engaged to occasionally mobilized when action is needed, and you rest and digest when the action is over. Life, however, isn't always that simple. It's not uncommon for people living in the modern world to experience continuous moderate stress. As a rule more than an exception, we are busy, always racing against the clock. We're constantly looking at our phones, reacting to alerts or scrolling through timelines. People hold their breath or breathe more shallowly when they are responding to a text or an email. While texting, they tighten their neck and shoulder muscles. This has become so normal that we don't even notice anymore that our sympathetic nervous system is always switched on. We're living in a twilight zone where we virtually never experience life-threatening stress, but we also never find complete relaxation. When you're in that zone, it's hard for your nervous system to effectively switch between the gas pedal and the brake.

While the sympathetic nervous system can be activated in a fraction of a second, we don't usually take enough time to calm down afterwards and allow the parasympathetic functions to return. Moreover, people who are under too much stress for a long time, have lived through trauma, or are naturally overexcitable, might notice that finding the break after stepping on the gas pedal takes even longer than it does for the average person. Such people's sympathetic response mode remains activated long after the stress is gone. As a result, their breathing stays fast and shallow, keeping the stress response going on and on. Fight-or-flight has become a vicious circle that keeps reacting to itself. Remember Jamie from Chapter 5, the young man with intense psycho-motor overexcitability? His sympathetic response mode was always activated and consequently he took fast, shallow breaths in the chest.

When this goes on for too long, your body will accept all these stress symptoms as the new normal. It will come to feel normal to have a high heart rate and fast, shallow breathing. This means that hyperventilation has become chronic. Such chronic stress enhances feelings of anxiousness, restlessness, and difficulties focusing. It can also cause high blood pressure, depression, and chronic disease, as well as generally weakening your immune system.

You already know that your body plays a role in how emotions come into being and develop. Your breathing pattern is part of that. Scientists have found that by changing your breathing pattern, you can induce emotions and reduce symptoms of arousal, anxiety, depression, anger, and confusion. When you're in ventral vagal response mode, you breathe slower and deeper. What's striking is that, when you're stressed or anxious, or even sad or angry, breathing slower and deeper can actually switch you into ventral vagal, quickly making you feel calmer and more relaxed. You can also go for the opposite effect, breathing in a fast and shallow way to become more active and alert.

Try it Yourself: **Calm Yourself with Your Breath**

When you're preparing for a presentation, performance, difficult conversation, or some other stressful event, you can tap into your social engagement response mode by doing the following:

- 15 to 30 minutes before you have to perform, find a place where you can sit down quietly, preferably alone.
- Put your phone on silent mode. Don't check your messages. When you're nervous, you'll probably be tempted to pick up your phone because it distracts you from your nerves. But, as you've already learned, looking at your phone will activate your sympathetic nervous system and will only enhance your stress.
- Close your eyes and start following your breath. Notice its pace. You might even notice your heartbeat or other physical sensations.
- Do you experience signs of nervousness like a racing heart, tight muscles, or a restless mind? If so, don't try to push these sensations away. They don't need to be fixed. Let them come into being, paying gentle attention to them. Notice what happens when you do this.
- If you breathe high in your chest, see if you can send the air deeper, without lifting the chest. Put a hand on your belly and notice what you feel.
- Slow down your inhalations and exhalations until your breathing pattern approaches a count of five in and a count of five out. Continue for a couple of minutes.
- After a while, observe your heart rate and the activity in your mind. Have they decreased?
- Take a short inbreath and say "one" while you are aware of your breath-voice connection. After that, let go of the air you have left in your lungs and prepare your inbreath for the next number. Then say "two," carrying on until you reach ten.
- Open your eyes. Can you can take that calmness and breath-voice connection with you onto the stage or into the meeting?

Even if you are with other people, you can easily check in with your breathing when you don't have to speak. While listening to others, you can simultaneously focus on breathing more slowly and deeply through the nose. Nobody has to notice you doing this. When it's your turn to speak up, make sure that you exhale deeply and then inhale consciously before you start.

Breathing as a Tool to Become Self-Aware

Although my music lessons as a teen taught me about breath support, I wasn't truly a conscious breather until a few years ago. Before that, I would automatically shift to deep breathing when I sang, but after I finished, I stopped noticing my breathing. As I came to recognize later, I tended to hold my breath after inhaling, especially when I was focused on a task or caught up in my thoughts.

It was only after I had been doing meditation and contemplation practices for some years that I really became aware of my breathing pattern. I started to notice my breathing a few times per day, reflecting on whether it was deep and slow enough. After a while, I could integrate these moments with tasks like watching television, walking, reading, or typing on my laptop—all excellent occasions to focus on breathing more slowly and deeply. Today, I spend about half of my waking hours being aware of my breathing pattern during activities like listening, walking, writing, dancing, singing, and speaking.

Ania is a woman who came to see me because she felt she wasn't in charge of what she was saying, and she was not the public speaker she wanted to be. She thought she spoke too much, which she did because she was afraid people wouldn't listen otherwise. She wanted to be able to speak so that people would listen and take her seriously.

Ania told me later that it was the breath techniques from our first session that helped her the most. Breathing correctly made her focus on her sensory experience, getting her out of her busy head. By breathing more slowly, she managed to lower the pace of her thoughts, actions, and speech as well. She came to realize how fast and chaotic she had been—a way of living that she now recognizes in other people.

By focusing on the breath, you become more aware of your body, emotions, beliefs, thoughts, conditioned behavior, and your environment. It's therefore no surprise that ancient teachings like the Hindu and Vedic scriptures have endorsed breath techniques as an important part of their practice.

Nowadays, the benefits of breath techniques are spreading into the mainstream of the Western world via yoga, meditation, mindfulness, tai chi, chi kung, and similar practices that all teach conscious breathing.

Practicing yoga can support your voice not only with healthy breathing, but also with self-awareness. According to the philosophy of yoga, the mind and the breath are closely connected. Breath techniques are called pranayama (*prāṇa* = life force, *āyāma* = mastery). Yoga sutra 2.52 says about pranayama: "Thus the covering of brightness is removed." Experts generally interpret this as saying that pranayama will gradually lift the veil that usually covers the mind to reveal the light of clarity. The veil represents darkness, suffering, ignorance, and conditioning. Awareness arises when you lift this veil. It is your direct experience of the present moment—the here and now. By following your breath, your direct experience will intensify and thought activity will decrease. Thoughts about past or future events—things that happened earlier or that you'll need to do later—diminish or even disappear. When your mind inevitably drifts away from the breath, you notice this and redirect your attention again to the breathing. Some people think that they're failing the practice when their mind keeps on drifting off. But it's actually in the moments you notice your mind has drifted, that awareness unfolds. So please allow yourself to drift off—it is a vital part of the practice. This practice is extremely valuable to improve your voice if too much thought activity gets in the way of expressing yourself calmly and clearly. You'll read more about self-awareness in Chapter 12.

Breathing to Boost Your Immune System

Chronic stress weakens your immune system and is linked to a variety of diseases. We've learned that slow, deep breathing contributes to reducing stress and relaxing your nervous system, and that oxygen plays an important role in the immune system. We can therefore predict that slow, deep breathing will benefit your immune system.

But this is where things take a surprising turn. As we discussed in Chapter 2, some people intentionally use fast and heavy breath techniques to deliberately turn on their sympathetic response, helping them to feel focused and energized. Similarly, controlled and acute stress—as in working out or playing sports—is also known to boost immune responses. Though the scientific consensus has long held that it was impossible to manipulate the autonomic nervous system, Tibetan Buddhists devised a practice that suggested this was not the case. This practice, known as Tummo breathing, gave them control over their bodily processes like heat production, metabolism and pain experience. Studies on Tibetan monks and Western control groups have confirmed this effect.

Today, Tummo breathing is having a popular revival through the Wim Hof Method. You might have heard about Hof, also known as the Dutch Iceman, taking ice baths and running a half marathon barefoot along the Arctic Circle. Hof's cold exposure training and Tummo-inspired heavy breath techniques are now known worldwide. The Dutch Radboud University ran tests on Hof and twelve other healthy men who had mastered his technique, comparing them to a control group. Like the Tibetan monks, the men who practiced the Wim Hof Method were able to turn on their sympathetic response mode and control their body temperature, heart rate, and even immune response to an injected *E. coli* endotoxin. The combination of cold exposure, mindset, and heavy breath technique apparently gave these men the ability to release adrenaline on command. The release of these hormones was responsible for the impressive boost in immune responses their bodies showed.

Quite a few of my clients practice Hof's breathing method, so I decided to try it out myself. For about four weeks, I practiced the Wim Hof Method daily: thirty fast and deep inhalations followed by an exhalation that you hold as long as possible. Then you inhale once deeply and hold your inhalation for 15 seconds. You repeat the cycle two more times. Though I was already feeling energized and focused at the time, after Wim Hof, my focus was so strong that I felt more restless than usual and impatient to get things done. I think I got *too* goal oriented. Now I clearly had more sympathetic energy in my nervous system, but I didn't particularly like this uptight version of myself. So I didn't consider these effects an improvement. I do, however, recognize these breathing exercises as a powerful tool that I can use in certain situations, like when I'm tired or not motivated and need to get things done—in other words, when I need to mobilize.

Although the research results from the Radboud University are impressive, there are some things to consider if you start experimenting with heavy breathing. Most importantly, all the participants in this experiment were men. Of the many physiological differences between men and women, the brain's response under the influence of stress is one of the more significant ones, probably because of the role that the testosterone-adrenaline axis plays here. Men have access to testosterone more readily than women, so women have to produce more testosterone during periods of stress. It will also take them longer. Sometimes they fail to do so, resulting in an adrenaline level out of balance with their testosterone, which can lead to anxiety and depression. So until the Radboud University experiment is repeated with women, we won't know for sure if the Wim Hof Method is as beneficial for them as for men—or even whether it's safe for women's health.

We also don't fully understand how heavy breath techniques affect people who are under continuous (unconscious) stress, have lived through trauma, or are overexcitable. Their nervous systems already produce a lot of sympathetic energy, and they might struggle to keep ventral vagal response mode in the lead. If you have a sensitive nervous system, the line between acute and chronic stress is a narrow one. Instead of enhancing your immune response with heavy breathing, you could develop chronic stress. In a Q&A session with therapist Deb Dana, I asked her if she thought it was safe for those people to include heavy breathing in their daily routine, and her answer was a clear "no." She explained that breathing is a powerful tool to influence the nervous system, and that you should always be careful with extreme practices in this respect. Therefore, if you are someone who takes fast or shallow breaths in the chest by default, stay away from heavy breathing. First you need to learn what healthy breathing is and how you can use it to calm yourself.

Keep in mind that people are wired differently and that there is no panacea that works for everyone. While some people thrive by intentionally activating the sympathetic response mode, it is my guess that most others will benefit far more from reducing stress and learning to intentionally activate their ventral vagal response mode. In order to know where you are on this spectrum, you must know your body and listen to its particular needs. This is what the next chapter is about.

9. Feel into The Body

Because speaking is central to their work, teachers often come to me for help. Take Nadim: When he stood in front of his classroom, his shoulders would get sore and he would breathe too high in his chest. Sometimes he even held his breath. If he needed to raise his voice, it would sound and feel cramped. While Nadim's colleagues told him he didn't come across as nervous, on the inside, he always felt tense in front of a class.

Nadim came to me because he wanted to figure out how to relax his body. In our sessions, we discussed how he struggled to regulate his emotions and didn't do much to release his tension after work. Consequently, the stress got stuck in his body, resulting in many physical complaints. It took three months of concerted effort, but eventually, Nadim reached a place where he could finally relax while teaching. He had learned to truly *connect* to his body and his breath. Whenever his old habits reemerged, he would now notice them and adjust.

The key to achieving this was Nadim's growing body awareness. By now, you know that if you want to work with the voice, you have to work with the body: breathing, recognizing bodily sensations, knowing your autonomic responses, identifying your emotions, and training the muscles in your face. In other words, to use your voice well, you have to know your body well. You need to recognize the signals it sends you, understand them, and respond accordingly.

When you're connected to your body, you intuitively know what you need to do to use your voice to its full potential. If my clients speak quickly and restlessly without finishing their sentences, I ask them to slow down, close their eyes, focus on breathing, and notice their body. Afterwards, when I ask them to speak again, they always sound more grounded, well-paced and intelligible. In this chapter you will learn how to feel into your body, thereby developing more awareness of and agency over your voice.

9.1. Confidence is a Physical Experience

When people sign up for voice coaching, more often than not, they essentially want to become more confident. Either they don't feel confident and their voice reflects that, or they sense that their voice doesn't convey the confidence they do feel inside.

Here's the thing: Confidence is not a mindset. It's not a trick you can learn with cognitive tools or positive affirmations. Confidence is a *physical* experience—something that you embody with your whole being, from head to toe. You cannot fake it. People who are not comfortable in their own bodies don't come across as confident, while those who are comfortable in their bodies radiate it. When they enter a room, you can positively *feel* that they're content, calm, and relaxed. They breathe slowly. Their muscles aren't tensed. They're not afraid to take up space, and they allow you to take up space, too. If you want to become more confident, you will find the solution in your body.

Some people are blessed with automatic body awareness. Others find the concept utterly perplexing. *What should I feel? Where should I feel things? Is there something wrong if I don't feel anything? How do I know if I'm feeling the right things?* For a long time, I was one of those people—but I didn't realize I was missing anything. "You spend so much time in your head. You should connect with your body more," people used to tell me. But I didn't have a clue what they meant or how to do it. This lack of body awareness was one reason I struggled with my voice for so long.

Just as we discussed with breathing habits, we're all born with body awareness, but some of us lose it, for different reasons. If you're overexcitable, you will have a stronger response to stimuli at a lower threshold. You may then respond strongly to your own bodily sensations—including those that indicate emotions. This can make you feel so uncomfortable that you want to avoid feeling them. In order to feel less, you might shift your attention to external stimuli, away from bodily sensations. As a result, you are continuously drawn outside of your body, toward what you hear and see. This especially includes other people, with whom you empathize while gauging their reactions to you. Unfortunately, this all comes at the expense of your internal, interoceptive awareness.

A busy mind is another reason people lose body awareness. If you're overexcitable, it's also possible that you distract yourself from feeling bodily sensations by dwelling in your mind. Sometimes this happens when you're actively working on solving a problem, a complex mental task. At other times, however, you might just have a lot of random thought activity going on, such as during daydreaming. Do you recognize similar situations in your own life? Do you enjoy your random thought activity, or does it keep you from getting things done? In some ways, a busy mind is part of human nature. You might even value the busyness if it involves interesting thoughts and creative ideas. But a busy mind can be disruptive when we want to speak or listen actively. That's why most of us will benefit from learning how to quiet our minds and connect more with our bodies.

No matter where you are on this spectrum of body awareness, you can increase it. Some will achieve this by adding simple exercises to their daily routine for a couple of months, while others will need in-depth professional guidance. For everyone, however, it will be a gradual process, taking time before you notice any changes. But I promise you this: If you persevere, your efforts will be rewarded.

Before I introduce you to some exercises, however, I have to address one other important factor: modern communication technology. Today, you can find an incredible assortment of technical tools for analyzing your physical health—from apps to watches and rings that track key signals from your body, monitoring things like your heart rate, steps, sleep, workouts, and menstrual cycles. Although these technical devices can give us some useful data, we must be careful not to outsource our ability to perceive our own bodies. The data these devices provide are just that: data. Apps are designed by people and contain those people's biases and assumptions. The data they provide are therefore only an interpretation of reality, not a literal representation of your personal experience of your body. Technology can never replace feeling into your body with your own senses. Your own body awareness will always be your most reliable source of information about what's going on with you—and the more you learn to notice and interpret it, the more reliable it will be.

9.2. The Basics of Body Awareness

If you feel daunted by the whole idea of this practice, I completely understand. Contemporary society doesn't encourage us to take an interest in our bodily sensations. Rather, we're taught to neglect them. For the sake of performance and efficiency, we deny ourselves rest, relaxation, sleep, and food. At the times when we actually need these things, we put them off. We skip meals and trips to the bathroom because meetings are planned too tight. We neglect bedtime because we still want to reply to some emails at 11 p.m. In the morning, we don't allow ourselves to have a lie in because we want to be productive or finally spend time with the kids on the weekend. We go to our uncle's birthday party because we promised we would, even though a headache signals that we should stay home. Instead, we take a pain killer.

As a result, feeling into our body can give rise to a powerful resistance. If you feel this, then body awareness is *exactly* what you need. Your mind doesn't want to go there because it's not used to navigating with the body. It's used to navigating through sheer willpower, and it's happy to continue like this. It's true that considering bodily sensations will make life more complicated—at least in the beginning. Years of neglecting signals from the body, however, comes with a price. It can lead to chronic stress, which in turn can lead to high blood pressure, depression, burnout, chronic diseases, and a weakened immune system. On the level of voice, neglecting signals from your body will turn you into a talking head, with less vocal power and expressiveness as a result.

Try it Yourself: **Identify Bodily Sensations**

We all start at different places with this practice. The following is a very basic exercise for those of you who feel completely disconnected from your body. To restore the connection and build the foundation for the rest of the exercises in this chapter, try this every day for a couple of weeks:

- Lie down on the sofa or your bed for at least 15 minutes.
- Put one hand on your belly and focus on your breathing.
- Use your hand and your breathing to become aware of the sensory information coming from your body. Do you feel any sensations? Are there any body parts that draw your attention? Do these sensations evoke any thoughts or emotions?
- If you feel anything in particular, can you stay there with your attention, instead of drifting away from it?

Choosing a Practice

Once you have a basic foundation of awareness of your bodily sensations, you're ready to move on to a regular practice designed to increase your skill. In general, low-impact activities work best because they allow the gentle attention and open curiosity needed to note bodily sensations without any distracting focus on performance.

Yoga is the most popular activity in this genre. I've practiced yoga for about ten years now, starting my day with it a few times per week. As little as 15 minutes of yoga will give me a completely different focus and intention than I have if I rush to my day without it. Other movement practices you can try include tai chi and chi kung; you could also simply take a walk in nature. What's especially valuable about yoga, tai chi, and chi kung, however, is that they not only make your body more flexible, they help your mind become more flexible as well. Mindfulness practices help with body awareness as well, as I'll discuss in later chapters.

Some formal practices can help in this area, too. I am personally most familiar with Rebalancing. It's a form of emotional body work that is executed by a Rebalancing practitioner. This practice is physically passive. You sit still or lie down and focus on direct experience in the body. On top of the exercises you will find in this chapter, Rebalancing enabled me to restore my disrupted connection to myself, thereby helping me unblock my voice as well. The treatment starts with the viewpoint that all our emotional experiences, whether we deny them or cling to them, settle in the body in the form of pain, stiffness, or inflexibility, causing imbalances and blockages. During the treatment, the practitioner helps you to release physical and mental tension, clearing the blockages. Rebalancing helps you to shift from *thinking*, to *conscious feeling*, to *being*. The more you are consciously present in your body, the less you are overwhelmed by unhelpful, anxious thought activity.

From that state of conscious presence, you will be able to use your thinking mind as a practical tool, attuned to what your body needs.

You can also work on developing body awareness without the guidance of a professional. One of your first goals as you develop this skill, will be to improve your posture.

Posture

Speaking confidently starts with good posture. A relaxed, open throat in line with your spine allows air to flow in for deep belly breathing. Removing tension from your upper body frees your diaphragm to move up and down while you breathe. The front of your body should feel soft, like you're a puppet on marionette strings. You trust those strings to pull you wherever they want, without resistance. Your spine should be straight and firm, giving your soft front a strong foundation. Overall, you're stable and flexible.

How do you know if you've got good posture? If you can walk around with a book on your head, you've passed the test.

Try it Yourself: **Check In With Your Body Before You Use Your Voice**

You can do the following exercise as a physical warm up routine before a concert, presentation, important phone call, or meeting. Basically any time you want to calm yourself and feel confident.

- Do a couple of full, circular neck rolls, clockwise and counterclockwise. Roll your shoulders backwards and forwards. Stretch your whole body as much as you can, then release your muscles by shaking your arms and legs.
- While standing, place your legs directly under your hips without locking your knees. Seek balance between your left and right leg.
- Notice sensations in your legs and feet and how they contact the floor. Wiggle your toes if you like.
- Notice sensations in your upper body. Your neck and shoulders should feel low and relaxed by now; if they don't, repeat the first step in this exercise. Your arms should also be quite heavy and the muscles in your jaw and face should be relaxed, too.
- Now focus on the lowest part of your spine. Make it as long as possible by extending it with the top of your head. You should probably also press your chin down just a tiny bit. Imagine that you can touch the ceiling with the crown of your head. This way, your neck becomes long and spacious without tension on your larynx. Your posture should feel relaxed and neutral.

- Closing your eyes, breathe slowly and deeply from the belly.
- As you continue to breathe, relax the front of your body. Do you notice any tension in your muscles? Are your shoulders low and relaxed? Is your jaw relaxed? How about the muscles in your face? Is your belly expanding and contracting while you breathe, or do you tend to hold it in? Are your hands hanging loose along the body? Can you feel your heartbeat?
- Allow yourself a few moments of silence.
- After checking in with your body one more time, open your eyes. Enter the stage, sit down at your screen, or walk into the room. Make sure you take this heightened body awareness with you. Don't hurry; slow your movements down. Keep on feeling the ground under your feet, and continue to feel connected with your body through your feet.
- When you speak, don't focus on your voice and its sound. Instead, bring your attention to your audience and to the intentions and emotions you want to convey to them with your message.

When you start with training in body awareness, you'll notice that you go in and out of contact with your body while you speak. When you notice that happening, consider this a good thing! The act of *noticing* that you lost contact with your body is the first sign of your growing body awareness. It's to be expected that you will lose this connection from time to time, returning to your head as you've always done. Don't expect to master this skill on day one.

There are, however, several exercises you can do to maintain body awareness while you rehearse a presentation or a song. They will help you engage your whole body—not just your head—while speaking or singing, and stay connected to your body while you use your voice. Here are some suggestions:

Try it Yourself: **Three Exercises to Stay Connected to Your Body While You Speak**

Exercise 1: Engage Your Core

- Do you have workout weights at home? Take one in each hand while standing up, hold them in front of you with your elbows bent at a ninety-degree angle, keeping the elbows tight by your sides. The weights should be at the same height as your diaphragm, thereby activating your core.
- Begin to speak or sing, and then engage your core. Feel how the engaged core enables breath-voice connection and supports your voice.
- You can get the same effect if you stand facing a wall and push against it with your hands.

Exercise 2: Give Your Mind a Task

Moving around slowly while speaking and singing is generally a good strategy to stay connected to your body. Try giving your mind a simple task while you move. A directed task allows less space for self-conscious thoughts about your performance. This opens more space for intentional body awareness.

- Place a big pile of books on the floor.
- Start practicing your song or presentation. Walk to the pile of books, bend over, and take one of the books. Walk to the other side of the room, bend over again, and put the book down. Walk back to the pile and start moving all the books to the other pile, one at a time.
- When you finish one pile, start moving the pile back again.

Exercise 3: From Head to Toe

The following exercise is taken from *Find Your Voice*, a book by voice coach Caroline Goyder, and you can do it standing or sitting. Which foot do you lead with when you walk? Press the big toe of this foot into the floor.

- Speak or sing. Feel how this engages your core and enriches your voice.
- Now take the pressure off the big toe and rock onto your heel. As you continue to speak or sing, notice how your voice loses some energy.
- Press the big toe back into the floor and notice the power return to your voice.

Embodied Listening

When we speak, we want others to listen to us. But frankly, how good are we ourselves at listening to others? Making a sincere effort to truly listen is a complementary practice that can help you as you work to develop awareness of your own body, as it makes use of some of the same skills.

Listening is becoming harder and harder in the twenty-first century. Most of us are surrounded by noise all the time—traffic, background music, or conversations we don't take part in. We also have a sense that we don't always need to listen carefully to what's been said. After all, we can always look things up again in the newspaper, on Youtube, or on Wikipedia. Most significantly of all, modern media doesn't exactly encourage deep, meaningful listening. As we get more and more of our information from people broadcasting quick sound bites of their feelings and opinions, we become less receptive to longer videos, let alone lengthy essays that focus on the bigger picture and add nuance. And so we become impatient listeners.

One of the greatest gifts you can give someone is to actively listen with full attention. Too often, we're just waiting for the other person to finish, using his speaking time to think about what we're going to say next. If we continue like this, we never establish a true connection where we both feel heard. After all, if you haven't truly listened to someone, your response is meaningless. That's why, to understand each other in this over-stimulating world, it's worth paying extra attention to how we listen.

Body awareness can help you establish this connection. Being present while you're having a conversation means being present in your body, not being caught up in thought activity. Focus on your body and breathing while you're listening to someone. You'll notice that it makes it easier to listen, as conscious breathing draws you into the present moment and away from your thoughts about the past or future.

Try it Yourself: **Focus on Your Body while Listening**

While listening to someone else, try the following:

- Relax your posture. Do you notice any tensed muscles in your body? Are you able to release this tension?
- Focus on sense perception: What do you hear, feel, and see? What cues do you get from this person's tone of voice and facial expressions?
- Within your own body, focus on your breathing. With a little practice, following your breathing pattern will make it easier to listen to someone else.
- Allow the words of the other person to sink in. Try to resist the habit most of us have to immediately formulate advice or a counter-opinion. Stay open and nonjudgmental to what is being said.

- Slow down. This will give you time to feel what's truly happening within your body and to digest what's being said.
- Allow silence into the conversation. You don't have to react immediately. When you're comfortable with silence, you allow yourself time to respond from a place of conscious awareness instead of habitual reactivity.

9.3. Building Confidence

When we work with our voices, we tend to dwell on how they sound. The way the listener perceives the sound coming out of your mouth is what matters most, right? When it matters most, our inner critic goes on high alert. We become judgmental about our voices and lose ourselves in unimportant details. The thoughts in our heads absorb us, and we lose contact with our bodies—especially when we don't want to be the center of attention. Consequently, our speech becomes flat, monotonous, and far too fast.

To calm that inner critic, Goyder says that we should *feel* our voices rather than listen to them. Becoming aware of the resonating qualities of your body can help you overcome any negative reaction to hearing your own voice:

> *Feeling your voice is fundamentally simple. Your voice is vibration. You may have tuned that vibration out of your awareness because your thoughts have been whirling around in your head. But when you feel your voice, you bypass all of that self-consciousness. You bring yourself into that pure sensation of your voice in the present moment and so your voice releases and becomes more expressive, more conversational.*[34]

Try it Yourself: **Feel Your Voice**

Here is an exercise by Goyder that I have slightly modified for my practice. Its purpose is to enable you to feel your voice in your body.

- Say a word and hear it through your ears. Focus on its sound, not its meaning. Hear your voice as you speak. Become aware of what it's like to listen to your voice through your ears as sound, rather than feeling the buzz of it in your body.
- Say the same word again, and this time, focus on your body. What do you physically feel when you speak? Where do you feel buzzing sensations? Where in your body does the sound resonate?

---

34   C. Goyder *Find Your Voice: The Secret to Talking with Confidence in any Situation* (2020, Vermillion, London) p. 113.

- If you don't feel any buzzing sensations, try some exercises for resonance from chapter 4, or try making more space in your throat by yawning. Then say the word again. Put your hand on different parts of your body. Where do you feel the vibrations? In your lips, cheeks, nose, forehead, throat, mouth or chest?
- Experiment with different pitches. Notice that high tones vibrate in a different place than low tones. When you speak, let your attention settle down into the *feeling* of your voice rather than the sound.
- If you want to find your most naturally buzzy note, say "mm-hmmmm," as if you are agreeing with someone. This is usually your most comfortable speaking pitch. Say "mm-hmmmm" a couple of times and feel the buzz it creates. Notice where you feel the buzz in the body.
- Now say the word you originally chose with the same pitch as your "mm-hmmmm" and put a hand on the place where you feel it in your body. This can feel comforting and grounding. Staying in the feeling of the sound, rather than assessing it by ear, is an excellent sensory foundation for speaking with confidence.

The Challenge of Judging Your Own Voice

Another common trigger for our inner critic is hearing our own voice on recording for the first time. This comes as a shock for almost everyone. The recorded voice always sounds so different from how you think it should—and not in a positive way. Most people perceive their recorded voice as higher and thinner than what they hear in their head while speaking. This can lead to disliking of your own voice—even to the point of disgust. It certainly doesn't boost anyone's confidence.

So what exactly is going on in this common experience? When you speak, you hear your own voice in two different ways. The first is through the sound waves that leave your mouth and enter your ears again, the same way you hear everyone else's voice. But the second way applies only to your own voice: It's the resonance of your voice in your skull. Your skull works like a subwoofer, amplifying low frequencies to produce the deeper, warmer layer you hear in your own live voice. While you can hear your subwoofer, everyone else just hears your voice the way as you hear it through your ears.

Another thing the subwoofer does is amplify the volume of your voice as you perceive it. That's why there's often a discrepancy between how loudly a person believes she is speaking and her voice's actual volume in the ears of others. I meet many people in my practice who tell me that they have a very soft voice and find it hard to make themselves heard. When I challenge them to speak just a little louder, they look alarmed. "But now I'm shouting!" they insist. To my ears, however, they're not shouting at all. For the first time, they're actually speaking at a regular volume. When I make a quick recording of what they perceive as shouting, they always agree with me that the playback of the recording sounds much quieter than they expected. They perceive their own voices as much louder than others do. That's how powerful the subwoofer is.

When you listen to your voice on a recording, you hear it without the subwoofer—maybe for the first time. That's why you're shocked. Know that you're not alone here. In the ears of others, we all sound thinner and higher than we think we do. When you realize this, please don't try to sound deeper or lower.

Try it Yourself: **Record Yourself**

There's only one way to overcome your dissatisfaction with your voice in this area: You must record and listen to yourself as much as possible. If you already struggle with confidence, this can be tough. It might feel like torture. But it's a matter of biting the bullet on this one. To defuse from this negative charge, you must make a short, one minute recording of your voice and listen to it. Then listen to your recorded voice again. And again. And again, and again, and again. And again. It's essentially exposure therapy: You'll get used to the way you sound and, gradually, the things that bothered you won't stand out so much. There will no longer be a contrast between what you expect and what you hear.

Taking Up Space

Sharice, who described herself as humble and introverted, came to me with the goal of becoming a better communicator. The voice exercises I gave her in order to achieve this, however, made her uncomfortable and self-conscious. Speaking louder and with higher intonation made her feel vulnerable. She told me that she'd rather not take up a lot of space. But her goal remained the same, so despite her discomfort, she kept on practicing. After some weeks, she started to notice that people reacted differently to her when she spoke with more expression. They were actually *listening* to her. As she realized, this was because she was finally allowing herself to take up space with her voice and body. She was less hesitant to draw attention to herself.

Do you abhor being the center of attention? When all eyes are focused on you, do you want to run away? It's not always easy to take up space and to be comfortable with that. Most of us experienced situations where our presence was unwanted. We've all been in situations where we were not allowed to speak up or express what we needed. Or when we did speak up, we may not have been heard. This was probably during childhood, but it could have been later in life as well. The situations in which we are unwanted, or where we are not seen or heard, leave deep impressions on us. Later in life, when we are purposely asked to bring attention to ourselves by speaking up or contributing in other ways, we deal with the residue of those earlier rejections. It's become difficult for us to take up space.

Fortunately, you can learn to take up space with your presence, your body, and your voice. I recommend you aim to keep about fifty percent of your attention with your own body and fifty percent with your surroundings, including other people. This equal balance is essential. If you are too focused on your own body, you'll lose contact with what's going on around you. If you don't consider the subtle cues coming from other people's bodies, you won't allow enough space for them, and you'll come across as dominant or insensitive. On the other hand, if you're too focused on your surroundings, you're not taking up space for yourself. Then you won't be seen or heard, even if you say something relevant. Being too caught up with what's going on around you often goes hand in hand with a lot of thought activity about the self, including worrying about what others might think of you and fears of being judged. As we discussed earlier, such thoughts don't help with body awareness; they count as getting trapped in your mind.

> *Try it Yourself:* **Allow Yourself to Take up Space**
>
> If you want to learn to take up space in a balanced way, you can combine all of the exercises above in these five steps:
>
> 1. Check in with your body and relax your posture.
> 2. Engage your core, breathe from your diaphragm and slow down your breathing.
> 3. Bring your attention to sense perception: What do you hear, see, feel, and smell around you?
> 4. Be aware of other people and objects around you. Listen consciously while others take up space.
> 5. When you speak or sing, feel your voice inside your body. Direct fifty percent of your attention to your body and the intentions and emotions you want to convey with your message. Direct the other fifty percent to your surroundings.

10. Make Sense of Your Emotions

Working with your emotions is the key to strengthening your voice. This is fundamental for everyone, but especially for those with emotional overexcitability. If you experience everything so intensely, what can you do about it? After all, it can feel like you're trapped on that emotional roller coaster, doomed to always broadcast your emotions through your voice.

The first thing people like this typically try is to suppress their emotions. As I mentioned in Chapter 5, such suppression can result in one of two seemingly opposing outcomes:

1. Your emotions become *too* controlled. Your voice lacks overall expressiveness, and you sound flat, impersonal, or insincere.
2. Your emotions sound through *too much*. They go into overdrive easily—and always reveal themselves through your voice.

Both of these outcomes indicate a failure to become aware of, express, and regulate emotions. I myself belong to the first category. In the past, I got so good at suppressing my emotions that no one could tell what was going on—neither others nor me. Most of the time, I wasn't even aware of the nerves I felt before I went on stage. This was partially because I wasn't in contact with my body and partially because my mind suppressed my nerves, thereby convincing itself it had everything under control. The result was that, on the outside, I appeared to be doing fine. But when I started to sing, my voice was tight and strained—clearly affected by those suppressed nerves. While my conscious mind thought it was in control, my autonomic nervous system was signaling that I didn't feel safe. The body never lies.

Unfortunately, my experience isn't all that uncommon. Most people are just as good at ignoring the bodily sensations that reveal their emotions. Children are often forced to unlearn their direct emotional expressions of anger and sadness because adults teach them that these emotions are too intense or otherwise unwelcome. Only rarely do they teach these kids socially appropriate, effective ways to handle the turmoil of emotions. Even children's joyful enthusiasm is too much for many grown-ups. So as you grow older, you learn to suppress yourself, and that behavior gets rewarded by society—at least at first.

Sometimes, people with this problem focus on the emotions of others at the expense of their own. Imagine that you're giving a presentation and instead of thinking about your topic, you're focused on how your audience feels: *What are they thinking? Am I boring them? Am I offending anyone?* When you try to get into other people's heads, you usually fail to identify what you feel yourself. Empathy is generally a positive trait, of course, but not when you use it to hide from your own emotions.

If you want to actively regulate the emotions expressed through your voice, you must first be aware of what you feel. As you know by now, your emotions emerge from a highly complex process that involves your whole physical and mental being. Being fully aware of them will not be easy, especially in the beginning, but it's possible to make sense of your emotions. If you struggle with this, you can learn by breaking the process down into several steps that you can practice:

1. Read your body's cues
2. Become introspective about what your feel
3. Accept what you feel
4. Don't react, regulate
5. Identify your unmet needs and values

10.1. Read Your Body's Cues

As we discussed in Chapters 2 and 7, the body and mind are not separate. Our autonomic nervous system detects cues of safety/comfort and danger/discomfort from our own body and our surroundings, including other people. It then activates a response mode that directs us to either protect ourselves or engage socially. These response modes are the origin of our emotions, leading our mind to create narratives that try to explain what's going on. The thing is, these don't necessarily reflect reality. To make it even more complicated, we have such strong minds that even a single thought or memory can activate a response state on its own.

The solution to regulating your emotions therefore lies in the body. It begins with eating healthy, exercising regularly, and getting enough sleep. Of course, we all know we should do those things, and yet, so many of us struggle here. It goes beyond the scope of this book to discuss all the hurdles to a healthy lifestyle. For now, just keep in mind that diet, exercise, and sleep affect more than just your physical health; they also influence your overall level of *emotional* well-being. When you eat well, exercise, and get enough sleep, you'll experience less moodiness and irritation, replacing them with more positive, less overwhelming emotions.

Of course, even when you're eating right, you'll still have to deal with challenges in your life. What can you do to regulate your emotions during stressful or unpleasant moments? Therapist Deb Dana developed a method for active regulation of your autonomic response states based on the polyvagal theory. In Dana's method, you begin by identifying the response state you're in, then identify the cues that brought you there. This is the first step in the process of effectively regulating emotions and vocal expression.

Try it Yourself: **Identify Your Autonomic Response Stage**

Remember the three stages of response of the autonomic nervous system? The ventral vagal response enables you to engage socially, the sympathetic response enables you to fight or flee, and the dorsal vagal response causes you to freeze. Can you identify which state you're in at the moment? Evaluate your physical sensations, emotions, and thoughts before finally turning to the information encoded in your voice as the final clue to identify where you are on the spectrum between comfortable and uncomfortable:

- Do you feel irritated, stressed, anxious, or worried? This is the sympathetic response mode. Now, turning to your voice, is it fast, loud, and defensive? That's a fight response. Is it fast, soft, and unintelligible? That's a flight response.
- Do you feel lonely, ashamed, hopeless, or numb? This is the dorsal vagal response mode. Now, how is your voice? Is it soft, unexpressive, and monotonous—or maybe you're unable to speak at all? That's a freeze response.
- Do you feel energized, curious, creative, confident, and resourceful? Does your voice sound engaging, with lots of variety in rhythm and intonation? You are in the ventral vagal response mode, and ready to socially engage.

Remember, it will take practice to make this a habit. You are retraining your nervous system, and that takes time and effort. If you do this exercise when you're only mildly stressed, eventually you'll find the practice accessible to you in those high-stress situations when you need it the most.

Try it Yourself: **Identify What Brought on this Response Stage**

After you've identified your current response stage, try to figure out what triggered it. What did your body unconsciously detect that made you feel comfortable or uncomfortable? These triggers are personal, so you need to become aware of your particular cues. Here are three categories of cues you can search for triggers of fight, flight, or freeze responses, with some examples of each:

- Cues from others: An unfriendly look. Someone looks away when you're talking. A sharp and defensive voice. Someone doesn't respond when you try to make contact.
- Cues from your five senses: A noisy environment. Bad lightning. An unpleasant smell. Rainy weather. Badly brewed coffee.
- Cues from your body: Your heart rate. The rate and depth of your breathing. Sensations in your organs and limbs, like pain. Tiredness.

10.2. Become Introspective About What You Feel

Observe what happens to your feelings after you identify your response stage and its trigger. There are times when simply acknowledging the trigger is enough to alleviate an unpleasant emotion. Maybe you were just hungry or cold, or maybe something on the news upset you. It's easy to address these situations.

Other times, of course, your emotions point you toward something that's harder to address. Maybe your emotions stem from an ongoing stressor. Maybe they have their origin in past events when you felt uncomfortable. You'll recall from Chapter 7 that this is what Antonio Damasio calls a negative somatic marker.

To make sense of your emotions, you need to become introspective about what you feel and find the right words to describe it. Discern between feelings and primary emotions. As explained in Chapter 7, primary emotions are how we understand and give meaning to our most basic physical sensations in the form of fear, anger, joy, sadness, and disgust. Feelings are consciously felt emotions, blended with thinking. Usually, they are more refined than emotions; you can feel connected, insecure, sentimental, lonely, satisfied, etcetera. A feeling can emanate from an emotion, but it can just as well emanate from a thought.

Try it Yourself: Identify What You Feel

After you've identified your autonomic response state and its trigger, investigate a bit more into what this means with this self-inquiry exercise. You can also do this when you can't identify your response state and your feelings are a big blur.

- Sit down with your eyes closed. Take a couple of breaths and check in with your body. Identify your bodily sensations, taking care not to get carried away by the story your mind wants to tell you about these sensations.
- See if you can find the vocabulary that describes how you feel. Are you anxious, irritated, excited, ashamed, helpless, restless, worried, nervous, or something else?
- Now inquire more deeply. One way to do this is to connect your feeling to a primary emotion. Is there anger at the core of your irritation? If you are nervous, does that point to something you're afraid of? Are you restless because you feel sad? If you'd rather not conceptualize what you feel, try imagining what your feelings would *look* like by picturing a color, form, or texture.[35]
- When you inquire about your feelings, does that trigger a certain memory? Does it trigger a somatic marker from a previous situation when you've felt like this before?

---

35 Labelling one's personal emotional state and talking about this is not a universal phenomenon. This is predominantly common in Western countries, while people in other countries speak less in terms of feeling 'sad' or 'afraid'. They rather literally describe their physical sensations, while Western people interpret these sensations as *emotion concepts*.

- Keep your attention on these physical sensations. Try to allow them to just be there, without trying to get rid of them. What happens if you give them your full attention? Do they become larger or smaller?
- Ask yourself this question: Are you willing to accept the fact that you have these physical sensations and emotions, that they are yours? Can you feel compassionate towards yourself for the fact that you feel like this? If you are not willing to accept these sensations, can you simply experience them? Remind yourself that they will eventually pass and that they are not who you *are*.

10.3. Accept What You Feel

As you know by now, it used to be my strategy to suppress my emotions, disconnecting from my body and ignoring its sensations. Over time, as I developed more body awareness, I suddenly started to notice my nerves before a gig. At first, this was annoying because I didn't want to accept that I was nervous. I tried to fight them the way I always had, to "control" my nerves with my mind, but this was no longer effective. The signals my body sent overruled the mental story I was telling myself and demanded I listen to them. My voice revealed more nerves than ever before.

For a while, this frustration sucked the joy out of performing. Eventually, however, I realized that this was an essential part of developing awareness—thereby presenting an opportunity to solve the problem. I learned to accept my stage fright. This was a gradual process that happened during many sessions under the guidance of a Rebalancing practitioner and other self-reflections and meditation exercises I was doing at the time. When I became friendly with my emotions, accepting them and feeling them fully, I gave up the fight against them that was the real source of my struggle. It was only after I did so that their impact on my performances diminished.

Oddly enough, the solution for dealing with both overwhelming and suppressed emotional experience is the same: stop resisting. Allow yourself to feel what's going on. Remember that our autonomic nervous system doesn't make moral meaning and has no other agenda than to keep us safe and ensure survival. Since you know that there is no bear chasing you down, it's safe to accept all that you feel. This approach, which is used in Acceptance and Commitment Therapy (ACT), teaches us not only to allow, but to *actively invite* uncontrollable and even painful events in our life. Our goal is not to feel *better*, but to *feel* better. Respond actively to your feelings, including the unwelcome ones, by feeling them as much as possible.

Let me add that this approach doesn't simply end with feeling unpleasant feelings; rather, that's the means to a more hopeful end. By actively feeling these feelings, you can use the energy that you would spend suppressing them to *direct your life toward what you value as important*. You see, acceptance isn't the same as complacency. It doesn't mean letting others have their way with you or that you shouldn't do anything to change your situation. Sometimes, after accepting your feelings about a situation, you need to act. You may need to confront your friend about her behavior, leave your job, or file for divorce. Accept how you feel about a certain situation and make changes accordingly.

As for those many occasions when we do not have the power to change our situation—say, bad weather during an outdoor concert or getting ill with the flu on the day that you were supposed to do your TED Talk—your best shot at dealing with the situation is still accepting both reality and your feelings about it. Then there are those times when we *can* change a situation, but we *choose* not to. Although you *can* leave your job, you may not be willing to do so because the financial insecurity would cause you more stress than the job itself. In those cases, acceptance means realizing that it is your conscious choice: You *can* make the change but you are not *willing* to make the change. This will make it easier to fully accept what is and how you feel about it.

Accept What You Feel

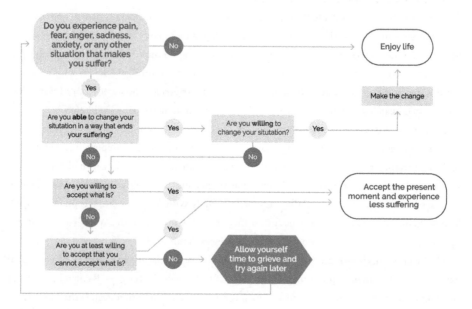

10.4. Don't React, Regulate

So you've read your body's cues, been introspective, and accepted how you feel. This may be all you need. Sometimes, however, you need to actively regulate your emotions. This is especially important when your feelings stem from something someone else said or did.

My client Charlie told me that he applied for a promotion at work for which he was by far the most competent candidate. But he didn't get the job. They told him he was way too intense (overexcitable) and that the way he spoke undermined his credibility as a leader. Charlie was devastated by this feedback and took it personally. His instinctive first reaction was to snap at his manager, telling him that it was unprofessional to deny him the job based on his communication style. This, of course, didn't improve the situation, and left both Charlie and his manager uncomfortable with each other.

There are many ways to express and manage feelings, some of which are more effective than others. When you react immediately to what you feel, you vent those feelings into your environment, which might not be what you would choose to do if you gave yourself some time to think about it. Once you become aware of your emotions, you can choose to process them within yourself first, and respond later.

When someone's behavior has stirred your emotions, start by sitting with those emotions for a moment. You can do this alone, in an introspective moment, or you might choose to talk about it with someone you trust. Remember how relieved you can feel right after having a good cry with a friend! On the other hand, you may need to process them on your own first, so the things that need to come to the surface get your full attention, unaffected by anyone else.

Emotions are not fixed states; they are ongoing processes. They will come and go. They will settle when you've fully felt them and processed them through your awareness. Charlie, for example, discovered that his intensity at work is related to the extremely high expectations he holds for himself. He has the same high expectations of his co-workers, but they're not always able to live up to them. As a result, Charlie often feels disappointed and frustrated. He believes that he is shouldering more responsibility than his colleagues, especially when it comes to delivering excellence. He realized, however, that he can't change his co-workers. He can only change his attitude towards them.

When you address such a personal emotion on your own first, you allow yourself an opportunity to respond in a more constructive way. Instead of snapping at your manager, you give yourself time to think about what you truly want to say to him—including regulated emotional expression, *if* you actively choose it. Charlie started to practice these moments of introspection, and after some time, he was able to develop some agency over the intensity that sounded through his voice.

Others Ways to Regulate Your Emotions

There are many other ways to regulate your emotions, like inviting more cues of safety into the moment. This will activate your ventral vagal response mode. In Chapter 2, we discussed some ways you can regulate your autonomic nervous system. Below are some additional ideas that will stimulate multiple brain areas. You can regulate emotions by becoming active, creative, comfortable, connected, or introspective.

Over time, if you diligently and consciously practice regulating your emotions, those of you who were too controlled will learn to connect with the emotions that you used to suppress. You will begin to speak from the heart, becoming more expressive and livelier as a speaker. As for those of you whose emotions had been in overdrive, with conscious practice, you will gradually develop the ability to allow the right amount of emotional expression into your communication. You will come to feel comfortable with those feelings, thereby empowering yourself to convey your message in a purposeful manner. In other words, you will learn to express your emotions on your own terms.

Get Active

Have you ever watched a wildlife documentary where a prey animal is being chased by a predator? If the prey animal survives the chase and doesn't get eaten, she always shakes off the stress that's been building up in her body by movement. Just like this animal, you will need to release the emotional energy that has been built up in your body in order to fight or flee—even when you never really needed to do either. This is the right time to work out, go for a walk, or dance. Movement not only releases surplus energy; it also activates ventral vagal response mode. On top of that, according to neuroscientist Lisa Feldman Barrett, moving your body can change the predictions you make about your environment, thereby changing your experience. Movement may also bring other, less bothersome concepts to the foreground of your mind.

Get Creative

Creativity is an excellent tool for regulating emotional tension. As I described in Chapter 6, creative expression is one way to deal with the states of mind that are part and parcel of personality development through inner conflict like nervousness, disquietude, depression, and anxiety. Try painting, drawing, making music, writing a story, or making something with your hands. For an added benefit, try singing or playing a wind instrument, which (as you'll remember from Chapter 2) improves your breath technique and consequently helps you to regulate your emotions at their physical root.

Get Comfortable

Making yourself more comfortable helps make your nervous system feel safe. Take a bath. Get a massage. Undertake an activity that you like, just for fun. Make your house cozy and listen to comforting music.

Connect to Others

Co-regulate with another nervous system by asking your friends and family for support. Pick up the phone and call a friend. (Don't just text them—you want to hear their voice!) Cuddle with a loved one or with a pet. Connect with a specific, trusted person, or go to a place where you feel particularly safe.

Go Deeper

Getting introspective helps you to digest emotions. Write about what you feel, letting that ongoing stream of consciousness out on the paper. Listen to music while you let your thoughts wander, without doing anything else that might distract you. Engage in meditation or contemplation practices. Chapter 12 is devoted to these types of activities.

10.5. Identify Your Unmet Needs and Values

I have to warn you about something: When you start accepting your emotions, their impact may at first grow worse. When you're used to fighting or suppressing them, allowing yourself to feel what you feel can be overwhelming. When this happens, hang in there. They will become manageable eventually if you stick with these practices. The process of welcoming and accepting your emotions will ultimately make strong ones less overwhelming. These emotions are also an indication of the things you value highly. Consider them an invitation to explore your values in this area.

This is what Lisette experienced. Lisette was a young student with apparent emotional overexcitability who was studying to become a primary school teacher. Because she would be standing in front of a class every day, she wanted to gain more control over her voice, like Nadim, the teacher I told you about in Chapter 9. So she came to me for voice coaching. She talked quickly and softly with a high-pitched voice, using mostly short vowels, which made her sound like a child. When we did voice exercises, Lisette was surprised to find out that she could use a much lower intonation than she thought she could. We also did articulation exercises to slow down her speech, and as she spoke lower and slower, she also sounded louder. She quickly got the hang of it all, and everything seemed to fall into place with just a couple of exercises.

Immediately after the exercises, however, Lisette's voice became faster and higher again. This happens with many of my students: While they're reading sheets that tell them what to do, they perform flawlessly. Then, as soon as their attention leaves the sheet and they're again expressing their own thoughts and feelings, they're unable to continue using the technique they've just learned. It's so much easier to focus on your voice when you're reading something off a paper than when you're finding words to express your inner world. The moment your emotions or thoughts get the upper hand, the techniques you've practiced so dutifully will no longer be of use to you. In Lisette's case, there was a lot happening in her inner world, and when she began to express this, her voice became fast and chaotic.

Later on, we discovered during an introspection exercise that while she didn't get very nervous when she was teaching the children, she did when she was presenting in front of others teachers. That's when her nerves would overwhelm her—and the voice techniques would abandon her. Deep down, she feared that she wasn't good enough to teach. She was afraid of failing at her job. She also came to recognize that during moments of nervousness, she would move away from the emotion of that situation and get preoccupied with the future, when it would all be over. This made her speak faster, and because she was dwelling on how she would do better *next* time, it prevented her from making genuine contact with her audience *this* time.

What brought Lisette to my practice—wanting to be a better speaker in front of the classroom—turned out not to be the real problem. It only became one when others were listening in and she felt she was being judged. As she discovered, she lacked confidence. Deep down, she doubted that she could succeed in her mission to care for children, to contribute to their future and to a better world.

That was one of Lisette's core values—and that made her especially vulnerable to criticism in that realm. It was the reason why a sense of safety had eluded her.

It helped Lisette to become aware of the reason why teaching is so extremely important to her and how that made her so vulnerable to criticism. She was aware of how her physical sensations influenced her behavior, but had never thought about how this was connected with her needs and values. Once Lisette became aware of the role of her key values, she realized why success as a teacher was so important to her and why in turn that made her so vulnerable to criticism. This was the context she needed to address her nerves when her qualities as a teacher were being judged.

Nonviolent Communication

Once you identify the values and needs that lie behind what you feel, you can take actions to fulfill those needs and live up to those values. In the 1960s, psychologist and mediator Marshall Rosenberg developed a conflict resolution method that he called nonviolent communication. According to Rosenberg, "self-judgments, like all judgments, are tragic expressions of unmet needs [...]. We are compassionate with ourselves when we are able to embrace all parts of ourselves and recognize the needs and values expressed by each part."[36]

The following exercise is taken from Rosenberg's nonviolent communication program. Going a step further than accepting emotions, it is an exercise in cultivating self-empathy. Self-empathy is about being present with your thoughts and feelings in order to realize what you need in a given moment. It allows you to formulate a request designed to fulfill that need. Whereas empathy involves connecting with what it's like to be someone else—to paying attention and really listening to them—self-empathy is the same, but directed at yourself. It means really listening to yourself, connecting with what's alive in you. It's a helpful practice when you're experiencing emotional discomfort, especially if your tendency is to avoid your emotions or distract yourself from them.

Note that you don't have to apply self-empathy in the heat of the moment. It's powerful enough to be helpful before or after a discomforting event. If you practice self-empathy after, for instance, a presentation that didn't go well because you were so nervous, you can make sense of your emotions in retrospect, becoming aware of what you might feel and need during future presentations. Then you can formulate requests to yourself and others in accordance with those needs.

You can also choose to rehearse a challenging presentation with self-empathy. When you vividly imagine this future event with all your senses, your mind will behave as if it is really taking place. Remember how, as we discussed in Chapter 7, we are constantly predicting and creating our own emotional reality? This is what you should actively do in this exercise. When you use your imagination to become aware of future uncomfortable emotions and accept them, they won't take you by surprise when they occur in reality. Then, when you identify your needs and formulate requests accordingly, you'll create a positive somatic marker for this event. There is a good chance that when the real moment arrives, your nerves will be considerably calmer.

---

36 M.B. Rosenberg *Nonviolent Communication: A Language of Life*. (2015, Encinitas: PuddleDancer Press) p. 132-135.

Try it Yourself: **Self-empathy**

The first two steps of this exercise are similar to the earlier steps in this chapter: Read your body's cues and identify what you feel. Only after that, you'll inquire a bit deeper into the unmet needs that lie behind your feelings.

Close your eyes, turn your attention inward, and ask yourself the following questions:

1. What am I observing in my body and my mind?
What kind of physical sensations do you feel? What thoughts about yourself are coming up? Are they assumptions, judgments, or fears? Do you have these thoughts often?

Example: I experience heart palpitations, pressure on my chest, and my breathing becomes superficial. I'm having the thought that I'm not good enough doing this performance, and I'm worrying about what other people would think of me.

2. What am I feeling?
What are the feelings that are connected to your thoughts and physical sensations?

Example: I feel insecure. I'm afraid of being judged. I feel fear.

3. What do I need at this moment?
Connect your feeling to a need that is not being met.

Example: I need acceptance and safety.

4. Following my needs, do I have a request for myself or someone else?
Acknowledge that this need is important to you. What can you do yourself to meet that need, or what can you ask others to do?

Example: I am willing to accept that I am afraid of being judged and to feel compassion for myself. In order to feel safe and accepted, I can ask my colleagues to make eye contact with me and smile when I'm giving a presentation.

Because it can be challenging to identify your unmet needs from scratch, I have included Rosenberg's list of basic human needs below.[37]

Autonomy

To choose one's dreams, goals, values

To choose one's plan for fulfilling one's dreams, goals, values

Celebration

To celebrate the creation of life and dreams fulfilled

To celebrate losses: loved ones, dreams, etcetera (mourning)

Integrity

Authenticity, creativity, meaning, self-worth

Play

Fun, laughter

Spiritual communion

Beauty, harmony, inspiration, order, peace

Physical nurturance

Air, food, movement, protection, rest, sexual expression, shelter, touch, water

Interdependence

Acceptance, appreciation, closeness, community, consideration, contribution to the enrichment of life, emotional safety, empathy, honesty, love, reassurance, respect, support, trust, understanding, warmth

Connecting Compassionately to Others

Nonviolent communication goes beyond identifying our own feelings and needs. Its primary purpose is to nurture greater connection with others. To use its full toolkit, then, we not only ask ourselves what we feel and what we need, we also tune into the needs and feelings of others. If those are unclear to us, we can ask them directly. As Rosenberg writes:

[Nonviolent communication] guides us in reframing how we express ourselves and hear others. Instead of habitual, automatic reactions, our words become conscious responses based firmly on awareness of what

---

37 M.B. Rosenberg *Nonviolent Communication: A Language of Life*. (2015, Encinitas: PuddleDancer Press) p. 54-55.

we are perceiving, feeling and wanting. We are led to express ourselves with honesty and clarity, while simultaneously paying others a respectful and empathic reaction. In any exchange, we come to hear our own deeper needs and those of others.[38]

When we open up and communicate from a place of compassion for others, radical change is possible in our relationships. As you'll recall from Chapter 2, when you are socially engaged in a conversation and open to the needs of others, your voice reflects this with rhythmic, melodic speech. In return, your pleasant voice offers an opportunity for others to co-regulate their autonomic state. Your voice then helps them to feel safe and socially engaged as well, with the result being more empathic and compassionate communication for all those involved.

One of my clients, Walter, was a highly intelligent, fast-thinking young man. At work, he was tasked with creating a series of webinars in which he had to appear and speak on camera. This turned out to be a challenge for him, as he struggled to sound engaging and interesting. One particular flaw he noted was that he used a lot of filler words. In a self-empathy exercise, we revisited a meeting that he had attended that morning. First, he observed what had actually happened in the meeting without expressing judgments or evaluations. Next, I asked him how he had felt when sitting in that meeting room. As he returned to that space in his memory, he noticed that he was uncomfortable doing the webinar: He felt unappreciated, disappointed, angry, and frustrated. But—as he immediately recognized—he normally suppressed or rationalized those feelings. He feared he'd tear up if he didn't.

In Chapter 7, I spoke about how feeling unappreciated is not a true feeling in the sense we've discussed, but a feeling mixed with assumptions about the situation. Was it true that Walter's colleagues didn't appreciate him? Looking objectively at the situation, we assessed that this was not true. It was merely his subjective assumption. Feeling unappreciated is what Rosenberg calls a "pseudo-feeling." The good thing about these pseudo-feelings is that they often clue us in to our unmet needs. And Walter had a need for recognition—to be heard and to be seen. This was a powerful realization for him. It felt like a truth that had been hidden away for a long time had finally come to light. He had been suppressing his emotions for more than twenty years. Because of his quick mind, he was always ten steps ahead of his colleagues, and they could not always follow him. That was why he didn't feel recognized. Allowing himself to feel this and connect to his needs was transformative. When we came to the part of the exercise that involved a request, he decided that he could ask his colleagues to trust his strategies for the company, even though his vision might not be immediately clear to everyone.

Next, we discussed the possible feelings and needs of Walter's colleagues. When he explained things too quickly for others to follow, what would they feel? With his highly empathic nature, Walter quickly noted that they probably felt insecure and confused. They might need more reassurance, careful explanations, time, attention, or support from him. He could offer them these things

---

38   M.B. Rosenberg *Nonviolent Communication: A Language of Life.* (2015, Encinitas: PuddleDancer Press) p. 3

during the webinars by asking questions that would signal this connection and keep them on board: *Is everyone still able to follow? Do I need to slow down? Do I need to clarify something?*

What started as a coaching request for help to sound more interesting and engaging turned out to be a request for help with honest, compassionate communication. Walter realized that his giftedness did make him meaningfully different from others. He now recognizes that he needs to provide more explanation and context for what he says and thinks. He also realized that he's more sensitive than he had thought because he'd suppressed this talent for years.

After our sessions together, he sent me this email:

> *I am happy with the unexpected aspects that the sessions have brought me. I realize now that I think differently from many others. The space that has arisen for myself to look at my emotions in a different way, has brought about a change for me. This will help me enormously in the coming period to continue growing and to develop on a personal level.*

11. Step Back from Your Thoughts

Do you think faster than you speak? Are you carried away by many thoughts at the same time, taking you in all different directions? Do you take mental leaps and lose your train of thought? Does the whole process seem unstoppable? These are signs of excessive thoughts, and they're often the primary challenge for people with intellectual and imaginational overexcitability.

For speaking, this typically leads to one of two outcomes:

The Improvisor: You are comfortable with speaking on the fly in conversational or informal situations. When you have to take the stage for a rehearsed presentation, however, self-conscious, unhelpful thoughts sabotage your performance.

The Prepared Performer: You are comfortable in the spotlight when you can convey your message in a controlled, rehearsed way. You struggle, however, in group conversations or when you need to respond to questions or improvise. Sometimes self-conscious, unhelpful thoughts prevent you from communicating in a relaxed and engaged manner.

Note that even though excessive thought stems from intellectual and imaginational overexcitability, it is rooted in emotion as well—whether consciously felt or not. In Chapter 10, we've already explored the emotions that come with stage fright when all eyes are on you. In this chapter, we'll explore how you can work with your thoughts as another tool to regulate emotions.

11.1. Don't Think While You Speak

In Chapter 10 we talked about stage fright, and how it can sabotage the performance of the improvisor. Let's have a look now at the challenges of the prepared performer. Are you one of them? Consider that when you give a staged presentation, you speak in a controlled environment where you have permission to take up space, making you feel safe and comfortable. You're prepared and in the present moment. You don't have to anticipate questions from other people that require you to think about how to answer, and you won't be interrupted. Compare this to unrehearsed, informal situations. In those environments, you have so many thoughts that they get in the way of direct communication—and this shows up in your voice. When someone asks you a question that you're not prepared for, you try to edit yourself as you speak, and you come across as chaotic and insecure. There's a good chance you prefer writing to speaking. When you write, you can read and reread your own words, editing your text until your email, text message, or article is perfect.

Unfortunately, when you speak, you can't take the time you take in writing to make things perfect. Voice coach Caroline Goyder aptly describes this phenomenon:

> *Self-editing and the quest to be perfect stop you from speaking up because you are worried you don't know enough, or that others know more. They stop you from speaking well because you're too busy listening to your inner censor trying to edit you mid-speech — "You shouldn't have said that." They stop you from trusting your instinct and responding in the moment. If you want to speak up and stand out, forget perfect.[…] Be prepared, be present, trust your instinct and then commit to your choice.[39]*

You can tell when people are thinking while they speak. Their voice has the rising inflection at the end of a sentence known as *uptalk*. This style smashes the whole message together as one long sentence, rarely allowing for natural pauses. It sounds like one extremely long sentence with many commas, and that's hard for the audience to digest. Another problem that comes from thinking while you speak is *tailing off*. These speakers' voices become weak and unintelligible at the end of a sentence, because they've already moved on to thinking about the next sentence without concluding the previous one.

Uptalk and tailing off both suggest that your mind is not present with what you are saying. Instead, it's busy judging your performance or preparing what to say next. If you want to make a point but your attention is not present with that message, you'll fail to make an impact. You'll appear less confident and therefore less competent. To avoid this, you'll have to practice keeping your attention present with the words you're saying in the moment. You'll want to come to trust that you can rely on your knowledge to be available for yourself, especially when you've prepared. This will help your nervous system activate social engagement, away from fight, flight, or freeze— which has the benefit of making your store of knowledge more readily accessible to you. If you can learn to be present and trust yourself, you will find the right words for the right moment.

Try it Yourself: **Get Concise**

If you have a tendency toward uptalk or tailing off, try the following exercise while you practice a presentation or conversation. It will also help you get rid of crutches or filler words like "um" and "like." This will make your message more concise, and therefore more effective.

---

39   C. Goyder *Find Your Voice: The Secret to Talking with Confidence in any Situation* (2020, Vermillion, London) p. 162.

- As you begin to speak, break your message up in simple, short sentences, like you're reading from a children's book.
- After each sentence, take a pause as you take a breath.
- Prepare what you will say next, but just the next sentence or two, in the silence of these pauses.
- As you speak, put one hand in the air. Use it to direct the inflection pattern of your voice. If you tend to uptalk, begin with your hand low, letting it rise in the middle and descend again at the end of the sentence. Follow the movement of your hand with your eyes and your voice.
- If you tend to tail off, signal the same inflection pattern with your hand, making sure that you stay present with your final words. Pronounce them carefully.
- Repeat this until you're comfortable using short sentences with powerful endings.
- Now return to your natural speaking style, using regular sentences. Alternate between sentences you'd write using commas and short ones you'd conclude quickly with periods. It's normal to use uptalk as a sort of verbal comma, but as you come to a period, be sure to use descending inflection, unless you actively intend to signal a question mark or an exclamation point.

The previous exercise will help you become aware of your speech patterns and develop new habits. Still, if you experience excessive thought activity, you'll probably face challenges applying these habits to your daily life, outside of this deliberate exercise. "Don't think while you speak" is easier said than done, right? If you've ever tried to control your thoughts, you've probably found that this only seems to make more of them arise. Your voice will reflect this. Your speech will start to speed up—maybe so much that people will struggle to follow you. Your focus shifts towards your thoughts and the content of your message and away from your voice and its delivery. Learning to step back from your thoughts can help to structure this process.

11.2. What Are Thoughts?

What are our thoughts, really? Only this: the active response of memory. They're electrical pulses, created in our mind and manifested through language or images. There's not much more to it than that. On the one hand, these thoughts can be useful; they help you create, organize your life, and get things done. However, even positive, creative thoughts can hinder you if ten or twenty overwhelm you at the same time.

The good news is that, if you're easily absorbed by thought activity, you can learn to identify less with your thoughts when they aren't helpful. Your thoughts are not who you are, nor do they represent objective reality. They are impermanent. And as they come and go, you have the opportunity to choose which you act upon and which you allow to pass by. You don't have to believe everything you think and you should not take your thoughts too seriously. They're like waves in the ocean; one comes up and then disappears again, followed by another. The thought is merely one piece of content from your life, while you are the ocean—the space in which the thought unfolds.

I also want to point out that "having thoughts" is not the same as "thinking." Theoretical physicist and philosopher David Bohm says that when thought functions on its own, it imposes its own generally irrelevant and unsuitable order, drawn from an individual's memory. In this context, thought is a mechanical process—and not intelligent. "Thought is, however, capable of responding," Bohm explains, "not only from memory but also to the unconditioned perception of intelligence that can see, in each case, whether or not a particular line of thought is relevant and fitting."[40]

In keeping with Bohm's observation, I've concluded that *thought plus intelligence equals thinking*. Intelligence is the ability to perceive a new order of information, which is not simply a modification of what already was present in memory. Intelligence is able to judge the significance of particular thoughts, and create new information from them.

Your Thoughts as the Cause of Suffering

In Chapter 7, we explored how suffering is caused by the mind, when we blend feelings with thoughts about how we feel. Now let's follow a child's course, Susan, as she develops the capacity for thinking, paying attention to how suffering arises along the way.

You'll recall that we enter this world without concepts and predictions, and that we first rely on sense perception to understand the world around us. Because of her physical sensations, as a baby, Susan knows when she's uncomfortable and needs food. She has not, however, developed a sense of self yet that's separate from the rest of the world. In her mind, there is not an "I" that can think "I am hungry." Whenever the mother is available to feed her child, Susan's biological impulses are satisfied and the need for food disappears. The uncomfortable physical sensations are instantly replaced by the physical sensation of satisfaction, without any conscious memory of the previous distress.[41]

In contrast to a baby, a toddler has a conscious mind with a developed sense of self. This means as a toddler, Susan has quite a different experience. She has short- and long-term memory and has developed language to think and communicate. When she wants ice cream but her parents don't give her any, she gets angry. Where she differs from her younger self is that, on top of the physical sensations of anger, she's also familiar with the *emotion concept* of anger. She can verbally express anger to her parents, shouting "I want ice cream!" as she bangs on the table with a frown. She can also think to herself, using language, "I'm angry because Mommy and Daddy won't give me ice cream."

An important consequence of this cognitive ability is that even when Susan's exhausted parents give in and give her some ice cream, she still retains a conscious memory of her previous distress, including the emotions she felt back then. This will happen with any distress she might feel over

---

40   D. Bohm *Wholeness and the Implicate Order* (1980, Routledge & Kegan Paul, New York, NY) p. 67.
41   Please note: Distressful situations can of course cause trauma in babies. These traumatic experiences are stored in the autonomic nervous system and can trigger sensations of fear later on, without having any conscious memory of the previous experience.

the course of her life. When Susan gets bitten by a dog, she retains the memory of the distress that dog caused her, possibly leading her to fear any dog she encounters in the future, even if it gives off only signals that it's friendly and wants to play.

This is where suffering starts. Although there's no direct threat to Susan when she meets a friendly dog, she can still experience distress, derived from earlier memories when the situation was different. She can think *relationally*, connecting an event in the past to her feelings in the present moment or projecting them on to a future event. In this way, memory contributes to her suffering.

Memory, thoughts, and language are aspects of the mind. They are powerful cognitive abilities for learning, reflecting, planning, organizing, and so much more. But they have a downside: These capacities also allow you to experience distress in the present due to situations that happened in the past, situations yet to come, or even imagined situations that will never happen at all. In all these examples, you can experience the imagined distress as if it were happening right now, in the present moment. At its worst, this type of distress can cause trauma (directed at the past) and anxiety (directed at the future).

Defuse from Your Thoughts

Here's some good news: You can use your intelligence to choose to identify only with your most salient thoughts in a given situation. Those are the thoughts that give you useful information for addressing threats—like whether a dog really looks like he'll bite you or just wants to lick you—without sending your mind into overdrive. This is the path to calming your mind and your speech.

But how do you step back from unhelpful thoughts in a practical way?

Acceptance and Commitment Therapy (ACT) offers exercises that separate verbal and cognitive processes from your experience of the world; they call this approach "defusing from thoughts." These exercises reveal that words exist separately from their meanings. This in turn will help you develop what I call an observer view, from which you look at the content of your mind as something separate from yourself. With defusion techniques, you do not fight thoughts. Instead, you decide how much attention you want to pay to them.

Try it Yourself: **Defuse Through Writing**

- Take a recurring thought that's not helpful when you need to contribute to a discussion or speak in public. For example:
  I am never going to be able to do this.
- Write this sentence down. As you look at it in written form, notice what it's like to look at the words, experiencing that the thought exists outside of you.
- Then write down your thought in the following form:
  I am having the thought that I am never going to be able to do this.
- Look at this sentence and observe whether your relationship to the thought has changed.
- Finally, write it down in this form:
  I notice that I am having the thought that I am never going to be able to do this.

How did your perception of the thought shift during the course of the exercise? This is one way to learn how to look at your thoughts rather than at the world from your thoughts.

Try it Yourself: **Defuse Through Using Your Voice**

You can combine defusion techniques with voice training techniques. Here's what you can do if you want to defuse from an unhelpful thought or a particular hurtful word:

- Repeatedly say the thought or word out loud, in all kinds of different ways: high, low, slow, fast, funny, sad, angry, or scary, like a Minion, Darth Vader, Mickey Mouse, or any other fictional creature.
- Keep on doing this for at least a minute. In the beginning you might feel foolish, but bear with me.

After the minute passes, what happens with the spoken language of your thought? Is it still tightly connected to its meaning, or do the words turn into abstract sounds? Does your thought itself seem foolish now, or at least less serious than before?

The Outcome of Defusion

To see the power of this simple intervention, consider Jason's story. He was a young man who came to me struggling with social anxiety. He thought he had terrible communication skills, telling me that every aspect of his life was dictated by this fear. He overthought everything he said. When he didn't perform well at work or in social life, he thought over and over about what went wrong and what he should have done differently. Naturally, he felt awful with these thoughts constantly repeating in his head. They also took him out of the present. Once he was so absorbed with his thoughts that he didn't recognize a friend walking by on the street.

To address this, we began by defusing from his thought "I'm socially awkward." After we finished, he began to laugh. He had realized the absurdity of this thought—and that allowed him to put some distance between his mind and that particular bit of content. Without any further directions, his voice sounded more cheerful, louder, and spontaneous. For the first time during our sessions, he was in touch with the present moment and his sense perceptions.

For Jason, defusion literally changed his relationship with his thoughts. When we finished working together, he told me that he felt five times happier than he had at that time the previous year. He could see how his thoughts came and went—and that they weren't always accurate. He was less concerned about the future and had fewer assumptions about what others thought of him, contributing to a quieter mind overall.

As all of this was happening, his communication skills improved immensely. He no longer overthought everything he said, leading to a much freer and more expressive voice. Defusion in particular played an important role in this process. He resolved to keep practicing it daily.

Sounds and Their Meaning

Some of us are particularly attached to the meanings we attribute to the sounds we call words. The verbal defusion exercise, however, reveals how readily these meanings can fall away. To demonstrate how defusion works, I often start defusing from a random word like *milk*, letting go of the meaning we attach to it and focusing instead on its phonetic qualities.

This can be a challenge for people who especially appreciate language. As such clients have rightly observed when I suggest this exercise to them, the fusion of meaning with sound gives rise to so much of what is beautiful in literature, poetry, and song. The meanings we attach to words carry emotions, and those emotions can be powerfully fulfilling. They can also utterly derail us. That's why the people who get the most joy out of language, and who therefore are most resistant to it, are the ones for whom it's the most powerful.

The process of infusing sounds with meaning and emotion begins in infancy. As we grow from babies into children, we start to make sounds that we associate with language. In our earliest years, we make sounds that are outside our native language, but as we grow, we drop those sounds. As adults, we tend to get uncomfortable if we're asked to make sounds that have no meaning. I notice this often in my clients when I ask them to make sounds to practice resonance: "Mmoom, mmoam, mmoum, mmoim." This makes them feel extremely awkward and self-conscious. Voice coach and singer Yinske Silva says that we feel vulnerable when making sound without linguistic meaning because it exposes our voice in its purest form. The pure voice doesn't lie. It cannot hide behind the roles you play in life—employee, father, daughter, husband, etcetera.

My experience as a singer means I don't feel this awkwardness when making random sounds. I sang along phonetically to songs by Whitney Houston and Michael Jackson well before I knew any English—"Keep on with the force, don't stop, don't stop till you get enough!" I had no clue about what I was singing. During my classical training, I was still singing in languages that I didn't speak, like Italian and Russian, and I also did vocal exercises every day that consisted mainly of sounds without meaning. Later on, I participated in a group called the Genetic Choir that composes music with improvisational vocal sounds. After all these experiences of separating sound from meaning, I don't attach a lot of importance to the meaning of words. I once discussed this with Yinske, a fellow member of the Genetic Choir. Like me, she acknowledged the major difference between the world of sound and the world of language. We had both experienced how improvising with only vocal sound contributes to self-acceptance and self-confidence. It really sets your mind free.

Try it Yourself: **Defuse Through Singing**

If certain words or thoughts make you feel sad, upset, or self-conscious, then my advice to you is to start singing them.

- If an unhelpful thought is troubling you, turn that thought into a song. Sing it, repeat it, make it absurd, and let its meaning fade away.
- If you're practicing a spoken presentation or speech and you can't shake off your self-consciousness, try singing your speech. Sing the words to the melody of a song you know or make up a melody yourself. Then practice the speech without the melody again. Does it feel lighter?
- For singers, however, songs can themselves be a source of self-consciousness. If your mind gets in the way when you sing, try adjusting the song in a playful or even silly way. Can you do any accents? Can you do an imitation of your favorite movie or cartoon character? Sing your song with that accent or as your character of choice. Enjoy your own silliness and observe how your experience of the song changes.
- You can also try accents or imitations while practicing a speech or presentation. Remember, the ultimate goal is to defuse from self-consciousness, so don't take yourself too seriously.

Try it Yourself: Give Your Thought Producing Process a Name

Another tip from ACT is to give your own thought producing process, your mind, a name. Once you name your mind, it's easier to treat it as an entity that you can choose to listen to, or not. When that named entity chatters on, repeating the same useless or negative thoughts to you, you can distance yourself from it the same way you'd distance yourself from a human entity who said such tiresome things to you.

Try it Yourself: Slow Down Your Speech

When you're talking rapidly and unclearly, you're probably doing so to express the large volume of thoughts running through your rapid mind. As you start practicing with defusion techniques, you might discover that you can choose to let certain thoughts pass by without expressing them. This bottom-up approach creates more time and space to determine the essence of your message and deliver it at a slower pace. Simultaneously, you can practice slowing down your speech with a top-down exercise. If you master this technique as well, it will gradually become easier to find the right words to express yourself clearly and intuitively, taking people along with your enthusiasm without losing your connection to them. As a way to practice this, I suggest recording yourself. This exercise can help to increase your awareness of your speaking pace.

- Switch on your recording device and slowly read a written passage from a book or magazine. Be sure to articulate and take pauses during periods and commas.
- When you're done, play this back to yourself. Evaluate your voice while listening to the recording and notice if your speech is as slow as you perceived it to be while you were reading aloud.
- If your recording suggests you tend to trip over words or otherwise struggle to articulate well, take a pencil and bite down on the eraser end with the tip pointing out of your mouth. Say a sentence a couple of times while looking in the mirror. Then take the pencil out of your mouth and say the sentence again. Has your articulation improved?

Why Not Defuse from Emotions?

Sometimes clients ask me why we defuse from thoughts and not emotions. If you can make thoughts lose their impact, why not emotions?

From Chapters 2 and 7, you know that emotions are first and foremost cues from your body about comfort and arousal. Before emotions become conscious experiences—before they become *emotion concepts* and feelings—they are physical sensations. Defusion is a technique that separates words from their meaning. Emotions, however, are more than conceptualized language. They are feelings in your body that signal you are in danger or in pain, and you *don't* want to defuse from that!

As we discussed in Chapters 9 and 10, it's important to recognize emotional cues, listening to your body to identify what you need. If your thoughts get entangled with your emotions, however, the result is feelings that are expressed in language. It's as part of this knot that thoughts cause additional suffering on top of emotional pain. Moreover, feelings we label with language like *abandoned*, *criticized*, or *neglected*—that is, passive verbs—make someone else responsible for what you feel. Pseudo-feelings like this, connected as they are to what you think that others *do*, *don't*, *should*, or *shouldn't*, are best approached with the techniques from nonviolent communication from the previous chapter, not with defusion. With pseudo-feelings, the key is to get to the pure feeling first (like feeling lonely or insecure) and then to determine how you can meet the unmet need it springs from. Defusion is best when your negative thoughts don't involve another actor: *I feel worthless, useless, not good enough, stupid, ugly.* It's your own mind that comes up with these, so defusion can help reveal when these thoughts are nothing but silly waves that will pass.

11.3. Three Senses of Self

Imagine two fish, swimming around in the sea. One fish asks the other, "Hey, how's the water today?" The other answers, "What water? What are you talking about?"

Thought activity is to humans what water is to fish: We're so completely submerged in it that we aren't even aware of it. Because of this, we often fail to see it as something apart from ourselves. But unlike a fish who needs water to survive, humans can live just fine without thought activity. Not one hundred percent of the time, of course—thoughts are how we use our intelligence and navigate through life. But as I've explained, your mind is also accountable for distress about situations that happened in the past, situations yet to come, or even imagined situations that will never happen at all.

It's one thing to recognize that we're submerged in thought activity; it's another to make a change. What other options do we even have? One way to address this is to deepen our understanding of the concept of the self.

Although most of us perceive the self as an entity separate from others, some scientists now claim that "the self" doesn't exist. What we perceive as the self is something like a hologram that we learn to project after our infancy. It exists in one respect, but in another, it is an illusion.

That's interesting theory, but for something more actionable, consider the three ways of experiencing a sense of self as described in ACT:

The Conceptualized Self

This is the most familiar sense of self, in which you fully identify with the content of your life, your identity. It's the story you tell yourself (and others) about your life. For instance, you have a gender, a nationality, a professional role, and maybe a role as spouse or parent. You might also describe yourself as kind, sensitive, spontaneous, a little insecure, and prone to mood swings.

The Self as Ongoing Awareness

This is the self that becomes aware of the fact that it is describing itself with words and language. For instance: "Oh, now I am having the thought again that I'm insecure," or "I notice I start worrying again."

The Self as Context

This is the hardest sense of self to grasp in words because it has no content. It is simply being—*I am*. The self as context is the *space* where all your thoughts, feelings, and memories come and go. It's the part of you that notices you are *having* a thought or an emotion. Imagine your thoughts and emotions are the weather in the sky. Clouds, rain, thunder, and lightning suddenly come up, but they will always disappear again. The sky is the stage where the weather erupts and passes. The weather changes, but the sky itself remains.

The self as context has also been called *the transcendent self, presence*, or *pure consciousness*. Spiritual teachers like Eckhart Tolle don't even talk anymore about the self as a separate entity, teaching that the self as context exists beyond duality. In my own practice, I treat the self as context as something impersonal; that is, it cannot be reconciled with identity. This awareness of pure consciousness is the foundation of what we are. It is a state of peace to which we potentially can connect whenever we need to, no matter what's going on inside our bodies or in our surroundings. This state of peace feels not merely safe, but unbreakable.

The key to understanding the self as context is to practice ongoing awareness. When you begin to notice that you're having thoughts, you'll also notice the gaps between them. In these gaps, the mind is not active; you are simply present. Whenever new content arises in your mind—and it always will—you can observe it for what it is: mere thoughts that erupt and dissipate like the weather. As you grow more accustomed to this way of experiencing your mind, you can avoid becoming entangled in those thoughts and letting them affect your behavior in ways you don't like.

Note that this doesn't mean that you cannot engage in intense thought activity anymore. Sometimes it *does* serve you well. The goal is to choose it actively—to steer your thoughts rather than letting your thoughts steer you. Developing this skill is essential if you want to speak more calmly and clearly, without jumping from one subject to the other.

Try it Yourself: **Leaves on a Stream**

ACT therapist Russ Harris provides an excellent exercise to observe your thoughts, called *Leaves on a Stream* (2009). I often introduce this exercise to clients who struggle with overactive minds. It helps them to step back from certain thoughts that make them lose their train of thought.

- While sitting in a comfortable position, either close your eyes or rest them gently on a fixed spot in the room.
- Visualize yourself sitting beside a gently flowing stream with leaves floating along the surface of the water. Take some time to immerse yourself in this visualization.
- For the next few minutes, take each thought that enters your mind and place it on a leaf, allowing it to float by. Do this with each thought, painful, neutral, pleasurable, or even joyful. If your thoughts momentarily stop, continue to watch the stream. Sooner or later, your thoughts will start up again.
- Allow the stream to flow at its own pace. Don't try to speed it up or rush your thoughts along. You're not trying to rush the leaves along or to get rid of your thoughts. You're allowing them to come and go at their own pace.
- If thoughts arise along the lines of *This is dumb, I'm bored,* or *I'm not doing this right,* place those thoughts on leaves, too, and let them pass.
- If a leaf gets stuck, allow it to hang around until it's ready to float by. If the thought comes up again, watch it float by another time.
- If a difficult or painful feeling arises, simply acknowledge it. Say to yourself, *I notice myself having a feeling of boredom/impatience/frustration.* Place those thoughts on leaves and allow them to float along.
- If you get overwhelmed by this exercise, take a break from it for about twenty seconds.
- From time to time, your thoughts may hook you and distract you from being fully present in this exercise. This is normal. As soon as you realize that you have become sidetracked, gently bring your attention back to the visualization exercise.

11.4. Show Your Enthusiasm and Engagement to The World

Recall that if you have intellectual overexcitability, you might find it important to say things exactly as they are, leading you to focus on the content of your message at the expense of its delivery. Although you try to be specific when articulating your message, somehow, it often seems to lack impact.

I'd like to let you in on something here: Although you hold the truth in high regard, the majority of people are not moved by factual information. If they were, my guess is that people would not deny anthropogenic climate change or a round Earth. People connect with information that resonates with the moral intuitions that give rise to their personal values, fears, and beliefs; whether it's factual or not matters less in comparison. In this respect, you can learn from those who ground their message in something other than facts.

Claudia, a university researcher, approached me to rehearse an important presentation she needed to prepare in order to apply for research funding. Claudia was highly analytical and thought a lot while she spoke. On the level of content, her presentation was solid and perfectly prepared. However, her delivery was really boring.

I asked her what she wanted to convey with her presentation to the jury. Her answer? Enthusiasm for her research project. We therefore set about finding ways for her to connect to that feeling. Eventually, she found enthusiasm while she thought of her puppy dog. I asked her to talk about her research project while at the same time keeping images of her dog in her mind. Suddenly, Claudia's enthusiasm came naturally to her. Her eyes started to twinkle, and she became open and approachable.

What are you passionate about? What makes your heart pound and your tail wag? When you speak about something that you value highly, share the passion you feel in the way you speak. Don't focus so much on facts—those won't stay with people. They will mainly remember how you made them *feel*. Even if you're not sure that your story is one hundred percent correct, don't start questioning yourself. You have already shown that you value the truth, so you're unlikely to deviate too far from it. Focus on the delivery! This goes for speaking as well as singing. What your audience will remember is your engaged and inspiring enthusiasm, so feel free to show this.

Try it Yourself: Set Intentions

If you want to engage with passion, don't obsess about content or how you'll come across. Your content is solidly formulated in your mind, so think instead about the feelings and intentions you want to convey. This creates connection. Here are some questions to ask yourself to clarify your intentions:

- Why are you saying what you are saying?
- What do you feel? Wonder, excitement, empathy, melancholy? Connect to these feelings while you speak or sing.
- How do you want your audience to feel? Inspired, comfortable, amused, shocked, surprised, confident? Set an intention about the feelings you want to inspire in your audience.

11.5. Values as a Gateway to Feelings

While connecting to your feelings is simple for some, it can be challenging for others—especially those with imaginational and intellectual OE. There are many reasons why people block feelings or struggle to identify them. If you struggle to find words for what you feel, don't assume you're doing something wrong. In your case, it might be easier to connect to *values* first.

For people who spend a lot of time in their heads, values can be a gateway to identifying their feelings. If you know what your values are, you'll have easier access to identifying what you feel. Overall, identifying values is important for everyone who wishes to improve his or her voice. Knowing what you value will give you the courage to take up space and speak up for what you find important. When your values are at the foundation of your message or your song, it's not about you anymore. That means there's no reason to get self-conscious. You're contributing to something greater than yourself. When you temporarily transcend your conceptualized self, you can just function as the vessel that communicates this valuable message.

We should also distinguish between goals and values. While goals are about *what* we want to do, values are about *how* we want to do it. Let's say that you value creativity. Being creative isn't something that you can check off once you have accomplished it; it's something that you can extend, if you see fit, into everything you do. Goals can help you live up to a value; for example, to live a creative life, you can resolve to cook creative meals, apply for a creative job, or use your free time for artistic pursuits.

If you haven't thought about your personal values before, or if you're not really sure what they are, you can identify them in the following exercise. Prioritizing values is a practical first step in the process of developing a personal hierarchy of values.

Try it Yourself: **Prioritize Your Values**

1. Reflect on what matters to you
You can find the direction of your values by answering the following questions:

- As a child, what did you like most? What did you want to be when you grew up?
- If you were to die tomorrow, what would you regret most?
- Imagine you are 80 years old and you look back on your life. What would you be most proud of? How would you like others to remember you?
- What would you like to do if there were no limitations (financial, time, location, knowledge)?

2. Write down your finest moments

Your values usually have to do with the moments when you were happiest, which probably meant you felt like you had made the right choices for yourself and others. To get at these, answer the following questions, using situations from your work as well as your private life:

- What were the moments when you felt happiest?
- What were the moments when you felt most fulfilled and satisfied?
- What were the moments when you felt connected to something bigger than yourself?
- What were you doing during these moments? Who were you with? What other factors played a role? What are the similarities? Which desires were fulfilled, and how did this make your life meaningful?

3. Identify your values

Based on the moments when you felt most happy, fulfilled and connected, choose fifteen to twenty values from the list at the bottom of the next page, and write them down.

4. Find your core values

From your list of values, choose the ten with which you identify most. Write them down in the first column in random order:

Once you've completed this, think about which values are the most important to you and which are less important. Give each value a number, and write this number down in the second column, creating a personal Top Ten. No. 1 is the most important and No. 10 the least important. Use each digit only once.

If you find it difficult to decide which of two values is higher for you, imagine a situation where you have to make a choice based on the two values in question. Let's say that you value both creativity and leadership. Imagine you're offered a job that will come with significant opportunities for leadership but will allow for less creativity than your current job. Should you take it? If you've sorted out your personal values, you'll know whether you should prioritize creativity or leadership. While the society around you might insist that leadership should be on top, it's possible that creativity is more important to you, which of course would mean the new opportunity isn't the best choice for you.

Which values are your top three? These are your core values. Write them down:

1...

2 ....

3 ....

Values list
This list is only for inspiration. You are completely free to write down values that are not on this list.

freedom	modesty	drive	depth	openness
truth	autonomy	altruism	ambition	assertiveness
care	challenge	change	curiosity	expertise
awareness	discretion	diversity	gratefulness	fantasy
education	empathy	elegance	entertainment	knowledge
loyalty	focus	honesty	compassion	generosity
hospitality	diplomacy	humor	non-conformity	imagination
inspiration	independence	intelligence	self-reflection	intimacy

respect	sustainability	wisdom	perfection	power
patience	responsibility	passion	playfulness	fun
faith	thoughtfulness	peace	sympathy	pride
comprehension	pragmatism	desire	spontaneity	growth
structure	endurance	harmony	beauty	grace
trust	credibility	objectiveness	self-confidence	motivation
conviction	conservation	collaboration	conviviality	courage
self-respect	sensitivity	pleasure	optimism	variation
vision	dignity	vitality	consciousness	development
love	purity	impact	relaxation	integrity
strength	prosperity	success	kindness	alertness
eagerness	willingness	decisiveness	engagement	continuity
simplicity	vigorousness	consensus	effectivity	joy
recognition	expression	correctness	flexibility	nuance
hierarchy	equality	clarity	innovation	intensity
calmness	companionship	insightfulness	quality	boldness
loyalty	neighborliness	spirituality	accuracy	cleanness
entrepre-neurship	impartiality	professionality	righteousness	surrender
open-mindedness	togetherness	reason	relativism	quietness
sportsmanship	stability	stability	synergy	tolerance
transparency	faithfulness	patriotism	versatility	craftmanship
forbearance	reformation	wonder	progres-siveness	perseverance
benevolence	tenderness	self-reliance	conscien-tiousness	thrift
authenticity	balance	excellence	service	flow
helpfulness	reliability	uniqueness	leadership	influence
sensuality	determination	competition	connection	creativity
victory	support	solidarity	precision	decisiveness
enthusiasm	decency	sincerity	charity	austerity
dependence	resilience	devotion	appreciation	safety

12. Become Self-aware–
Then Transcend the Self

In the long term, attention to the self and inner growth improves a person's self-management and emotional well-being and promotes positive relationships with others. The latter is the first step to global awareness. Continued inner growth raises consciousness until we realize our common humanity with all people—the end of feeling separate.[42]

— Dr. Michael M. Piechowski

Your voice, as we have discussed, is most authentic and powerful when your attention is in the present moment. When you develop awareness of the present, you begin to speak from your intuition, bypassing unhelpful thought activity.

In this final chapter, all that I've explained so far—about the nervous system, about your breath, about the nature of thoughts and emotions—come together in a simple but powerful capstone: *awareness*. Cultivating your skills in awareness will help you notice your body's signals, welcome and regulate emotions, and look *at* your thoughts rather than *from* your thoughts. These are high-level emotional skills, and I've never met anyone who couldn't benefit from practicing them.

What's more, increased awareness will impact not only your voice, but also your overall well-being, connection with others, and global understanding, too.

12.1. How Developing Awareness Helps the Voice

Soraya, a passionate and ambitious manager, approached me because she wanted to feel more confident about her voice at work. Meetings and presentations were a big part of her job, but when she spoke in front of these groups, she thought she sounded like a robot. In these spaces, she'd get preoccupied with what she wanted to say; she had a strong desire for control, so she always memorized her scripts, word for word. Her memory was strong enough to pull this off, but it consumed her attention. Then there were the other thoughts that bubbled up while she was presenting! All of this, as Soraya recognized, meant she failed to connect with her audience.

To start, I advised Soraya to quit memorizing her scripts and instead improvise. She could use a

---

42   M.M. Piechowski *We are all cells in the body of humanity* (2010, Gifted Education International, Vol. 27) p. 9.

mind map or bullet list to structure her story, but otherwise, she would have to let go of her desire for perfect control. Unsurprisingly, this made her feel insecure.

Then I introduced Soraya to mindfulness, and things started to shift. I taught her something called *directive meditation*, a practice in which the meditator focuses her attention on a specific target that she can physically sense, most often the breath. We complemented this with *non-directive meditation*, a practice in which the meditator simply observes what passes into her field of awareness. One's own thoughts are a frequent subject for open meditation, and that's what Soraya observed in this exercise.

After some time practicing both directive and non-directive meditation, the first thing Soraya noticed was that her mind became quieter. With less thought activity, she could connect more readily with the present moment; this in turn made space for what she intended to convey to show through. In Soraya's case, that was her excitement. When she stayed in touch with her excitement about her topic while she spoke, she was less likely to get caught up with superfluous thoughts. While before she had feared that her excitement would come across as childish, she now found that the opposite was true: When she tried to present herself as serious and professional, she sounded detached and robotic, but when she allowed her natural excitement to resonate through her voice, she became an engaging, professional speaker.

At the end of her training, Soraya said that she had become more confident when speaking. Feeling comfortable with less control, she deliberately did not prepare her latest panel discussion, which was attended by two thousand people. Instead, she let go and relied on her latent knowledge and expertise to surface when needed, trusting what she would say in the moment. To her surprise, Soraya's mind remained quiet—and she herself remained calm. Present in the here and now, she spoke from her intuition and said just the right things. For the first time, she really connected with the other attendees, which made a world of difference. It was the meditation exercises, Soraya told me, that helped her the most.

Mindfulness, Yoga, and Meditation

There are many ways to develop self-awareness. The most popular practices nowadays are mindfulness, yoga, and meditation. Let me briefly explain each of them:

- Mindfulness is the practice of purposely bringing your attention in the present moment without evaluation. You develop mindfulness through training, of which, meditation and yoga are examples.
- Yoga is a group of physical, mental, and spiritual practices intended to quiet your mind and develop awareness.
- Meditation is a practice in which you either observe what passes through your field of awareness or focus your attention on a particular object or activity. This trains your attention and promotes compassion and emotional calmness.

Going forward, I will refer to yoga, meditation, mindfulness and the like collectively as mindfulness practices. If you commit to practice one of these regularly, you'll improve your ability to regulate yourself in the following ways:

- Learn to stay present and open in complicated situations without trying to avoid difficult emotions
- Make space to consciously decide how you want to respond to a stimulus instead of reacting automatically
- Develop the ability to choose whether to follow thoughts instead of getting caught up in them

There is much neuroscientific research available on the effects of meditation. In general, regular meditators have more mental plasticity and psychological flexibility. Moreover, while experienced meditators may respond to emotional stimuli as strongly as others, they are capable of recovering much faster from the emotional event than novice practitioners. Meditators can shift readily between brief moments of empathic distress into equanimity and compassion. These findings suggest that experienced mediators develop the capacity to regulate their nervous system.

According to clinical therapist Deb Dana, in meditation, the nervous system simultaneously activates both parasympathetic responses, with the inactivity and immobilization from the dorsal vagal response mode and the sense of openness and connection from the ventral vagal response mode. In this state, immobilization is no longer connected to fear, giving rise instead to stillness and self-reflection. You are then able to stay calm, tune into your intuition and trust that the right words will come without actively having to search for them.

The research results concerning mindfulness practice are also encouraging. David Vago, a PhD researcher and director of the Contemplative Neuroscience and Mind-Body Research Laboratory, has found clinical evidence that mindfulness practice can help decrease both the intensity and perceived unpleasantness of pain sensations. It does this, as Vago explained on *The Psychology Podcast*, by eliminating the emotional reactivity and replacing it with an open and accepting attitude to the pain. Other clinical studies reveal similar results in anxiety and depression symptoms as well as a positive effect on executive functions, contributing to sustained attention in those with attention deficits.

Another benefit of mindfulness practice is that it makes it much easier to adopt new habits and let go of those that don't serve you. Researchers at Duke University found that more than forty percent of our daily actions each day stem from habit rather than conscious choice. With increased self-awareness, we are able to replace habits with conscious choices in our daily life.

When you are working on changing the way you speak, this is vital. You have been using your voice in a particular way since you learned to speak, so this behavior is mostly unconscious. The more aware you become of your behavior, the less you do on autopilot, and the more you can choose to act—and speak—differently.

Mindfulness in the Brain

If you want to succeed at this, you'll need to pick a mindfulness practice that's right for you. To help with this, I'll offer several exercises that you can try out—but first, you should understand a little more about the networks in your brain that are involved with mindfulness.

The Central Executive Network

The central executive network processes content generated by our perceptions. It's the home of our executive functions—cognitive working memory, focused attention, task performance, thinking (but not having thoughts—see below), and fluid reasoning. If you experience problems with any of those, you should choose a practice focused on training your central executive network, which activates when we focus our attention on demanding tasks that require concentration. By focusing on our sense perceptions, we give this part of our brain direct experience, thereby helping to reduce mind wandering. This is the primary goal of Western directive meditation practices.

The Default Mode Network

You know from Chapter 11 that having thoughts is not the same as thinking. When we think, we're tapping into the central executive network, but when we have thoughts, they emerge from the default mode network. Psychologist Jonathan Smallwood defines those thoughts as self-generated mental content unrelated to the current environment. This includes all the language, images, ideas, and feelings that arise in your mind throughout the day. It's spontaneous and often unsolicited. You experience it in the form of daydreaming, ruminating, worrying, mind wandering, or mental chatter.

We only recently learned about the existence of the default mode network. As psychologist Scott Barry Kaufman explains in his book *Ungifted*, neuroscientists in the twentieth century weren't interested in researching inner chatter, considering it mere mental noise. Recent research into brain functions during passive rest and introspection, however, led to the discovery of a specific brain network—the default mode. In addition to mind wandering, this neurological network is also the source of creative improvisation and evaluation. It's where we imagine the future and exercise self-awareness. It also plays a central role in our emotional experiences, retrieving deeply personal memories, reflecting on the meaning of experiences, simulating the perspective of another person, evaluating the implications of our and other's emotional reactions, moral reasoning, and reflective compassion. When those twentieth century neuroscientists ignored mental chatter, it turned out that they were brushing off half of what the mind does.

It's worth noting that mind wandering can be positive or negative. Clinical psychologist Jerome L. Singer has identified three styles of daydreaming:

- Positive-constructive daydreaming, including playful and creative thoughts
- Guilty-dysphoric daydreaming, including obsessive, anguished fantasies and unhelpful negative beliefs

- Poor attentional control, which interferes with concentration on thinking or an external task

On its own, the default mode network is mainly responsible for unintended mind wandering and poor attention control. Increased default mode network activity has even been associated with depression, anxiety, and addiction, among other disorders. When you're caught up in thoughts or mind wandering, you aren't focusing on sense perception. As we discussed in Chapter 7, the less your brain depends on sense perception, the more it depends on simulations and predictions, and those have a greater chance of prediction errors. Essentially, you've created your own world based on self-generated mental content. And that world may be significantly unlike the real one that you would experience through sense perception. If your self-generated content is guilty-dysphoric and negative, it's not surprising that it leads to anxiety and depression.

Self-generated content that is positive-constructive, in which mind wandering furthers a goal, actually recruits *both* the default mode network *and* the central executive network. It needs both networks to work in harmony.

Connecting the Central Executive and Default Mode Networks

When these networks are working together, we seem to experience a four-part cognitive cycle in which our attention naturally ebbs and flows—our mind wanders; we notice it wandering; we shift our attention; and we sustain it again, until our mind wanders and the cycle begins again.

Consider a study that used fMRI scanning to observe the brains of fourteen experienced meditation practitioners as they performed directive meditation. When participants realized their minds had wandered, they pressed a button and returned their focus to the breath. The fMRI scans were able to see evidence of the four intervals in our cognitive cycle, with activity in brain regions associated with the default network during periods of mind wandering. When the meditators became aware of their mind wandering, the researchers noted activity in the part of the brain that modulates the switch between the default mode and central executive network (known as the salience network). During shifting and sustained attention, their central executive network was active. Meditation thus enables you to activate and switch between different brain networks. People who train in this style of meditation nurture their ability to monitor cognitive processes of attention and distraction, enhancing flexible attention and increasing awareness of what's going on inside of them and in their environment. In other words, they become more self-aware.

These studies show that if you frequently find your brain hijacked by unconstructive mind wandering, you can use focused attention to reduce activity in the default mode network and strengthen the central executive network. If you practice this regularly, your mind will wander less and less. You'll also increase your capacity to actively switch in and out of constructive mind wandering.

In the following exercises, I'll introduce you to some mindfulness practices that will help you accomplish these general goals. Note, however, that each exercise has a different purpose. Some will strengthen your central executive network; others will strengthen the positive-constructive function of your default mode network. In general, I recommend alternating between these two types of exercises; however, some people will benefit from extra focus on the central executive network, while others will benefit from extra focus on the default mode network.

I have one last note before we go on: practicing mindfulness is safe for most people. If you have untreated trauma or mental illness, however, you should not start practicing without support from a professional.

Tune into Your Central Executive Network: Directed Attention

If you are intellectually or imaginationally overexcitable and easily distracted by your own thoughts and ideas when you speak, you will benefit from training awareness by directing your focused attention away from the mind.

The following exercises will help you return to your original focus when you get distracted while you speak by strengthening your central executive network. If you *notice* that you're getting caught up in a new thought when you're telling a story, you'll be able to choose not to follow that thought. You'll stop losing your train of thought, and you'll notice when you relapse into old habits like speeding up and mumbling. With trained awareness, you'll notice this as soon as it happens, empowering you to immediately adjust the way you speak. You will also be less preoccupied with how you come across and more connected to your audience. In the present moment, you can rely on your expertise, knowledge and skills to be ready for you when you need them. This enables you to feel more confident about what you say or do—and therefore more engaged. This is a completely different attitude than continuously trying to use your knowledge and skills in a tightly controlled way.

Reconnecting with your own body is the first step to increasing self-awareness, so I'll begin with tips for inwardly-directed practice. This is especially important as a foundation if you lack body awareness.

Try it Yourself: **Directive Meditation with Internally Directed Attention**

When you focus inward, you direct your attention toward sensing bodily sensations instead of thoughts. This trains body awareness at the same time that it strengthens your central executive network. Here are some of the practices that can direct your attention inward:

- Gentle forms of movement like yoga, tai chi, and chi kung
- Breathing exercises
- Mantra singing
- Body scan meditations
- Guided, visualizing meditations
- All exercises from Chapter 9, Feel into the Body

Try it Yourself: **Directive Meditation with Externally Directed Attention**

Simple activities give you a good opportunity to practice sustained attention and direct experience. By "simple," I mean activities that leave you enough mental bandwidth for mind wandering. Any activity that allows you to shift easily from direct experience to mind wandering will work.

The exercise is simple too: Try to focus on the sensory experience of what you're doing. When your mind starts wandering, notice that and return to direct experience. Here are some things to try as you're practicing:

- Close your eyes and focus on what you hear. You probably notice sounds that are usually in the background, like a ticking clock or the refrigerator. Then open your eyes. What do you see? Look at your home with curiosity, as if you were seeing your house and your possessions for the first time. Maybe you notice things you haven't noticed before. Tune into other senses as well: What do you smell? What do you feel? Is the room warm or cold? Can you feel if it's dry or humid?
- Mindfully drink a cup of tea or coffee, allowing yourself to be fully absorbed in all your senses.
- Many people experience mind wandering while doing household chores, making it another excellent chance to practice sustained attention. When you fold the laundry, focus on the textures you feel. Experience the textures of the clothes. Fold carefully and precisely. When you cook, do the same. Carefully cut the vegetables, focusing on their texture, color and smell.
- Put some music on and listen to it. Don't do anything else. Which different instruments do you hear? What parts do they play?
- Stare at a candle flame in the dark for 20 minutes. Return to the flame when you notice your attention has wandered.
- Take a walk in nature. Maintain a moderate pace, resisting the urge to go faster. While you walk, actively engage your senses—look, smell, and listen. Be curious about what you perceive. Don't use your intellect to identify this flower or that bird, but rather, observe their characteristics. What colors do you see? What shapes? Enjoy all the beauty that nature has to offer your experience without labeling with concepts like oak, grass, woodpecker, etcetera. If you prefer, you can do this while gardening, too.

Tune into Your Default Mode Network: Emotional Processing

Try it Yourself: Experience Default Mode During a Simple Task

You can acquaint yourself with the working of your default mode network during the same simple activities I suggested for directive meditation. To do this, instead of focusing on what your senses perceive, engage fully in mind wandering. You can use the very same settings as you used to experience your central executive network:

- Sitting in your house, perhaps having a tea or coffee, without doing anything else
- Household chores like cooking and laundry
- Listening to music
- Taking a walk outside
- What do you notice about your mind wandering? Is it positive and creative, or negative and anxious? Maybe there's a little of both. Will the thoughts that you're having help you with some tasks, or are they only likely to distract and drain you?

While directive meditation practices like yoga, breathing, or body scans train you to focus your attention, non-directive meditation facilitates emotional processing by observing the emotions you encounter and the thoughts that occur to you. Noting that what you feel in your own body has a focus similar to that of making sense of your emotions. I recommend that if you practice directive meditation, you should always balance it with non-directive meditation. Later on, it will be clear why.

Non-directive meditation is beneficial for everyone, but especially for those with emotional overexcitability, whether internally or externally expressed. It can help if you bury or suppress your emotions when you speak, or if your concern for others or your surroundings tend to make you lose contact with yourself. The best type of exercise, however, will depend on where you are on the emotional spectrum. If you identify too much with what you feel, you'll want to learn to *observe* what you feel. If you're detached from your emotions, you'll want to *identify* what you feel.

Try it Yourself: Non-directive Meditation to Observe What You Feel

This exercise is for those of you who experience emotions as too intense and get carried away with them easily. During this practice, you'll relax your focus, permitting spontaneous thoughts, images, sensations, memories, and emotions to emerge and pass freely through your mind. This allows you to mentally process memories and emotional experiences, thereby decreasing the stress they cause you. Do the following exercise for five to ten minutes per day:

- Close your eyes. Breathe slowly five to ten times in and out.
- Notice the thoughts going through your mind and what is happening in your body. What do you feel?
- Observe these thoughts and feelings without labeling them as "good" or "bad." Don't try to change, ignore, or hold on to these thoughts and feelings. Just observe. If another thought draws your attention, notice that, too.
- Are you able to let these thoughts and feelings come and go without holding on to them? Are you able to take an observer perspective on what you think and feel? And if you can't help but keep clinging to a certain thought, can you accept that and be non-judgmental about it?
- In between your thoughts and feelings, are you able to experience occasional moments of mental silence? If you can't, can you accept that as well?

Some find it useful to alternate this exercise with the "leaves on a stream" practice from Chapter 11. Both help you to step back from your thoughts.

Try it Yourself: **Non-directive Meditation to Identify What You Feel**

To use the observer perspective, you need to be in touch with your emotions, so if you struggle with this, your first step is to master identifying what you feel. If you're a beginner in this area, return to the exercise in Chapter 10, "Identify What You Feel." If you only need a quick refresher (as most of us do), here's another version you can try. Do the following for five to ten minutes per day:

- Close your eyes. Slowly inhale and exhale five to ten times.
- Become aware of the thoughts going through your mind and the sensations in your body. What do you feel?
- Find language to describe your feelings. For instance, are they comfortable or uncomfortable?
- As you dig more deeply into what you feel, see if you can name a primary emotion.
- Focus on that emotion. Where do you feel it in your body? Does it trigger any thoughts or memories?
- Now return your attention to these physical sensations. Try to allow them to just be there without trying to get rid of them.
- Are you willing to accept the fact that you have these emotions—that they are yours? Can you feel compassionate towards yourself for the fact that you feel like this? Remember that they will eventually pass and that they are not who you *are*.

Try it Yourself: **Morning Pages**

In her book *The Artist's Way*, writer Julia Cameron offers a wonderful exercise for activating the positive-constructive function of the default mode network. The exercise, which she calls Morning Pages, is the bedrock tool for creative recovery. For three years, when I was struggling with a creative block, I began almost every day with Morning Pages, following it up with a directive meditation like yoga. I credit this regime for much of the shift in awareness I experienced during this period. My mind is now much quieter, with unhelpful thoughts relegated to the background and positive-constructive mind wandering strengthened. The exercise is simple:

Morning Pages are three pages of longhand, stream-of-consciousness writing, done first thing in the morning. There is no wrong way to do Morning Pages. They are not high art. They are not even "writing." They are about anything and everything that crosses your mind—and they are for your eyes only. Morning Pages provoke, clarify, comfort, cajole, prioritize, and synchronize the day at hand. Don't overthink them! Just put three pages of anything on the page, and then do three more pages tomorrow.[43]

Cameron calls this method meditation for Westerners. It's a form of observing your stream of consciousness, but the act of writing takes thoughts and feelings out of your mind, changing how you see and relate to them. This helps you to make sense of what you think, feel, and need. It also helps you to commit to activities during your day that are in line with those feelings and needs. Morning Pages thereby combine non-directive meditation with contemplation. Here are the rules:

- Make sure you write the Morning Pages by hand, not on the computer.
- Plan to spend about thirty minutes per day writing them.
- Don't re-read what you've written. Put them away, and start with three new pages the next day. If you want, you can re-read your previous pages several months after you've written them.

When Mindfulness Becomes a Coping Strategy

These days, many who practice mindfulness do so to "empty their minds." In line with the mainstream modern take, they sit quietly in the hopes they will build mental clarity and emotional calm, leading to lives with less stress and more efficiency. For these practitioners, mindfulness is nothing more than a coping strategy to avoid unpleasant and uncomfortable feelings.

---

43   J. Cameron *Julia Cameron Live*. 2022, juliacameronlive.com/basic-tools/morning-pages/

Although you *can* use mindfulness practices in this way, you'll miss several other benefits if relaxation and focus is all you seek. First, as we've already discussed, the acceptance of negative feelings is an indispensable step in personal development. If, when you're tired, sick, stressed, or short on time, you think, "I'll just skip meditation today," you're missing the best opportunities to practice—a chance to be with your pains without trying to get rid of them.

What's more, while a relaxation-focused approach to mindfulness *can* yield increased focused attention, it can also *decrease* creativity and constructive reflection. This happens when you neglect the default mode network and the contemplative emotional processing that goes on there.

Then there's a possible pitfall faced even by meditators who *do* sit with their painful emotions: When you practice "accepting what is," you risk becoming passive.

In Chapter 10, I argued that acceptance is not the same as complacency: *Accept what you feel, change what you can, and accept what you cannot.* The key, however, is knowing the difference between what you can and cannot change. To strike this balance, it's essential to connect the central executive and default mode networks in your mindfulness practice, alternating between meditation and *contemplation*. If you strike a balance between these two practices, you can decrease your guilty-dysphoric daydreaming and distractedness without losing your ability for positive-constructive daydreaming and healthy reflection on yourself and others.

12.2. Contemplation

So far, we've explored how mindfulness can help your voice, the way you speak and your overall well-being. In the final section of this capstone chapter, we'll look at how mindfulness practices can increase your sense of interconnectedness and lead to more global awareness.

In practices around the world, meditation goes hand in hand with contemplation. Contemplation is a form of non-directive meditation that seeks a direct awareness of the divine that transcends the intellect. Buddhists practice contemplation to become more aware of their environment and to accept physical and emotional feelings. The aim of this practice, according to Vago, is to dissolve the border between self and other and enhance human connection. The transformative power of contemplation lies precisely in this increased connection to others, so be careful not to bypass this.

You contemplate by connecting compassionately to yourself and others with an introspection exercise like non-violent communication from Chapter 10. You identify your values as well as your own feelings and needs, but you also contemplate what others feel and need. You can extend this exercise to contemplate what your community feels and needs—and beyond that, the world as a whole. If you connect to your compassionate nature on a regular basis, you'll have a much richer and more meaningful life than if you're forever a detached observer of yourself and the world. If you want to practice compassionate contemplation, I have developed an exercise that I call *The Terrestrial Overview Effect*. You'll find it in the appendix of this book.

Self vs. No-Self

Mindfulness without contemplation remains in the realm of "the self." I would argue that it even promotes individualism. Without contemplation, you risk detaching not only from your own feelings, but also from the world around you. In that case, mindfulness practices can actually make you egocentric. Some people develop a "spiritual ego" during their practices, believing themselves better than others because they're so accepting, mindful, and spiritual. You can imagine the caricature of this type—shutting themselves off from the normal world and its complicated problems, moving to a hippie island like Goa, Ibiza, or Bali.

The thing is, being enlightened in a community filled with like-minded spiritual people isn't really a challenge. These people are often simply *avoiding* unwelcome and complex emotions. The real challenge is to stay open, accepting, and compassionate in the real world, where a lot of people are not self-aware and things can get nasty. It's in this unfair, dirty world that you have the chance to contribute and inspire others to become more self-aware.

In her essay *The Problem of Mindfulness*, philosophy student Sahanika Ratnayake writes:

> In claiming to offer a multipurpose, multi-user remedy for all occasions, mindfulness oversimplifies the difficult business of understanding oneself. It fits oh-so-neatly into a culture of techno-fixes, easy answers and self-hacks, where we can all just tinker with the contents of our heads to solve problems, instead of probing why we're so dissatisfied with our lives in the first place. […] The focus tends to be solely on the contents of an individual's mind and the alleviation of their distress, rather than on interrogating the deeper socioeconomic and political conditions that give rise to the distress in the first place. Mindfulness follows the trend for simplicity and individuation. Its embedded assumptions about the self makes it particularly prone to neglecting broader considerations, since they allow for no notion of individuals as enmeshed in and affected by society at large.[44]

Ratnayake explains that mindfulness is originally grounded in the Buddhist principle of Anattā, or "no-self." As we discussed in Chapter 11, although we do perceive the self as a separate entity, some scientists argue that "the self" doesn't exist. Anattā is in accordance with this idea that there is no underlying subject of our own experience, thereby denying that there is an ongoing individual basis for identity. The Western view of mindfulness, however, holds on to that separate entity—the self to which all thoughts, emotions, and physical sensations are happening.

During their practice, longtime meditation practitioners usually have one or more periods with negative experiences including terror, fear, dissociation, or feelings of isolation. In Buddhist texts, this has been described as "the dark night of the soul." There are stages in the practice where these longtime meditators experience their selves dissolving, realizing that there is no permanent self. Their egos becomes less present in their awareness, sometimes even vanishing. To some, this is ultimately liberating, but others totally freak out. Western practitioners in particular might not be

---

44   S. Ratnayake "The Problem of Mindfulness" *Aeon* (2019, Aeon Media Group Ltd.) /aeon.co/essays/mindfulness-is-loaded-with-troubling-metaphysical-assumptions

willing to accept that there is no such thing as a permanent self. If you have a strong ego or are very attached to it, you might not want to go down that rabbit hole.

If, however, you accept that there is no self, you enter a completely new paradigm. Your personal identity becomes less important; consequently, you become less attached to your conceptualized self, including your accomplishments, belongings, and life story. For your voice, this can ultimately be liberating. Imagine that this presentation you give or that song you sing is no longer about you, it is about the message. You only function as a vessel to convey the message. In my experience and those of my clients, the concept of no-self helps a lot with performance nerves.

We live in a world that defines you by your identity, narrative, accomplishments, and belongings, making it especially difficult to turn around and start swimming against this stream. Being freed from your sense of self can be a burden as well as an epiphany. Day to day life in this world may not make sense to you anymore, and you may have a hard time fitting into your environment. This is often part of that dark night of the soul. But like everything in life, the dark night is not permanent, and you'll enter a new stage at some point.

The principle of Anattā is not acknowledged by everyone who researches personal development. Consider Kazimierz Dąbrowski. Although he endorses and promotes meditation as a practice, he firmly rejects the idea that there is no self. In an interview from 1975, he called this philosophy an annihilation of our individual personality—even dangerous and anti-human. From his point of view, the joyful, enlightened no-self that certain spiritual gurus were promoting at the time trivialized everything that makes human life worth living, including friendship, love, and the possibility for development through suffering. In his theory of positive disintegration, the self does not dissolve, it transforms.

Dąbrowski does have a point. If your goal is to reach a state of no-self through meditation before you really know who you are, you risk the danger of bypassing contemplation and the complementary emotional development.

Whether the self really exists or not, we all do have an experience of a *sense* of self with the potential to learn and develop. I therefore argue that, before we even consider experiencing no-self, we must first become thoroughly self-aware. A highly developed self with a personal hierarchy of values has the capacity to transcend egoic self-interest and to feel part of something greater. Transcending your "self" in that respect leads to greater feelings of connection and compassion, making room for a collectivism that still has space for authenticity and autonomy. In his book *Transcend*, Kaufman calls this a healthy self-loss:

> *Having a substantial quieting of the ego is strongly related to having a strong, not weak, sense of self and with increased, not weakened, authenticity. Indeed,* those with the quietest ego defenses often have the strongest sense of self. *As the Buddhist Harvard psychotherapist Jack Engler put it, "You have to be somebody before you can be nobody."*[45]

---

45   S.B. Kaufman, Ph. D. *Transcend: the new science of self-actualization* (2020, TarcherPerigee, New York, NY) p. 204-205.

Individualism vs. Collectivism

"If you learn that you are connected to all things before you learn that you have no self, you may not necessarily freak out." These are the words of Vago about a common hurdle faced by Western practitioners. Since the Enlightenment and the Romantic era, we in the West have embraced individualism as one of our highest values, encompassing autonomy of the individual, independence, personal freedom, privacy, and a clear awareness of "I" and "the self." An individual person is an entity in itself, separate from society and its surroundings. He or she is not connected to the environment by default, but can choose whether or not to engage with it. This sense of separateness is hardly ever questioned in the Western world. It's rare to find a renowned scientist like David Bohm, who treats the totality of existence as an unbroken whole.

In Asian societies, individualistic freedom is not a core value the way it is in the West. These collectivist societies emphasize the identity of the group over that of the individual, emphasizing cohesiveness among individuals and prioritizing the needs of the group over those of the individual. In the hierarchy of a Japanese business, for instance, we can see less of a sense of separateness among individual people. Within the organization, there is a clear hierarchical structure that makes the role of each person and their relationships well defined. As a result, everyone is acutely aware of each other's roles and strives to achieve goals and deadlines as a group. Maintaining harmonious relationships is vital in this process. Individuals tend to regard themselves as a representative of the company, and credit for achievement is shared as a group effort.

If you practice meditation from a collectivist perspective, you will enhance your sense of the interconnectedness of all things. You might lose your individualist view, but in return, you'll gain a growing experience of being part of something bigger than yourself—your community, nature, the Earth, or even the Universe. It will provide a safety net that is not available to those who experience no-self from an individualistic perspective.

Dualism vs. Non-Dualism

> Under heaven all can see beauty as beauty,
> only because there is ugliness.
> All can know good as good because there is evil.
> Being and non-being produce each other.
> The difficult is born in the easy.
> Long is defined by short, the high by the low.
> Before and after go along with each other.
> So the sage lives openly with apparent duality
> and paradoxical unity.
> The sage can act without effort
> and teach without words.

Nurturing things without processing them,
he works but not for rewards;
he competes but not for results.
When the work is done, it is forgotten.
This is why it lasts forever.

This is the second verse from the *Tao Te Ching* by Lao Tzu. It lays out what is sometimes called the principle of paradoxical unity, which presents duality as merely a concept, not something concrete or absolute. Every aspect of life is created from a balanced interaction of opposite forces. These opposites, moreover, are complementary, like yin and yang—two sides of the same coin which must come together to make the coin complete.

What are the implications of paradoxical unity for your meditation practice? On a philosophical level, the whole conundrum about self versus no-self disappears. There is a self and there is no-self. It is no longer necessary to question whether you are an individual or part of something bigger than yourself; you are both.

But there are also practical implications. If you look further than the limits of duality and embrace the principal of paradoxical unity, you can rise beyond inner conflict. Ambivalent thoughts and feelings become less and less disturbing. Consider how this belief would lead you to interpret the following situations: *You have a strong desire to perform in front of an audience, but are terrified of what people would say and think of you. You are ready for a new step in your life, but still not ready to let go of the old. You love your partner, but you fall in love with someone else.*

Paradoxical unity replaces "but" with "and." It helps you acknowledge that you have a strong desire to perform, *and* are terrified at the same time. You allow the apparent conflicting situations to exist side by side in your life without looking to resolve them. You are ready for a new step in your life, *and* still not ready to let go of the old. You love your partner, *and* you fall in love with someone else. By acknowledging and accepting paradoxical unity, you can go beyond simplistic *right* and *wrong*, integrating all emotions and ideas into your life without fighting against them.

It's not only in ancient texts that we find wisdom about paradoxical unity; it also comes from ordinary people doing the work of living their lives. A blogger by the name of Invajy put it this way:

In your day to day life, you will find oneness and unity within these paradoxes, within the happy and the sad, the good and bad, the negative and the positive. These opposites balance each other and are part of the same coin i.e. your life. In order to complete your incredible journey of life successfully, it is vital that you turn each and every dark tear into a pearl of wisdom, and find the blessing in every curse.[46]

In his words about paradoxical unity, I recognize the process of positive disintegration. It has been my experience that if you go through the inner transformation of multilevel disintegration, you'll start to live more and more according to the principal of paradoxical unity.

---

46 Invajy *How to use duality or paradoxical unity to understand the life?* (2022, Self Improvement Blog) www.invajy.com/how-to-use-duality-or-paradoxical-unity-to-understand-the-life

12.3. From Contemplation to Moral Development

Let's imagine the next stage. You've reached a point where you have experience with directive and non-directive meditation. You can flexibly switch between the brain networks, have more focused attention, and observe your thoughts and feelings as things that you have rather than who you are. You pay attention to the present moment non-judgmentally. You've found anchors for your nervous system that increasingly ground you in ventral vagal response mode. When you do become dysregulated (because this will always happen) you can regulate your emotions to find your way back to safety and social engagement. Tapping into the power of contemplation, you've gained true wisdom and insight, and you even experience deepening states of concentration and tranquility. You aren't *surviving* daily life anymore, but *living* it—maybe even *enjoying* it. In this state, you're able to reconnect with society at large.

If and when that's you, you'll have reached the right stage to take emotional development one step further by actively developing your morals. You recognize that you must go beyond the non-judgmental evaluation of the present moment—while also recognizing (in an instance of paradoxical unity) that judgment and evaluation are necessary to make the right decision or action in a certain context.

The Power of Extraordinary Voices: Dr. Martin Luther King, Jr.

The voice is the oldest and arguably most powerful medium to share our values, wisdom, insights, and ideas about a better world. People use their voices to speak essential truths, sometimes even risking their lives in the process. To conclude this book, we'll discuss a man with just such an extraordinary voice—and one that did indeed cost him his life. I mentioned him earlier as an example of intellectual overexcitability and as a role model for Marvin Gaye. Of course, I'm talking about Martin Luther King, Jr.

Besides being killed by gunfire, Dr. King and Gaye have many things in common. Both sons of preachers, each possessed a great developmental potential and felt a strong desire to spread the word of the Lord. Their personalities were complex, passionate and sensuous. But the second factor of development sets them apart. While Gaye grew up in an emotionally deprived environment, Dr. King grew up in a warm and loving family and enjoyed a healthy and stable environment when he was young. In his autobiography, he says that his childhood experiences made it quite easy for him to lean more toward optimism than pessimism about human nature.

There was, however, one particular disintegrative incident that heavily shaped the course of his development. Young Martin was friends with a white boy. The two played together until they were separated at the age of six—young Martin was sent to a school for black children, while his friend went to a school for white children. This was business as usual in Atlanta in the 1930s. Soon afterwards, the white boy's parents stopped allowing him to play with Martin. When Martin discussed this with his parents, he learned about racism for the first time. It came as a tremendous shock to him, and he resolved to hate every white person. His parents, however, told him that it was his Christian duty to love the white man equally. This led young Martin, aged only six years, to a major inner conflict. How could he love a race of people who hated him, and who had been responsible for breaking him up with his friend? It was only the first of the many injustices he would face as he grew up under the strict racial segregation of the American South.

Young Martin had always had a bright and critical mind. At the age of thirteen, he shocked his Sunday school class by denying the bodily resurrection of Jesus—a fine example of intellectual overexcitability. As he developed his questioning mind further, his voice became his main means of expression for his values and ideas. At fourteen, he won an oratorical contest in Georgia with a speech entitled *The Negro and the Constitution*. In college, he absorbed literature from all kinds of philosophers and thinkers; Mahatma Gandhi became his most important inspiration.

In college, Martin began to work with organizations that were trying to make racial justice a reality. The wholesome relations he had in the Intercollegiate Council convinced him that he could count many white persons as allies, particularly among the younger generation. Along the way, his resentment toward white people softened. Working together with white people instead of fighting against them, Martin came to believe that a nonviolent approach was the best way to reach his goal of a racially just world—a great example of *positive maladjustment* to the segregated world in which he lived.

Feeling an inescapable responsibility to serve society, Martin entered the ministry. He wanted to change church culture into something both intellectually respectable and emotionally satisfying. So when he matriculated at Boston University, he chose to study philosophy alongside theology, eventually earning a doctorate in systematic theology.

In his first position as a minister, Dr. King was placed in Montgomery, Alabama. There he was asked to take up a leadership role in the Montgomery bus boycott. And while his intellect and force of character surely contributed, his powerful voice was a major reason the organizers invited Dr. King to lead. As biographer Godfrey Hodgson describes it, Dr. King's voice was powerful, deep and thrilling; it "started low and could build up until he communicated an irresistible shared passion to his congregation in church or to his followers in the streets."[47] In an age when the radio brought voices into people's homes, Dr. King's voice turned him into a public figure—the spokesman of the civil rights movement.

That leadership role came with costs. He faced continuous stress, scorn, and danger for himself and his family. The FBI tapped his telephone line. He was repeatedly arrested and imprisoned. He faced several attacks and bombings, including a knife attack that nearly killed him. Nevertheless, Dr. King kept going, delivering speeches and organizing and leading non-violent marches for basic civil rights for black people until his assassination in 1968.

What Mastery of the Voice Looks Like

As a charismatic and gifted orator, Dr. King understood that it was not only his words, but his voice that gave his message its power. He was a master of the spoken word. Consider his vocal rhythm.

---

47   G. Hodgson *Martin Luther King* (2009, Quercus, London) p. 6.

He knew exactly when to pause, slow down, or accelerate for effect, leaving his audience hanging on his every word. He led them from climax to climax, as if he wrote his speeches with a musical score in mind. If you set a metronome to his speeches, his voice will fit the beat, revealing his strong tempo-based organization of words, syllables, and phrases. Great leaders ought to be great speakers, and there have been many great orators in American history. But according to Hodgson, none since Abraham Lincoln came as close to the sheer emotive power—the astonishing gift for reaching, touching, and arousing an audience—as Dr. King at his best. His *I Have a Dream* speech is regarded as one of the finest speeches in the history of American eloquence, and it played an important role in putting civil rights at the top of the agenda of the reformers in the United States.

In his career and his life, Dr. King accomplished things that were denied to many other African-Americans in the United States at the time. The circumstances of his upbringing surely contributed to this. His father was an exemplar for the strong and dynamic personality Dr. King himself became, while his mother modeled the gentle, nonviolent attitude he embraced in his teachings. This loving, nurturing youth, combined with his overexcitabilities, extraordinary talents, and intelligence, enabled Dr. King to develop self-awareness and his own hierarchy of values at an early age. A sense of moral obligation led him to employ his talents and privileges to serve the world. Not everyone has such a rich and nurturing youth, nor such natural talents. If Dr. King had been born in more materially or emotionally deprived circumstances, it's doubtful that he would have become a resilient leader capable of leaving such an indelible mark on history.

Contributing to a Better World

It's not everyone's calling nor responsibility to change the course of history. Many people are completely preoccupied with surviving their daily circumstances. Nonetheless, when I look around—whether at my own community at home or at the world at large—I see a desire for change. People everywhere are attempting to make the world a better place, in ways big and small. These contributions give them a sense of purpose.

As the cliché has it, if you want to change the world, you should start with changing yourself. Research shows that compassion for self and others requires an active ventral vagal response mode in human beings, and that both forms of compassion need regular practice. Only from a place of safety within a regulated nervous system can you have functional concern for the outside world, truly recognizing how others suffer and responding with compassion to their suffering. The more self-aware you are, the more you realize how everything is connected and how all of your actions have consequences. This awareness will lead you to take better care of other people, your environment, and the planet. Importantly, this isn't just about helping others; it also helps you, because the more regulated and self-aware you are, the less you will experience suffering, and—in a powerful virtuous circle—people who suffer less will in turn inflict less suffering on others.

Being emotionally developed, self-aware human beings, we can contribute to the development and self-awareness of other human beings, causing a ripple effect. I therefore argue that the process of "personal development" is in fact *not* personal, if personal means individualistic. If you engage in personal development from the perspective of collectivism and non-dualism, believing that it is possible to transcend self-interest, you develop universal awareness. When you reach this point, using your voice to create a better world will not feel like an insurmountable burden. Rather, it will have become second nature.

Appendix – Two Extra Exercises

1. Take the Musician's Approach

Imagine you're going to an opera. You expect the singers to have prepared themselves: they know the score, having studied it many times. First, they studied the musical notes, and after that, the dynamics, timing, phrasing, and interpretation. They sang the arias over and over, many, many times.

Now, imagine how the singers would sound if they had just read through the score twenty times without actually singing the music. How do you think that concert would sound? The director would probably fire them.

When I ask my clients how they prepare for their presentations, they usually go all out on preparing the content, getting the relevant information into the PowerPoint, and reading it through about twenty times. But that's not enough to give a decent performance. If you're preparing for a presentation, you should approach this in the same way the opera singer prepares for a concert, rehearsing the delivery as well as the content. Yes, that takes extra time—time you probably want to spend on other things—but if you want to manage your nerves and ace the presentation, proper, comprehensive preparation is the way to do it.

- First, prepare your content. This can be a PowerPoint file, a mind map, a list with key words, or a script.
- Read your presentation aloud, checking whether you can convey the basic content. Don't worry about having it memorized, and don't worry about stylistic things just yet; focus instead on whether you can deliver your key points.
- Once you're able to recall and deliver your key points, switch your efforts to your delivery. Read your presentation aloud, focusing on dynamics, timing, and phrasing. Use voice techniques such as pace, rhythm, intonation, and word stress (for more on these, see Chapter 4). Make sure that you rehearse where you will breathe.
- Once you're reasonably comfortable with the basics of delivery, add the level of interpretation. What is your intent for this presentation? What feelings do you want to convey? See if you can convey your emotions, adjusting your delivery as necessary.

If you find it difficult to apply pace, rhythm, intonation, and word stress on the fly, practice this first on paper:

- Transcribe one excerpt of the lecture on a sheet of paper, or type it on your computer and make a print. Ideally, this is the beginning of your presentation, and maybe the end as well.
- With a pen, mark the transcript with accents that will support your story. If appropriate, jot down how you will use your voice to convey those accents. You should also note where you want to pause and breathe in your text.
- Using your annotated script, practice reading out loud while focusing solely on separate vocal skills:
    - Breathing and making pauses
    - Word stress, pace, rhythm, and intonation
    - Engaged delivery

Good preparation also means knowing when to stop preparing. Overpreparing is a waste of time that will keep you from something that's just as important—rest. Remember that you can't control every aspect of your performance. You may get questions you're not prepared for, or the amplification may not work. You may trip over a few words or lose your breath at some point. Things hardly ever go perfectly, and it's better to stay open and accepting when this happens. Overpreparing won't help you with a flexible approach. If you struggle with this, here are some tips on how to know when to stop:

- Finish your rehearsals the day before your presentation. Do not keep preparing until the last minute.
- Have a quiet night in the night before your presentation. Relax and get a good night's sleep. This will allow the rehearsed content to settle into your subconscious.
- On the day of the presentation, allow yourself between 10 to 30 minutes before your performance to focus. If possible, withdraw for a while, and do exercises for mindfulness, breathing and body awareness from Chapter 8 to 12.

This practice will help your nervous system enter ventral vagal response mode. Next to feeling comfortable and safe, it offers other benefits, too. In ventral vagal mode, you'll have easier access to the neocortical brain lobes where higher cognitive functioning originates. Your knowledge will be readily accessible to you. Trust that you've already done the hard work—that you're prepared. You can be confident that you'll say the right things at the right moment when you're equally connected to your audience and yourself, in the present moment.

2. A Contemplation Exercise in Interconnectedness

Mindfulness is a powerful way to affect your voice, the way you speak, and your overall well-being. Contemplative mindfulness exercises also increase your sense of interconnectedness and compassionate understanding towards yourself and others. On the level of the nervous system, this facilitates co-regulation of your nervous system with those of others through facial expression and rhythmic, melodic speech. Consequently, you'll contribute to an environment where you and others can feel safe to speak up, get heard and genuinely connect with each other. You can practice contemplation with the exercise below.

Astronauts have reported that they experience a cognitive shift in awareness when they look at Planet Earth from space. They get overwhelmed by the unity—and fragility—of life on the globe, suddenly becoming profoundly aware of the big picture and how everything down there is connected. Viewed from such a distance, national boundaries vanish, and differences between people become less important.

Only a few people will have the opportunity to look at Earth from that perspective, but there's a way we can experience a similar terrestrial overview without leaving the surface of our planet. It requires you to use your imagination. I recommend you perform this exercise when you find yourself surrounded by people you don't know personally, such as on a platform waiting for a train, in the supermarket, or on a busy street.

The Terrestrial Overview Effect

Take a moment and look at the people around you. The humans you share public spaces with are usually minding their own business; there's not a lot of interaction and even less connection. Most likely, you know nothing about these people—they are complete strangers to you.

Now consider that each of these human beings is living a life, just like you. I know that this sounds obvious. But what if you imagine those other lives? That's the next step: Imagine their parents and siblings. Imagine their partners, children, and friends. Think of all the stages that you've been through in your own life—childhood, young adulthood, the years after that, and all the experiences you've had. Now imagine that those other people also started as little, helpless babies, completely dependent on caretakers for survival. They experienced exactly the same stages after that, steadily growing into autonomous individuals, just like you did.

Next, remember all the emotions you've felt in your life—joy, anger, jealousy, enthusiasm, desire, insecurity, sadness, surprise, and so on. Imagine how those other human beings experienced the very same emotions that you've had. Can you imagine them sad? Joyous? Angry? Consider that they have laughed, cried, loved, and felt disappointed, just like you.

As human beings, we not only share the same emotions, but also the same basic needs, including appreciation, respect, community, contribution, support, and understanding. Imagine the ways that everyone around you spends a great deal of his or her life trying to get those needs met. They might do this in very different ways, and maybe some of those ways will be hard for you to understand.

Consider, however, that whether people choose to take care of sick people, earn a lot of money, make art, or carry out a terrorist attack, all of their choices stem from the desire to meet their needs. Their strategies may or may not fit your values, but every action comes from the same universal human needs.

Next, consider the wide range of thoughts you've had in your life. Remember how you've fantasized about your future and how you've overthought your past. Recall your dreams, judgments, worries, reasons, and plans. Then imagine all the different thoughts going on in the minds of the people around you right now. They're constantly thinking, just like you. Maybe they're thinking about something that happened earlier that day or what they need to do this week. Be aware of all of this mind activity going on around you without you seeing or hearing it. Now imagine what it would be like if you could hear everyone's inner world out loud. All of those thoughts and feelings—that would be quite intense, wouldn't it?

Next, extend your awareness to all the human beings you are connected too. I don't mean just family, friends, co-workers, and neighbors—you're connected to many more than that. Try to recall some random activities on a given day. For instance, in the morning, maybe you wake up and take a shower. In many countries, you just turn on the tap and fresh water pours out. Now imagine the human beings working in water treatment who make it possible for you to have access to clean water every day. Imagine the lives of those water employees, with families, friends, thoughts, feelings, and needs—just like you. Think about the 7.9 billion other humans on Earth who need several liters of water per day to survive. Consider that in your country, there's a group of people taking care of this important task for you.

After your shower, you get dressed. What do you choose to wear? Every piece of garment is made for you by another human being. This person could be an independent tailor or an underpaid employee in a sweatshop. Imagine this other human being, probably living in a different country, but still with a family, friends, thoughts, feelings, and needs. He or she made these jeans or this shirt so you could wear them.

The same goes for your phone, laptop, cosmetics, furniture, kitchen utensils, and so on. All those things you own are made for you by another human being, who is thus connected to you. Imagine the house you live in and what it's made of. Other humans built this house for you out of wood, stone, brick, or concrete. Maybe those humans aren't alive anymore, but they had lives like yours, and thanks to what they did in their lifetime, you now have shelter in yours.

Think about what you had for breakfast. Where did it come from? Usually we only meet the people who sell us food in shops or restaurants. Imagine now where the food chain really starts. Is this tomato grown by a small farm or a multinational company? Imagine the food producers who tend those crops—how they grow and harvest, with machines or by hand. Imagine the people in the food industry and on farms living a life just like you, with everything that comes with it. Consider that without food producers, you would have no access to food, or at least access to a very limited number of products.

These are just some examples of your connections to other human beings—connections you may never have considered before. If you keep up the exercise, you'll find many, many more.

Now extend your imagination to all the human beings in your city, country, or even your planet. Imagine every one of them is living a life, like you. In total there are 7.7 billion people experiencing, feeling, needing, and thinking just like you. If you fully realize this, it can feel over-whelming—maybe even incomprehensible. On the other hand, it can feel reassuring to realize that you share the same human experience with so many others. Though the content of their particular lives—their stories—is different from yours, you're still exactly the same in many respects.

But it doesn't end there. It's not just human beings to which we're connected. Let's go back to our food. If you eat meat or animal products, think about the meat, milk, or eggs that you buy and the animals those things belonged to. Imagine the lives those animals live while being raised and fed to become or produce food. Maybe their circumstances are poor and they suffer, or maybe they're kept in better circumstances. Imagine how our farm animals—like animals in the wild—almost never die naturally of old age. They might feel frightened or confused and suffer pain while dying. I'm not stating a moral judgment against animal products; this is emphatically not the point. The exercise is about becoming aware of all the other living beings you are connected to—in this case, the animals whose lives have provided you with food.

Now imagine the grains, pulses, fruits, vegetables, and other plants you eat. Consider that they are living beings, too. Human beings have constructed moral borders between animals and plants. To other beings with sight, hearing, smell, taste, and touch, we attribute some of the same features we recognize in ourselves. We widely acknowledge now that animals have the ability for pain and suffering. Now, however, some are arguing that trees have friends, feel loneliness, scream with pain, and communicate underground via the "wood wide web".

Consider what this could mean for the plant-based food you eat. Have you ever thought whether plants suffer when they get cut and get eaten? I'm not sure they do, and I'm not sure they don't. We don't know what it's like to be some other animal species, but we have even less sense of what it's like to be a plant. With that in mind, try to imagine what it's like. Become aware of those plants you are connected to, grown in fields or greenhouses. They are living beings whose lives ultimately feed you, enabling you to keep living.

Let's stay with the plants for a bit longer. They also provide you with oxygen, the most important thing you need to stay alive. Imagine the trees around you, including trees in your neighborhood but also in the great forests. Include the seaweeds growing in the ocean. All around the world, these plants are connected to you, keeping you alive, ensuring you can breathe air with sufficient oxygen.

Now let's consider the Sun—that big, hot, gassy ball in the sky that is responsible for our daylight and for keeping all beings warm, energized, and alive on Planet Earth. Without the Sun, there would be nothing growing here at all. Every living being on Earth is connected to the Sun.

In fact, we're so steeped in interconnectedness that we don't notice it. Maybe that's why we often experience our lives, thoughts, and feelings as something separate from others. But although we may sometimes feel lonely or disconnected, it's impossible to be truly alone. We are always connected in this sense. Albert Einstein (who never went to space) called this an optical delusion of consciousness:

> *This delusion is a kind of prison for us, restricting us to our personal desires and to affection for a few persons nearest to us. Our task must be to free ourselves from this prison by widening our circle of compassion to embrace all living creatures and the whole of nature in its beauty.*[48]

If you consider the interconnectedness between everybody and everything throughout the planet, you will realize that you can never really be an independent individual. Your voice is not separate from your body, neither are your body and mind separate from your community. You can never be held single-handedly responsible for your accomplishments, nor your failures. Together, we contribute to the beauty and suffering on the planet. Every day, your fellow living beings on Earth make it possible for you to live another day of your life. With everything you say or do, with every choice you make, you too make an impact—whether big or small—on the lives of other beings throughout the globe. If you can feel into this interconnectedness, you can use your voice as a vessel to connect to something greater than yourself. You don't necessarily need to go to space to become aware of that.

---

[48] This is noted on Wikiquote as being found in a letter from 1950, which was quoted in The New York Times (29 March, 1972) and a few months later in The New York Post (28 November, 1972).

Acknowledgments

I like to write, but was convinced that I would never write a book. Yet, this project evolved from doing extensive research to writing blogposts to commissioned writing, leading up to the inevitable next step. The fact that I eventually wrote this book is because of some people in particular.

I would like to start with thanking Jessie Mannisto, my editor. Her magazine Third Factor offered me a platform to publish for an international audience. She challenged me to share my knowledge about the voice with her readers, and nurtured my confidence to write in English too. When the idea for the book was taking shape, I was determined that I should only proceed in English with Jessie by my side. I admire her eye for detail and clarity without ever losing sight of the big picture, and I'm blessed with the incredible commitment she put into this project. It's been such a meaningful and pleasurable experience to work together.

"If you put positive disintegration in the context of your expertise, the voice, then you've got something interesting going on". After my first meeting with Lotte van Lith, these words of her stayed with me and the seed for this book had been planted. My heartfelt thanks to Lotte: for her feedback and support from the early beginning till the end, and for being a beloved, likeminded cocreating colleague and such a knowledgeable and inspiring teacher of Dąbrowski's theory.

The scholarly works of Dąbrowski would never have been accessible to me without William Tillier, whom I thank for disclosing and maintaining the Dąbrowski archive and thereby keeping his legacy alive.

I am grateful to the scientists who generously shared their knowledge and gave me new insights and notes on my early drafts: Michael M. Piechowski and Krystyna C. Laycraft. And to my dear friends who gave me notes from their expertise as medical doctors, Caroline van Oene and Elles Bindels.

Sander de Haan deserves a special warm thank you, not only for his unending support in this project as my much-loved life partner, but also for the time and dedication he put into the design of this book.

I'm also thanking Joanna Boruc for her advice on linguistic terminology, Daniel Dugour for being the first person to encourage me to write this book and his support along the way, Roel Iken for the cover illustration, Alex Scheiwe, Margo van de Linde and Leila Anderson for being such knowledgeable and committed proof readers, and publisher Susanna Klaver for her guidance and advice.

Last but not least I'm profoundly grateful to all the people who have put their trust in me to guide them with their voices and other aspects in their lives. It is their stories and development processes through which the theoretical framework and exercises I describe here truly come to life and become meaningful. In the case studies I used, all names are fictitious and personal characteristics are made unrecognizable.

Notes

Foreword by Lotte van Lith

• K. Dąbrowski *Multilevelness of Emotional and Instinctive Functions* (1996, Towarzystwo Naukowe, Lublin)

Introduction

• D. Bohm *Wholeness and the Implicate Order* (2002, Routledge Classics, New York, NY)

Chapter 1. Vulnerability

• J. Haidt *The Righteous Mind (Why Good People Are Divided By Politics And Religion)* (2012, Penguin Books Ltd, England)

Chapter 2. Safety

• S.W. Porges *The Pocket Guide To The Polyvagal Theory – The Transformative Power of Feeling Safe* (2017, W. W. Norton & Company, Inc., New York)

• C. Goyder *Find Your Voice: The Secret to Talking with Confidence in any Situation* (2020, Vermillion, London)

• D. Dana *De Polyvagaaltheorie in Therapie – Het Ritme van Regulatie* (2021, Uitgeverij Mens!, Eeserveen)

Chapter 3. Personal Growth

• B.W. Hands *Finding Your Voice – A Voice Doctor's Holistic Guide For Voice Users, Teachers And Therapists* (2009, BPS Book, Toronto)

• Kenniscommunity Positieve Desintegratie www.positievedesintegratie.nl

• M.M. Piechowski *How Well Do We Understand Dabrowski's Theory?* (2002)

• K. Dąbrowski *Multilevelness of Emotional and Instinctive Functions* (1996, Towarzystwo Naukowe, Lublin)

• K. Dąbrowski, A. Kawczak, M.M. Piechowski *Mental Growth Through Positive Disintegration* (1970, Gryf Publications LTD, London)

• K. Dąbrowski, A. Kawczak and J. Sochanska *The Dynamics of Concepts* (1973, Gryf Publications Ltd. London)

Chapter 4. Developmental Potential

• K. Dąbrowski, A. Kawczak and J. Sochanska *The Dynamics of Concepts* (1973, Gryf Publications Ltd. London)

• W. Thomas Boyce *The Orchid And The Dandelion – Why Sensitive People Struggle And How All Can Thrive* (2019, Penguin Random House LLC, New York)

• S. van Moen *Stem in Transitie* (2018, Gent, Academia Press)

• P. Pandey *Indian English prosody* (2016, Cambridge University Press) www.cambridge.org/core/books/abs/communicating-with-asia/indian-english-prosody/0182AA9B0CE88C41E02F3E06B7F8A1FF

• E. Meyer *The Culture Map* (2019, Uitgeverij Business Contact)

- P. Firozi *Top Clinton surrogate: She should 'smile more' during the debates* (2016, The Hill) thehill.com/blogs/ballot-box/297288-top-clinton-surrogate-clinton-should-smile-more-during-the-debates
- M. Monk *The Soul's Messenger*, first published in Arcana V: Music, Magic and Mysticism, edited by John Zorn (Hips Road; New York, 2010)
- K. Dąbrowski *Multilevelness of Emotional and Instinctive Functions* (1996, Towarzystwo Naukowe, Lublin)
- Toastmasters International *Your Speaking Voice* www.toastmasters.org

Chapter 5. Overexcitabilities

- K. Dąbrowski and M.M. Piechowski *Theory of Levels of Emotional Development – Volume 1 Multilevelness and Positive Disintegration* (1977, Dabor Science Publications, New York)
- Positieve desintegratie at Wikipedia nl.wikipedia.org/wiki/Theorie_van_positieve_desintegratie
- R. van de Ven, M. van Weerdenburg & E. van Hoof *Working with intensity; The relationship between giftedness and sensitivity in working adults in Flanders and the Netherlands* (2016). Unpublished manuscript. Retrieved from riannevdven.nl/publicaties/working-with-intensity
- W. Tillier *Personality Development through Positive Disintegration – The work of Kazimierz Dąbrowski* (2018, Maurice Bassett, Anna Maria, FL)
- Anne N. Rinn & Marilyn J. Reynolds *Overexcitabilities and ADHD in the Gifted: An Examination* (2012, Roeper Review) www.tandfonline.com/doi/abs/10.1080/02783193.2012.627551
- D. Dana *De Polyvagaaltheorie in Therapie – Het Ritme van Regulatie* (2021, Uitgeverij Mens!, Eeserveen)
- W. Thomas Boyce, MD *The Orchid And The Dandelion – Why Sensitive People Struggle And How All Can Thrive* (2019, Penguin Random House LLC, New York)
- K. Dąbrowski *Multilevelness of Emotional and Instinctive Functions* (1996, Towarzystwo Naukowe, Lublin)

Chapter 6. Transformative Inner Forces

- K. Dąbrowski, A. Kawczak & J. Sochanska *The Dynamics of Concepts* (1973, Gryf Publications Ltd., London)
- K. Dąbrowski *Multilevelness of Emotional and Instinctive Functions* (1996, Towarzystwo Naukowe, Lublin)
- D. Ritz *Divided Soul: The Life of Marvin Gaye* (1991, Omnibus Press, London)
- DVD: *Marvin Gaye – Behind The Legend* (2004, Eagle Rock Entertainment Ltd.)
- Sound on Sound *Marvin Gaye What's Going On?* (2011) www.soundonsound.com/techniques/marvin-gaye-whats-going
- Janis Gaye *After the Dance: My Life With Marvin Gaye* (2015) publicism.info/biography/jan_gaye/30.html

Chapter 7. Emotions

- K.C. Laycraft *The Courage to Decide* (2015, AwareNow Publishing, Victoria, BC, Canada)
- J. Aufenanger *Prisma Filosofie* (1993, Prisma)
- L. Feldmann Barrett *How Emotions Are Made* (2017 Houghton Mifflin Harcourt, New York)
- A. Damasio *Descartes' Error* (2006 Vintage, London)
- K.C. Laycraft & B. Gierus *Acceptance: The Key to a Meaningful Life* (2019, Calgary, AB, Canada: Nucleus Learning)
- M.B. Rosenberg *Nonviolent Communication: A Language of Life* (2015, Encinitas: PuddleDancer Press)
- Rittenberg and Tregarthen *"Chapter 6" (PDF). Principles of Microeconomics* (2012)
- J. Haidt *The Righteous Mind* (2012, Penguin Books Ltd, London)

Chapter 8. Breathe

- J. Nestor *Breath: The New Science of a Lost Art* (2020, New York: Riverhead Books)
- L. Bernardi, P. Sleight, G. Bandinelli, S. Cencetti, L. Fattorini, J. Wdowczyc-Szulc et al. *Effect of rosary prayer and yoga mantras on autonomic cardiovascular rhythms: comparative study* (2001, BMJ) www.bmj.com/content/323/7327/1446
- C. Goyder *Find Your Voice: The Secret to Talking with Confidence in any Situation* (2020, Vermillion, London)
- P. Philippot, G. Chapelle & S. Blairy *Respiratory feedback in the generation of emotion* (2002, Cognition and Emotion) www.researchgate.net/publication/232965660_Respiratory_feedback_in_the_generation_of_emotion
- A. Zaccaro, A. Piarulli, M. Laurino, E. Garbella, D. Menicucci, B. Neri & A. Gemignani *How Breath-Control Can Change Your Life: A Systematic Review on Psycho-Physiological Correlates of Slow Breathing* (2018, Frontiers in Human Neuroscience) www.frontiersin.org/articles/10.3389/fnhum.2018.00353/full
- M. Kozhevnikov, J. Elliott, J. Shephard & K. Gramann *Neurocognitive and somatic components of temperature increases during g-tummo meditation: legend and reality* (2013, PLoS One) www.ncbi.nlm.nih.gov/pmc/articles/PMC3612090/
- M. Kox, L.T. van Eijk, J. Zwaag, et al. *Voluntary activation of the sympathetic nervous system and attenuation of the innate immune response in humans* (2014, Proc Natl Acad Sci U S A) www.ncbi.nlm.nih.gov/pmc/articles/PMC4034215/
- M. Mather, N.R. Lighthall, L. Nga & M.A. Gorlick *Sex differences in how stress affects brain activity during face viewing* (2010, Neuroreport) www.ncbi.nlm.nih.gov/pmc/articles/PMC2948784/
- J. McHenry, N. Carrier, E. Hull & M. Kabbaj *Sex differences in anxiety and depression: role of testosterone* (2014, Front Neuroendocrinol) www.ncbi.nlm.nih.gov/pmc/articles/PMC3946856/

Chapter 9. Feel into the Body

- C. Goyder *Find Your Voice: The Secret to Talking with Confidence in any Situation* (2020, Vermillion, London)

Chapter 10. Make Sense of your Emotions

- D. Dana *De Polyvagaaltheorie in Therapie – Het Ritme van Regulatie* (2021, Uitgeverij Mens!, Eeserveen)
- L. Feldmann Barrett *How Emotions Are Made* (2017 Houghton Mifflin Harcourt, New York)
- M.B. Rosenberg *Nonviolent Communication: A Language of Life.* (2015, Encinitas: PuddleDancer Press)
- Centre for Nonviolent Communication www.cnvc.org

Chapter 11. Step Back from your Thoughts

- C. Goyder *Find Your Voice: The Secret to Talking with Confidence in any Situation* (2020, Vermillion, London 2020)
- D. Bohm *Wholeness and the Implicate Order* (1980, Routledge & Kegan Paul, New York NY)
- N. Nicolai *Emotieregulatie als basis van het menselijk bestaan* (2016, Diagnosis Uitgevers, Leusden)
- S.C. Hayes, K.D. Strosahl & K.G. Wilson *Acceptance and commitment therapy: The process and practice of mindful change.* (2012, New York: The Guildford Press)
- The Psychology Podcast *Mind the Mindfulness Hype with David Vago* (2019) www.youtube.com/watch?v=iFzCg1yl5UI
- S.C. Hayes & S. Smith *Get Out of Your Mind & Into Your Life: The New Acceptance & Commitment Therapy.* (2005, Oakland: New Harbinger Publications)
- E. Tolle *The Power of Now: A Guide To Spiritual Enlightenment* (2001, London: Hodder & Stoughton)

Chapter 12. Become Self-Aware - Then Transcend the Self

- M.M. Piechowski *We are all cells in the body of humanity* (2010, Gifted Education International, Vol. 27)
- J. Halifax *Standing At The Edge – Finding Freedom Where Fear And Courage Meet* (2018, Flatiron Books, New York)
- D. Dana *De Polyvagaaltheorie in Therapie – Het Ritme van Regulatie* (2021, Uitgeverij Mens!, Eeserveen)
- The Psychology Podcast *Mind the Mindfulness Hype with David Vago* (2019) www.youtube.com/watch?v=iFzCg1yl5UI
- Duke Today Staff *Key to Changing Habits is in Environment, Not Willpower, Duke Experts Say* (2007, Duke Today) today.duke.edu/2007/12/habit.html
- S.B. Kaufman, Ph.D. *Ungifted – Intelligence Redefined* (2013, Basic Books, New York, NY)
- K.A. Garrison, T.A. Zeffiro, D. Scheinost, R.T. Constable & J.A. Brewer *Meditation leads to reduced default mode network activity beyond an active task* (2015, Cogn Affect Behav Neurosci) www.ncbi.nlm.nih.gov/pmc/articles/PMC4529365/
- W. Hasenkamp, C.D. Wilson-Mendenhall, E. Duncan & L.W. Barsalou *Mind wandering and attention during focused meditation: a fine-grained temporal analysis of fluctuating cognitive states* (2012, Neuroimage) www.ncbi.nlm.nih.gov/pubmed/21782031
- J. Xu, A. Vik, I.R. Groote et al. *Nondirective meditation activates default mode network and areas associated with memory retrieval and emotional processing* (2014, Front Hum Neurosci) www.ncbi.nlm.nih.gov/pmc/articles/PMC3935386/
- J. Cameron *The Artist's Way - A Spiritual Path to Higher Creativity* (2002, Tarcher/Putnam, New York, NY)
- Contemplation on Wikipedia en.wikipedia.org/wiki/Contemplation
- S. Ratnayake *The problem of mindfulness* (2019, Aeon) aeon.co/essays/mindfulness-is-loaded-with-troubling-metaphysical-assumptions
- Kazimierz Dąbrowski reflects on the concept of 'no-self' www.youtube.com/watch?v=lbqLIFuk-VIs
- S.B. Kaufman *Transcend: the new science of self-actualization* (2020, TarcherPerigee, New York, NY)
- Cultural Atlas *Japanese Culture: Business culture* culturalatlas.sbs.com.au/japanese-culture/japanese-culture-business-culture
- Invajy *How to use duality or paradoxical unity to understand the life?* (2022) www.invajy.com/how-to-use-duality-or-paradoxical-unity-to-understand-the-life
- The Martin Luther King, Jr. Research and Education Institute, Stanford University kinginstitute.stanford.edu/king-papers/publications/autobiography-martin-luther-king-jr-contents/chapter-1-early-years
- G. Hodgson *Martin Luther King* (2009, Quercus, London)
- Martin Luther King Jr. on Wikipedia en.wikipedia.org/wiki/Martin_Luther_King_Jr.
- D. Dana *De Polyvagaaltheorie in Therapie – Op Weg naar Veiligheid en Verbondenheid – 50 Oefeningen voor Cliënten* (2021, Uitgeverij Mens!, Eeserveen)

Appendix

- Peter Wohlleben, *The Hidden Life of Trees* (2015, HarperCollins)

Index

Lightning Source UK Ltd.
Milton Keynes UK
UKHW032122081122
411848UK00009B/487